Gerald Murnane

SYDNEY STUDIES IN AUSTRALIAN LITERATURE

Robert Dixon, Series Editor

The **Sydney Studies in Australian Literature** series publishes original, peer-reviewed research in the field of Australian literary studies. It offers engagingly written evaluations of the nature and importance of Australian literature, and aims to reinvigorate its study both locally and internationally.

Alex Miller: The Ruin of Time
Robert Dixon

Australian Books and Authors in the American Marketplace 1840s–1940s
David Carter and Roger Osborne

Christina Stead and the Matter of America
Fiona Morrison

Colonial Australian Fiction: Character Types, Social Formations and the Colonial Economy
Ken Gelder and Rachael Weaver

Contemporary Australian Literature: A World Not Yet Dead
Nicholas Birns

Elizabeth Harrower: Critical Essays
Ed. Elizabeth McMahon and Brigitta Olubas

The Fiction of Tim Winton: Earthed and Sacred
Lyn McCredden

Gerald Murnane: Another World in This One
Ed. Anthony Uhlmann

Richard Flanagan: Critical Essays
Ed. Robert Dixon

Shirley Hazzard: New Critical Essays
Ed. Brigitta Olubas

Gerald Murnane

Another World in This One

Edited by Anthony Uhlmann

SYDNEY UNIVERSITY PRESS

First published by Sydney University Press

© Individual authors 2020
© Sydney University Press 2020

Reproduction and communication for other purposes

Except as permitted under the Act, no part of this edition may be reproduced, stored in a retrieval system, or communicated in any form or by any means without prior written permission. All requests for reproduction or communication should be made to Sydney University Press at the address below:

Sydney University Press
Fisher Library F03
University of Sydney NSW 2006
AUSTRALIA
sup.info@sydney.edu.au
sydneyuniversitypress.com.au

A catalogue record for this book is available from the National Library of Australia.

ISBN 9781743326404 paperback
ISBN 9781743326411 epub

Gerald Murnane's poem "Green Shadows", from his collection *Green Shadows and Other Poems* (Sydney: Giramondo, 2019), is reproduced by kind permission.

Cover image by Zan Wimberley.
Cover design by Miguel Yamin.

Table of Contents

Acknowledgements — vii

Gerald Murnane: A Chronology — ix

Introduction — 1
Anthony Uhlmann

1. Scenes from Gerald Murnane's Golf Club — 9
Tristan Foster

2. To the Eye Untrained — 13
Luke Carman

3. Truth, Fiction and True Fiction — 29
Shannon Burns

4. "Images and Feelings in a Sort of Eternity": Gerald Murnane's Ideal Female Reader — 37
Samantha Trayhurn

5. Retrospective Intention: The Implied Author and the Coherence of the Oeuvre in *Border Districts* and *The Plains* — 45
Emmett Stinson

6. Stream System, Salient Image and Feeling: Between *Barley Patch* and *Inland* — 63
Brigid Rooney

7. Gerald Murnane's Plain Style — 85
Mark Byron

8   Landscape within Landscape: The Intertwining of the Visible and the Invisible in Gerald Murnane and Henry James   107
Suzie Gibson

9   Memory, Image and Reading Traces of the Infinite: *A History of Books*   125
Arka Chattopadhyay

10   Reporting Meaning in *Border Districts*   141
Anthony Uhlmann

11   What Kind of Literary History Is *A History of Books*?   151
Ivor Indyk

12   The Still-Breathing Author   163
Gerald Murnane

Contributors   179

Index   181

Acknowledgements

This book was produced as part of a project funded by the Australian Research Council's Discovery Program, called "Other Worlds: Forms of World Literature" (DP170101002), and the ARC is gratefully acknowledged here. Further work related to this project can be found on the project website (formsofworldliterature.com). We would like to thank other members of the project who assisted with elements of this book, in particular the project manager Melinda Jewell, Ivor Indyk (and Giramondo Publishing), Alexis Wright and Samantha Trayhurn, who contributed to the conference "Another World in This One: Gerald Murnane's Fiction" in Goroke in 2017. We would like to acknowledge the following: Gerald Murnane, who gave his blessing to the small conference in his home town of Goroke, and other members of the Goroke community who welcomed us on the day, fed us marvellous home-cooked cakes, and opened Goroke Golf Club to us; the support of the Writing and Society Research Centre and the School of Humanities and Communication Arts, and the Dean, Peter Hutchings, at Western Sydney University; Michael Heyward of Text Publishing (Murnane's other publisher) who offered advice and encouragement and attended the day; Andre Sawenko, who filmed and took photos on the day; and Melinda Jewell, again, this time for the work she put into the production of the manuscript. Finally, we would like to thank Robert Dixon, Susan Murray, Agata Mrva-Montoya, Denise O'Dea and the team at Sydney University Press for overseeing the book and its design.

We are grateful to *The Paris Review* for allowing us to reprint Tristan Foster's article in this collection, and to the *Sydney Review of Books* and its editor, Catriona Menzies-Pike, who published a slightly different version of Gerald Murnane's "The Still-Breathing Author", which also reappears here.

Gerald Murnane: A Chronology

This chronology draws upon and updates work done by Imre Salusinszky in his monograph *Gerald Murnane* (Melbourne: Oxford University Press, 1993), and *Gerald Murnane: An Annotated Bibliography of Primary and Secondary Sources* (Melbourne: Footprint, 1993).

1939 Birth of Gerald Murnane, Coburg, Melbourne, 25 February. His mother is Gwenneth Alberta Murnane (née Rooke) and his father is Reginald Thomas Murnane.

1944 Family moves to Bendigo.

1948 Family moves to the Western District.

1949 Family returns to Melbourne.

1956 Completes high school at De La Salle College, Malvern, a Catholic school founded in 1912 and run by the De La Salle Brothers, an order based on the teachings of Saint Jean-Baptiste de la Salle (1651-1719).

1957 February–May, studies for the priesthood at St Pius X Memorial College among the Passionist Fathers, an order mixing spiritual contemplation with missionary work, in St Ives, Sydney.

June, abandons his studies for the priesthood, returns to Melbourne and works as a temporary clerk in the Royal Mint.

1958 Attends Toorak Teachers' College to begin training as a primary teacher.

1960 Begins work as a primary teacher. Teaches in eight Melbourne schools between 1960 and 1968.

1963 Begins annual duties as an honorary lecturer in General Education at the Victoria Racing Club's Apprentice Jockeys' School.

Gerald Murnane

1965 Begins a part-time BA (majoring in English and Arabic) at the University of Melbourne.

1966 Marriage to Catherine Mary Lancaster, 14 May.

1969 Graduates from the University of Melbourne. Family moves to the Melbourne suburb of Macleod. Begins work as Publications Officer, then Assistant Editor, in the Publications Branch of the Education Department of the Victorian government.

Birth of the Murnanes' first son, Giles Francis Murnane, 16 January.

1970 Birth of twin sons, Gavin Edric Murnane and Martin Bevis Murnane, 29 May.

1973 Resigns from the Education Department to concentrate on his writing with his wife's support. Until he is employed full time again (in 1980) he works as a freelance editor, and receives some grants from the Australia Council for the Arts to support his writing.

1974 *Tamarisk Row* published by William Heinemann Australia.

1976 *A Lifetime on Clouds* published by William Heineman Australia.

1980 Begins work as a lecturer in fiction writing at Prahran College of Advanced Education (later Victoria College, later Deakin University).

1982 *The Plains* published by Norstrilia Press, Melbourne, a press that largely publishes in the genres of science fiction and speculative fiction.

1984 *The Plains* paperback edition published by Penguin Australia.

1985 *The Plains* published by George Braziller, New York.

Landscape with Landscape published by Norstrilia Press, Melbourne.

1987 Made an honorary member of the Victoria Racing Club. Receives tenured position at Victoria College. Convenes the judging panel for the Fiction Award in the Victorian Premier's Literary Awards.

1988 *Inland* published by Heinemann, Melbourne.

Inland published by Faber, London.

Is writer-in-residence at La Trobe University. Appointed fiction consultant for literary journal *Meanjin*.

1989 Documentary film, *Words and Silk: The Imaginary and Real Worlds of Gerald Murnane*, directed by Philip Tyndall, premieres at the State Film Theatre in Melbourne, 27 October. Broadcast on national Australian television (SBS), April 1992.

Gerald Murnane: A Chronology

1990 *Velvet Waters*, a collection of short stories, published by McPhee Gribble (Penguin). Wins the Barbara Ramsden Award of the Victorian Fellowship of Australian Writers.

Writer-in-residence, the University of Newcastle, NSW.

1991 Appointed to the Literature Advisory Panel of the Victorian Ministry for the Arts.

1993 Imre Salusinszky publishes *Gerald Murnane*, the first academic monograph on Murnane's work, with Oxford University Press, Melbourne. Imre Salusinszky publishes *Gerald Murnane: An Annotated Bibliography of Primary and Secondary Sources*, with Footprint Books, Melbourne.

1995 Retires from his position as lecturer in fiction at Deakin University. *Emerald Blue*, a collection of short stories, published by McPhee Gribble.

1999 Awarded the Patrick White Award for writers who have not necessarily received adequate recognition for their work.

2001 First major conference on Gerald Murnane's work held at the University of Newcastle, NSW, organised by Imre Salusinszky. Murnane presents a paper entitled "The Breathing Author". Ivor Indyk is present and asks to publish the essay in *Heat* magazine, leading to Murnane publishing with Indyk's imprint, Giramondo Publishing, a few years later.

2005 *Invisible Yet Enduring Lilacs*, a collection of essays, is published by Giramondo Publishing, breaking a publishing silence of ten years.

2007 Special Award for Lifelong Achievement, New South Wales Premier's Literary Awards.

2008 *Tamarisk Row* reissued in a revised edition by Giramondo Publishing.

2009 *Barley Patch*, a hybrid work of essayistic fiction confronting the question "Must I write?", published by Giramondo Publishing. *Barley Patch* awarded the Adelaide Festival Literature Award for Innovation. Murnane awarded the Melbourne Prize for Literature for lifetime achievement.

Following the death of his wife Catherine, Murnane moves to Goroke in rural Victoria to be near one of his sons.

2011 *Barley Patch* published by Dalkey Archive Press in the United States.

2012 *A History of Books*, a work of fiction, published by Giramondo Publishing. *The Plains* reissued by Text Publishing, Melbourne, in the Text Classics series.

Inland published by Dalkey Archive Press in the United States. J.M. Coetzee publishes an influential article in *The New York Review of Books*, "The Quest for the Girl from Bendigo Street", on Murnane's *Barley Patch* and *Inland*.

2013 *A Lifetime on Clouds* reissued by Text Publishing in the Text Classics series.

Inland reissued in a new edition by Giramondo Publishing.

2014 *A Million Windows*, fiction, published by Giramondo Publishing.

2015 *Something for the Pain: A Memoir of the Turf*, a non-fiction memoir related to Murnane's interest in horseracing, published by Text Publishing.

2016 *Landscape with Landscape* republished by Giramondo Publishing.

Awarded Victorian Premier's Literary Award for non-fiction for *Something for the Pain*.

A Million Windows published in the United States by David R. Godine, Publisher.

2017 *Border Districts*, fiction, published by Giramondo Publishing.

"Another World in This One", a one-day symposium on Murnane's work held in Goroke, Victoria, 7 December.

2018 Mark Binelli publishes the feature article "Is the Next Nobel Laureate in Literature Tending Bar in a Dusty Australian Town?" in the *New York Times Magazine*.

Border Districts published by Farrar, Straus & Giroux, New York.

Stream System: The Collected Short Fiction of Gerald Murnane published by Farrar, Straus & Giroux, New York.

Wins Prime Minister's Literary Award for Fiction for *Border Districts*.

Collected Short Fiction published by Giramondo Publishing.

Grenzbezirke (Border Districts) published by Suhrkamp Verlag, Germany.

Border Districts shortlisted for the Miles Franklin Literary Award.

2019 *Green Shadows and Other Poems* published by Giramondo Publishing.

Border Districts published by And Other Stories in the UK.

Tamarisk Row published by And Other Stories in the UK.

A Season on Earth (the full version of Murnane's second work of fiction, from which *A Lifetime on Clouds* was excerpted by his 1976 publisher) published by Text Publishing.

Border Districts shortlisted for the New South Wales Premier's Award for Fiction.

Introduction
Anthony Uhlmann

Gerald Murnane has long been thought of as a writer who has been unjustly neglected. Writing in 2009, Paul Genoni outlined some elements of this neglect, noting that the main awards Murnane had received up until that time had been "special awards" intended for writers who have been unfairly passed over.[1] Yet even in writing this, Genoni noted that Murnane's work had captured the attention of the Swedish Academy, so that Murnane had been given odds of 33/1 by the betting house Ladbrokes to win the Nobel Prize for Literature in 2006. Evidence of this international interest can also be found in Swedish scholars such as H.W. Fawkner, Lars Andersson and Ulf Eriksson. As I write, Murnane critics can no longer point to neglect as something that characterises the reception of his books. In recent years, both his writing and his eccentric persona have drawn attention and led to the publication and even republication of his writing, and high-profile reviews in the United States, the United Kingdom and beyond. He is again being spoken of as a possible Nobel Laureate, and his works, which had all but gone out of print at one point in his career, are now more widely available than they have ever been.

There is, then, a strong and seemingly growing interest in the unusual style Murnane develops in his fictions, which cannot easily be classified as "novels", and often move between the spaces of the essay form and fictional form. Critics have made distinctions within and between Murnane's works, suggesting they fall into three periods. The first distinction made is between the first two books, *Tamarisk Row* (1974) and *A Lifetime on Clouds* (1976), which have third-person narrators, and those that follow, beginning with *The Plains* (1982), which have first-person

---

1 Paul Genoni, "The Global Reception of Post-National Literary Fiction: The Case of Gerald Murnane", *JASAL: Journal of the Association for the Study of Australian Literature* 9, Special Issue (2009), 3.

narrators.² Yet even within this distinction, as Imre Salusinszky shows, it is notable that, from the very beginning, Murnane seems to have a well-developed store of images or iconography already worked out in *Tamarisk Row*: marbles, plains, grasslands, calendars, colours, horseracing, and so on, and further, that these images are associated with autobiographical elements of Murnane's life such as his Catholic upbringing, his father's and his own passion for horseracing, and his desire to create imagined worlds through games with marbles.³ Such images are linked together into sets of meaningful associations that resonate throughout Murnane's entire oeuvre, leading to the question as to the extent to which the oeuvre can be understood as some kind of whole. Genoni makes the strong claim that "Murnane's fiction is of a piece, instantly being recognisable as being the product of a single creative vision".⁴ Yet the essays of Shannon Burns, and Emmett Stinson in this collection, along with comments made by Murnane himself in "The Still-Breathing Author",⁵ add complexity to this view, showing how, especially with his early writing, Murnane was at the mercy of the opinions of his editors, who, for example, excised the published versions of *A Lifetime on Clouds* and *The Plains* from longer works.⁶ That said, the shift Genoni and Salusinszky identify, from third-person narrators and named characters to first-person narrators, is clear, and entrenched from *Landscape with Landscape* (1985) on (with *The Plains* involving a point of transition).⁷

The third stage of Murnane's fiction also appears to involve a stylistic shift, as the voice that narrates now seems still closer to the implied author "Murnane", yet to date little has been done to interrogate the stylistic differences between the texts up to *Inland* (1988) and those after *Barley Patch* (2009). In any case the break is apparent in the long hiatus between the publication of his last collection of short stories, *Emerald Blue* (1995), and his return to writing fiction with *Barley Patch* (2009). In his essay "The Breathing Author", Murnane himself points to a break, which involves a deliberate decision to stop writing,⁸ and aspects of the need for this break are the subject matter of *Barley Patch*, which begins with the question,

---

2 Paul Genoni, "Gerald Murnane", in *A Companion to Australian Literature Since 1900*, ed. Nicholas Birns and Rebecca McNeer (Rochester, NY: Camden House, 2007), 293-304.
3 Imre Salusinszky, *Gerald Murnane* (Melbourne: Oxford University Press), 15-16.
4 Genoni, "Gerald Murnane", 294.
5 Gerald Murnane, "The Still-Breathing Author", first delivered at "A World within This One: Gerald Murnane's Fiction" Symposium, Goroke, Victoria, 7 December 2017, published in the *Sydney Review of Books*, https://sydneyreviewofbooks.com/the-still-breathing-author-gerald-murnane/, and republished in this collection.
6 The full text from which *A Lifetime on Clouds* was drawn has now been published by Text Publishing under the title *A Season on Earth* (Melbourne: Text Publishing, 2019).
7 Although, as Salusinszky notes, a few of the short stories revert to the third person; Salusinszky, *Gerald Murnane*, 40.
8 Gerald Murnane, "The Breathing Author", *Heat* no. 3 (new series) (2002), 9-31.

"*Must I write?*".⁹ The works that follow *Barley Patch* seem to offer, in Murnane's own view, a meditation on the nature of his own mind and its functioning, which involves the connection of images as a means of creating meaning. While this focus is already apparent in *Inland*, one might argue that there it is presented within a fictional frame, whereas the addresses the narrators make to readers from *Barley Patch* on seem more directly to relate more closely to the experience of a narrator somehow aligned with "Gerald Murnane".

J.M. Coetzee, in his extended engagement with *Barley Patch*, underlines the nature of this interest in a network of images that comprises the mind:

> The activity of writing ... is not to be distinguished from the activity of self-exploration. It consists in contemplating the sea of internal images, discerning connections, and setting these out in grammatical sentences.¹⁰

Seemingly taking issue with Murnane, Coetzee suggests that Murnane is a "radical idealist", yet Coetzee's careful analysis also underlines the seriousness of Murnane's project. This seriousness, and the particular style Murnane develops in tending rigorously to his obsessions, plays a large part in rendering them fascinating to readers and scholars. While, as he makes clear, he is not interested in situating his own writing in relation to theoretical systems (though he does, as Stinson underlines below, occasionally refer to literary theorists), Murnane's project nevertheless offers a sustained engagement with internal mental processes of relation and understanding, which is not without interest to literary critics, and even to philosophers and cognitive scientists.

This collection began life as a one-day conference I organised on Murnane's writing, held in Goroke on 7 December 2017, called "Another World in This One". In late April 2016, I had arranged to meet Murnane in Goroke. While there I suggested that I would like to organise a conference dedicated to his writing. Murnane reminisced about the first important conference on his work, which had taken place in 2001, organised by Imre Salusinszky at the University of Newcastle. That event included Murnane as a keynote speaker, and his address, mentioned above, was entitled "The Breathing Author". This essay was later published by Ivor Indyk in his journal *Heat* (2002), and in Murnane's collection of essays *Invisible Yet Enduring Lilacs* (2005). In "The Breathing Author", Murnane touched upon his reasons for giving up writing, yet some years later he began again to write fiction. In our discussions of April 2016, however, Murnane made it clear that he would

---

9   Gerald Murnane, *Barley Patch* (Artarmon, NSW: Giramondo, 2009), 3.
10 J.M. Coetzee, "The Quest for the Girl from Bendigo Street", *The New York Review of Books*, 20 December 2012. https://www.nybooks.com/articles/2012/12/20/quest-girl-bendigo-street/.

no longer travel for a conference of this or any other kind. I quickly suggested that rather than asking him to travel to Sydney or Melbourne, we could ask those attending and presenting at the conference to travel to Goroke. Murnane eventually agreed.

Well before the conference, Murnane's writing had begun to be better noticed, as reviews had appeared in major outlets related to the publication of some of his works in the United States. Adding to J.M. Coetzee's 2012 article in the *New York Review of Books*, Ben Lerner wrote a major piece for the *New Yorker Magazine*,[11] and these articles helped to begin a groundswell of international interest. The small conference in Goroke served to amplify this reception still further. Soon after the conference one of the audience members, Tristan Foster, a Sydney-based writer, wrote a review of the Goroke conference, "Scenes from Gerald Murnane's Golf Club", which appeared in the online version of the important literary journal the *Paris Review*, published in New York.[12] In order to give both the general and academic reader an idea of the flavour of this event, we have republished Foster's fine review in this collection. A few months later a major feature article by Mark Binelli was published by the *New York Times Magazine* on 27 March 2018, entitled, "Is the Next Nobel Laureate in Literature Tending Bar in a Dusty Australian Town?" The article begins by mentioning our small conference:

> Goroke, Victoria, a former stagecoach stop in southeastern Australia, pop. 200, is not the sort of place you would expect to host a daylong academic symposium. About five hours from Melbourne by car, the town has the feel of an evacuation nearly complete. Empty storefronts line the main street; the local pub closed two years ago. Drive a few minutes outside Goroke, and the only signs of life arrive at dusk, when the kangaroos emerge from the brush to stare down passers-by from the edge of the road. But last December, about 40 scholars, critics, editors and general readers made the journey for a series of lectures on the work of Gerald Murnane. The author, who has lived in Goroke for the last decade, prefers not to travel, and he had suggested the scholars convene at the local golf club, where he plays a weekly game and also regularly tends bar.[13]

After the conference, I sent Murnane a letter including photographs of the day. On 19 March 2018, he wrote back, "I'm very grateful for the pics of our memorable

---

11 Ben Lerner, "A Strange Australian Masterpiece", *New Yorker*, 29 March 2017. https://www.newyorker.com/books/page-turner/a-strange-australian-masterpiece
12 Tristan Foster, "Scenes from Gerald Murnane's Golf Club", *Paris Review*, 26 January 2018. https://www.theparisreview.org/blog/2018/01/26/scenes-gerald-murnanes-golf-club/
13 Mark Binelli, "Is the Next Nobel Laureate in Literature Tending Bar in a Dusty Australian Town", *New York Times Magazine*, 27 March 2018. https://www.nytimes.com/2018/03/27/magazine/gerald-murnane-next-nobel-laureate-literature-australia.html

conference. May it become a legend, and may those who travelled there cherish their memories of it".

In developing this edited collection, I am aware of two potential audiences: an audience of general readers, and an audience of students and academics, who are interested in studying Murnane's writing. This collection does its best to accommodate both, and in doing this, I am conscious that at times it will run the risk of outraging the expectations of either or both of these two sets of readers. In an effort to pre-empt any such feelings, I will begin by underlining that Murnane is sufficiently difficult and sufficiently compelling a writer to sustain both kinds of reading, and that the reading an interested general reader might bring can inform a literary critic's reading, just as that interested reader might find, if they attend with genuine interest, that literary critical readings can deepen their appreciation of Murnane's works.

The back and forth between the two styles of reading will be apparent in some of the editorial decisions to follow. There is a context which brings these essays together, and that context involves engagement with the actual author in his home town, bringing with it the sights, sounds and sensations of the small town of Goroke in rural Victoria. Such contexts are often excised from literary critical discussion. The decision has been made, here, to allow them their power and bring them to the fore, because they allow us to better understand the works, as well as offering a way into them, through anecdote and felt descriptions. It is also apparent in the different styles contributors bring to the essays. This collection includes reflections from Ivor Indyk, who is both a major literary critic and Murnane's publisher, Murnane's biographer Shannon Burns, and another creative writer inspired by his writing, Luke Carman, as well as literary critics writing in more academic prose.

The essays that follow consider many aspects of Murnane's works. Foster's article outlines and reviews the conference "Another World in This One". Luke Carman is a highly regarded young writer, and his essay, which offers a writer's rather than a literary critic's response to Murnane, offers insights into the particular kind of writing Murnane develops. Shannon Burns is currently writing a biography of Murnane, and his essay here reflects on that process. Samantha Trayhurn turns to the question of Murnane's ideal reader, whom he indicates in a number of places to be female, and considers her nature. Emmett Stinson provocatively argues that, rather than forming a clear whole imagined in some way at the outset, Murnane's late works develop retrospective understandings of the previous ones, reimagining and reshaping the oeuvre as a whole. Brigid Rooney considers Murnane through the prism of two image-ideas suggested by his writing: topology, and the "stream system", adding depth to the general awareness of Murnane's interest in landscapes and plains. Mark Byron approaches the idea of the plain from another angle, focusing on questions of Murnane's literary style. Suzie Gibson also considers the nature of style, focusing on the encounter between Murnane and Henry James alluded to by the title of *A Million Windows*, and examining what is at stake and what is particular about Murnane's style. Arka Chattopadhyay takes seriously Murnane's overt interest in his own mind, and in tracing what occurs within that mind, links images, memory and reading and writing practice. My own chapter focuses on the idea of the reporting of images in *Border Districts* and how meaning is constructed through the relation of images. Ivor Indyk's essay retains the flavour of his spoken presentation in Goroke, since it involved, in many ways, a direct dialogue with Murnane the author and man, who was in the room at the time. Indyk speaks both as a publisher and a critic, teasing out the contradictions involved in the dialogue from each position, and addressing what is provocative and new in Murnane's work. The collection ends with Murnane's presentation, which was delivered at "Another World in This One". This essay forms a bookend with his earlier essay, "The Breathing Author". Whereas "The Breathing Author" marked a moment when Murnane felt that he had stopped writing fiction but would, a few years later, begin again, "The Still-Breathing Author" announces a new retirement. It remains to be seen if Murnane has indeed written his final book. Those who have contributed here and those who take the effort to read these essays will no doubt hope that a new moment with further writing awaits.

References

Andersson, Lars. "Troubled by Impossible Dreams: Fantasy and Desire in Gerald Murnane's *A Lifetime on Clouds*", *Antipodes: A North American Journal of Australian Literature* 27, no. 2 (December 2013): 189–93.

Binelli, Mark. "Is the Next Nobel Laureate in Literature Tending Bar in a Dusty Australian Town?", *New York Times Magazine*, 27 March 2018. https://www.nytimes.com/2018/03/27/magazine/gerald-murnane-next-nobel-laureate-literature-australia.html.

Coetzee, J.M. "The Quest for the Girl from Bendigo Street", *New York Review of Books*, 20 December 2012. https://www.nybooks.com/articles/2012/12/20/quest-girl-bendigo-street/.

Eriksson, Ulf. "En värld inne i världen-några fragment med anledning av Gerald Murnane", *Vagant* no. 2 (2006): 49–55.

Fawkner, H.W. *Grasses That Have No Fields: From Gerald Murnane's Inland to a Phenomenology of Isogonic Constitution*. Stockholm: Stockholm University Press, 2006.

Foster, Tristan. "Scenes from Gerald Murnane's Golf Club", *Paris Review*, 26 January 2018. https://www.theparisreview.org/blog/2018/01/26/scenes-gerald-murnanes-golf-club/.

Genoni, Paul. "The Global Reception of Post-National Literary Fiction: The Case of Gerald Murnane", *JASAL: Journal of the Association for the Study of Australian Literature* 9, Special Issue (2009): 1–13.

——. "Gerald Murnane", in *A Companion to Australian Literature Since 1900*, edited by Nicholas Birns and Rebecca McNeer. Rochester, NY: Camden House, 2007, 293–304.

Introduction

Lerner, Ben. "A Strange Australian Masterpiece", *New Yorker*, 29 March 2017. https://www.newyorker.com/books/page-turner/a-strange-australian-masterpiece

Murnane, Gerald. *A Season on Earth*. Melbourne: Text Publishing, 2019.

——. *Barley Patch*. Artarmon, NSW: Giramondo, 2009.

——. "The Breathing Author", In *Invisible Yet Enduring Lilacs*. Artarmon, NSW: Giramondo, 2005.

——. *Invisible Yet Enduring Lilacs*. Artarmon, NSW: Giramondo, 2005.

——. "The Breathing Author", *Heat* no. 3 (new series) (2002): 9-31.

——. *Emerald Blue*. Ringwood, Vic.: McPhee Gribble, 1995.

——. *Inland*. Richmond, Vic.: William Heinemann Australia, 1988.

——. *Landscape with Landscape*. Carlton, Vic.: Nostrilia Press, 1985.

——. *A Lifetime on Clouds*. Melbourne: Heinemann, 1976.

——. *The Plains*. Carlton, Vic.: Norstrilia Press, 1982.

——. "The Still-Breathing Author", *Sydney Review of Books*, 6 February 2018. https://sydneyreviewofbooks.com/the-still-breathing-author-gerald-murnane/.

——. *Tamarisk Row*. Melbourne: Heinemann, 1974.

Salusinszky, Imre. *Gerald Murnane*. Melbourne: Oxford University Press, 1993.

Zawacki, Andrew. "'Inner Experience' in Gerald Murnane's *The Plains*", in *Imagining Australia: Literature and Culture in the New New World*, edited by Judith Ryan and Chris Wallace-Crabbe. Cambridge, MA: Harvard University Press, 2004, 107-119.

1
Scenes from Gerald Murnane's Golf Club

Tristan Foster

The Australian writer Gerald Murnane is a man of profound contradictions. A recluse who craves attention. A Luddite who uses his smartphone to google himself. An author who retired long ago, then went on to produce his richest work. He was recently treated for prostate cancer, and yet he's still the sprightliest person in the room.

The room on this occasion was a small golf club in Goroke, Murnane's rural home town in Victoria, Australia, not far from the state border. We had gathered from faraway places to attend "Another World in This One", a one-day symposium on Murnane's fiction, and to mark the publication of what is by every account his final novel, *Border Districts*.[1]

The club was furnished with vinyl chairs and tables with the covers tacked on. It had views of the golf course, the flags for each distant hole waving between spindly gum trees. The attendance for the symposium was capped at forty people – the club is cosy and the kitchen only able to turn out so many scones and sandwiches. Attendees included Murnane's tireless publisher at Giramondo Publishing, Ivor Indyk; Alexis Wright, another of Australia's major writers; academics; poets; and passionate readers. Rumours abounded that noted fan J.M. Coetzee was due to make the drive from Adelaide. That he had other engagements was perhaps for the better – his presence would have been too much for the little golf club to bear.

The Wimmera, the district the town of Goroke is a part of, is the furthest point on the plains of Murnane's fiction. It is the kind of place where the men in the

---

This article originally appeared in the *Paris Review Daily* and we gratefully acknowledge their permission to republish it. We have used Australian spellings here. Tristan Foster, "Scenes from Gerald Murnane's Golf Club", *Paris Review*, 26 January 2018. https://www.theparisreview.org/blog/2018/01/26/scenes-gerald-murnanes-golf-club/

---

1   Gerald Murnane, *Border Districts* (Artarmon, NSW: Giramondo, 2017).

pubs can tell at a glance that you're not from around here. So can the frogs – the night before the symposium, we drank on the main street of a nearby town, and one jumped into my lap. Before the conference, the organisers at Western Sydney University emailed to say the region's cellular network was down and that we should study the map before setting out. The land smooths over long before Goroke, but it isn't till Goroke that it turns the colour of straw and seems to unfold.

The symposium began with organiser Anthony Uhlmann reading out a prepared statement from Murnane while the writer stood by tight-lipped; he would be present during the breaks and at the end of the day but was under no obligation to stay for the papers. Murnane didn't stay, at least not for the first session. During the second session, he lingered in the bar, pretending to read the newspaper. During the third, he collected empty beer glasses and tinkered at the sink. He seemed to be ignoring references to his presence until, during Indyk's paper, the publisher mispronounced *Feversham's Fag*, a novel by John Mowbray referenced in *A History of Books*. Murnane called out to correct him.

Even though his oeuvre demonstrates a deep unity, Murnane's writing life can still be split into two distinct parts. Underlying the first part is instability – his first seven books were published locally by different publishing houses, each more baffled and antagonistic to the writing than the last. The lack of attention to his artistic vision both from publishers and from the Australian reading public prompted Murnane to retire from writing for publication altogether. His obsessive and distinctive literature, created almost entirely out of personal "mental imagery" that ranges from marbles and the silks of racehorses to Catholic iconography and the rolling plains of his home state, would have disappeared into obscurity entirely if not for the promptings of Indyk at Giramondo. The second part, then, is characterised by certainty – with the support of a trusting publisher, Murnane could explore in full the images that preoccupy him. This narrow yet entirely unexpected body of work has finally started to find readers around the world.

Murnane's biographer Shannon Burns presented Murnane's literature as one of failure, proposing this as a source of humour in his writing but also the thing that keeps him writing. Or, more correctly, kept him writing. Murnane hasn't written anything new since 2015 and stated, in his paper and in private, that he again has lost the desire to continue.

During the lunch break, Murnane opened the bar and served drinks: $2.00 for a can of Coke, $4.50 for a bottle of Carlton Draught. He is the club's barman – an ideal position for receiving horseracing tips – as well as its secretary. On the end of the bar were copies of two items lifted from his archives, to be consumed in the breaks with tea and cake: an exam he sat during his undergraduate degree and a palindrome of 1600 words beginning, "Do good, dog-god! Do, o god! Do!"

In his presentation, Uhlmann observed that Murnane's images are not just images but are laden with meaning. Though Murnane is repelled by psychoanalysis and doesn't believe in the idea of the unconscious, his fiction is full of the slow uncovering of the secret meanings hidden in the imagery. When it was Murnane's turn to speak, he stood at the lectern with his hands behind his back and offered an updated reading of "The Breathing Author" titled "The Still-Breathing Author". The original paper, delivered in 2001, marked both his return to publishing and the beginning of his post-break career. The symmetry was not lost on anyone in the room, least of all Murnane. As he did back then, he used this occasion to reinforce some of the Murnane mythologies – the young author of *Tamarisk Row* never planned to retire as the old author of *Border Districts*; academics and critics complicate his simple ideas; he doesn't go in search of images, they come to him. Murnane doesn't like being put into a category but stated that, if pushed, he would call himself a "technical writer". As if for proof, he held up a diagram illustrating one of his stories – a wobbly parallelogram with lines from the elements on each corner linking to one major element in the centre. It could have been a map of the nearest horseracing tracks as much as a plan for a piece of fiction. To reiterate that his writing was finally finished, he quoted Thomas Hardy: "I have been delivered of my books". During Murnane's talk, it started to rain.

In the documentary *Mental Places*, Murnane quotes the name of a file in his archive: "I am a very strange fellow".[2] Which he is – as strange as a literary symposium in a country-town golf club, but not so strange that he was blind to the importance of what was taking place here. As the end of his paper approached, Murnane's chin quivered, his voice rose, and he shook a fist like a jockey clenching a riding crop. When it was over, he thanked us for coming, then went back behind the bar to serve drinks and sign the odd book.

The rain continued to fall as we went back across the plains. It didn't feel like a goodbye, nor the last time we would see the old writer. We had all begun our prayers for a third act of his career coming sooner rather than later.

References

Murnane, Gerald and Ivor Indyk. "Mental Places: A Conversation with Gerald Murnane".
    Artarmon, NSW: Giramondo, 2016. https://www.youtube.com/watch?v=5PqzX4TC1BE.
Murnane, Gerald. *Border Districts*. Artarmon, NSW: Giramondo, 2017.

---

2   Gerald Murnane and Ivor Indyk, "Mental Places: A Conversation with Gerald Murnane" (Artarmon, NSW: Giramondo, 2016). https://www.youtube.com/watch?v=5PqzX4TC1BE.

2
To the Eye Untrained

Luke Carman

My first Murnanian encounter was of a humiliatingly Bloomian stripe. On a visit to my editor's office to discuss the second draft of what was then a slip of a manuscript, I was offered a long list of books, collections and anthologies he felt were in my interest to investigate. When the question of which of Murnane's books I had read was raised, I confessed not only to having never read a word Murnane had written, but also to never having heard his name before. To this my editor recoiled as though I'd hocked a golly in his direction. Murnane, my editor informed me, was not only a major author in Australian letters, despite what is often referred to as his "lack of wider recognition", but more to the point, was one of the brightest stars in my editor's stable, and as such, my editor had every right to take my inattention to this important author as a personal and embarrassing failing on both our accounts.

I was immediately led to a room down the hall where my editor kept his vast stock of publications, and five titles, the latest of which was *Barley Patch* (2009), were pressed into my hands. "You'll like these", my editor announced in a voice as ominous as prophecy.

Despite the weight of this exchange, by the time I got around to reading even the first few pages of any of these titles, the years had run like rabbits. The short manuscript I'd been working on had long since been published as a brief collection of fiction, and Murnane had brought out at least two further publications. Unsurprisingly, when I came knocking on the office door, declaring to my editor that I'd read the opening pages of *Barley Patch* and had come to discuss the marvels I'd encountered there, the look on his face expressed a perplexed wonder at what it was he'd ever done to deserve such unsolicited and unintelligible harassment. I cannot now recall what it was I said that morning to my editor, but the gist of it was that I'd discovered in the pages of Murnane's work a textual doppelganger of my own mind. My editor showed nothing but impassive patience with the youthful diatribe I provided, and allowed me to go on making clear that this Murnane fellow, whoever he was, had written in *Barley Patch* not merely a facsimile of the thought-being I believed myself to be; he had, in his eccentric modes and bold assertions of style, shown me the writing entity I had privately, even unconsciously, dreamed one day to become.

Encounters of this kind are, I understood even at the time, not especially unknown among writers and readers of fiction, and I considered past discoveries of influence in Kerouac, Whitman, Bernhard and Salinger to have been approximate to this experience, but it had always been a notion of style or form that had caused me this feeling of false proximity. In the case of Murnane, the uncanniness went beyond style or voice: there seemed to me a form of thinking so closely resembling my own in those opening sentences of *Barley Patch* that I could imagine no means by which to separate what was printed on the page from what I thought, felt and hoped to be.

The reader to whom *Barley Patch* is a familiar work might rightfully wonder how it is possible that a young, developing writer could see themselves in the reflections of the narrator provided by Murnane in the opening pages of that work. The book begins with the narrator relating a letter from Rilke to an aspiring poet named Franz Xaver Kappus, quoting the former's response from his work *Letter to a Young Poet*:

> Nobody can counsel and help you, nobody. There is only one single way. Search for the reason that bids you write ... acknowledge to yourself whether you would have to die if it were denied you to write. This above all – ask yourself in the stillest hours of your night: must I write?[1]

The narrator then relates that when he had first read this epistolary exchange between master and apprentice he was a teacher of "fiction writing" at a "college of advanced education". As soon as he read the above passage, he typed it "onto a clean page and then put the page into one of the folders of notes" he kept at hand for his classes in a unit called "Advanced Fiction Writing", sharing it with his students each year thereafter, and supplementing the quote with an injunction to his students that they ask themselves, in the stillest hours of their nights, whether they themselves would die if writing were denied to them, adding that if they should come to the conclusion their own answer to this question was "no" then it would be "no bad thing" for the world to lose their attempts at fiction. It's true to say that I was myself a creative writing lecturer when I read this passage in *Barley Patch*, which offers some rationale for why I might have seen in this narration a bolt of my own inner being, but the narrator's pedagogic reflection is immediately folded up by an account of a

---

1   Gerald Murnane, *Barley Patch* (Artarmon, NSW: Giramondo, 2009), 3. All subsequent references are to this edition and appear in parentheses in the text.

"bustling afternoon" years later in his life where, without even consciously reflecting on the exchange between Rilke and the young poet Franz Xaver Kappus, the narrator discovers he desires not only to cease his fiction writing, but then stakes even the narrative he is presently generating on the answering of another, related question: *Why had he written?* From this provocation, the narrator looks back on the origin of his works – some eight or so single-authored books of fiction, and some thirty years' worth of unpublished material stored in filing cabinets – and begins his answer by expressing a long held antipathy to what is commonly called "imagination".

How can a writer who is only just beginning to "emerge" into the world of fiction-for-publication recognise his or herself in a narrator looking back over a long life in letters, contemplating the reasons for extinguishing and then reviving his narrative energies? The question is a naive one, in some ways, since fiction does not rely on a biographical facsimile between reader and narrator for the registering of its effect – but there was something seductive about this apparently dissatisfied, older man's reflections. It somehow resembled a pleasing projection of the ideal author-to-be, who has maintained, lost and regained his capacity to write; who has become exhausted and found himself incomplete in his work, and has returned to the practice by looking back with a final and dwindling sense of desire to recreate and be revised in words and pages, to create some new meaning for his own experiences as author, and to reflect with an artistic faithfulness on the history of the body of work attached to the author who is this narrator's creator.

It is true that at a fundamental level, Murnane's narrator, like Murnane as author, represents a sustained and accomplished record of publication – a writer whose fiction is admired by a discriminating few, while remaining heroically uncorrupted by the stain of celebrity or commercial appeal. A writer's writer, read chiefly by writers the way contemporary poetry is read only by other poets. The intensity of the experience of recognition was no doubt lent a charge of ecstasy out of sheer admiration for this conception of the incorrigible author, and what this author's trodden path might offer a young writer dreaming of some romantic fantasy of the writing life ahead – but the response I felt in reading Murnane for the first time was about more than seeing an ideal future self in the mythology of the Murnanian narrator's account of the writerly life. It was not simply an admiration or envy of style either, though Murnane's monologic metaphysical narratives can swallow readers whole in their concentric technical obsessiveness. Reading, as some would have it, is essentially a kind of writing, and writers are readers whose eyes are trained for ways of being to be borrowed – but there was something about the recognition I felt in encountering Murnane's narrator that was categorically deeper than the usual identification of a grammatical dynamic or technical ingeniousness.

To explain this sense of depth it may be necessary to address an intersection between the subjective and the sociocultural which is of some significance to the above dialectic between master and apprentice. For the "developing" Australian fiction writer who aspires even remotely to the level of the "serious" writer – to use a Murnanian term I was not familiar with when I first encountered *Barley Patch* – it is difficult to remain unsullied by the mythology that serious authors ought to be walking encyclopaedias of high culture, whose every sentence ought at least to glimmer with an effortlessly referential signalling of the author's breadth and depth of reading. Where a great American author, a Fitzgerald, for instance, might advise an apprentice writer that "a good style simply doesn't form unless you absorb half a dozen top-flight authors every year", a learned Australian author, a Clive James for instance, recognising that Australians, being born to a kind of nowhere, and therefore at home only in the dream of a global culture, might advise that an apprentice writer ought to learn entire novels by rote in order to pay their dues. In his much maligned almanac on the humanities, *Cultural Amnesia*, James suggests that the young writer should memorise both *The Great Gatsby* and *Tender Is the Night*, in order to understand where Fitzgerald was coming from. In the same collection, James suggests that any serious critic will speak at least three Romance languages, and anyone capable of confusing obscure mythological characters ought to be categorised as having "read almost nothing". It might be unfair to use poor Clive to make this case for an inferiority complex, especially using a work that is itself an address to the student of culture as my evidence, but that particular work was one I'd read only recently before I first came around to Murnane's fiction in *Barley Patch*, and the aphoristic account James gives of the humanities and the serious student's duty to cultural memory was one I could not square easily with my own inadequacies of knowledge and my desire to write.

Had I read with even a whiff of the diligence James recommends in *Cultural Amnesia*, I would have been able to make the case about an Australian sense of cultural insecurity driving young writers to consume every available canonical artefact without leaving the topic of Murnane's work at all. As I'd come to discover many years after my first encounter with *Barley Patch*, Murnane, too, was once in the thrall of this cultural imperative to arm oneself against the charge of an innate parochial culturelessness. As Murnane puts it in his essay "In Praise of the Long Sentence":

> For much of my life, I felt an obligation to "keep up" with what was being published in other countries, as though having been born a fourth-generation Australian ... had made me, by definition, a tailender or an also-ran in an interminable race for some such vague prize as to be called well read or up to date in literary matters.[2]

---

2   Gerald Murnane, "In Praise of the Long Sentence", *Meanjin Quarterly* 75, no. 1 (2016), 56.

Beginning the essay with this confession, Murnane then provides an anecdote about coming across a review of Thomas Pynchon's *Vineland* by the critic Frank Kermode in a copy of the *London Review of Books*, in which Kermode apparently demonstrates Pynchon's love of long sentences by supplying a large example from the novel which Murnane also supplies, abridged, in his essay. After reading this example of Pynchon's work, Murnane reports putting the review down and immediately writing a letter to the editors of the *London Review of Books* explaining that Kermode's example of Pynchon's long sentences is in fact "a sentence of sixty-six words followed by a comma and then a sequence of clauses and phrases that is neither part of the sentence preceding it nor a sentence in itself".[3] The short letter to the editors was published in full in the following issue of the *London Review of Books*, and Murnane "dropped out of the race mentioned above", being satisfactorily convinced that there was nothing worthwhile to be won in the running.

"In Praise of the Long Sentence" reveals Murnane's Wittgensteinian belief in the capacity for the sentence to generate more meaning than any other syntactical arrangement: "a sentence is the natural repository of meaning while a non-sentence is able to contain only a rudimentary sort of meaning".[4] But anyone who had read the opening pages of *Barley Patch* and supposed the narrator they encountered there to share sentiments about reading and writing with his author would likely conclude, without reference to the above account of Murnane's having been disillusioned by reading Kermode on Pynchon, that the author felt no shame in having failed to read and retain every great book ever written.

Having begun his reflection on a life of fiction by attending to the question "Why had I written?" (3), Murnane's *Barley Patch* narrator proceeds to describe his limitations as both reader and writer, particularly in relation to the claims of "voraciousness" made by many "writers of novels, short stories or poetry" (5-6). Murnane's narrator describes himself, in contrast, as an "erratic" reader, not only because he "failed to read many of the books most admired by readers and writers of my generation" but also because much of what he read he was soon to forget, and moreover, that which he managed to retain is largely restricted to a few short sections and passages from books of little or no literary significance (6). In this confession of his limitations as a reader, there is no hint of embarrassment for Murnane's narrator, who explains that in his experience "[a] person who claims to remember having read one or another book is seldom able to quote from memory even one sentence from the text" (7). Of greater significance to Murnane's narrator is the memory any given reader has of part of the experience of having read

---

3   Murnane, "In Praise of the Long Sentence", 56.
4   Murnane, "In Praise of the Long Sentence", 58.

one or another book. The narrator reports that after having read some thousand books between 1960 and 1990, he now discovers, in the paragraphs that follow the discussion of the detailing of his deficiencies and limitations, that of the mere twenty or so books that have left any lasting impression on him from these thousand recorded titles, he can recall only eleven. To be certain of this, he pauses between paragraphs for two days, during which time no further titles come to mind. Discovering such an absence, the narrator next describes a decision he made not long before deciding to give up writing sentences. The decision he made was to cease reading any book "of a sort that could be called literature", and confine his reading only to those few books that he had never forgotten. It is this decision that perhaps leads to his next decision to stop writing altogether and he soon comes to the resolve that he will evermore only concern himself "with those mental entities" that came upon him while he read or wrote. He has decided that the contents of his own mind, where the "essence of all my reading and my writing" reside, are enough (8).

For the apprentice writer, Murnane's narrator's deconstruction of the mythological image of the serious writer as an ambulatory encyclopaedia internalising libraries of literary data points might offer an unburdening of existential proportions, not least because it follows directly from the narrator's admission that he is bereft of "imagination", a capacity typically understood to be an essential talent for fiction writers. Having explained in an early passage his ever-growing distaste for the categories "short story" and "novel" – most readers and publishers apparently believing the narrator's works belonged in one or the other genre – Murnane's *Barley Patch* narrator next describes his antipathy towards the "antiquated" assumption that the writing of fiction is essentially an expression of "imagination", explaining, "Long before I stopped writing, I had come to understand that I had never created any character or imagined any plot. My preferred way of summing up my deficiencies was simply to say that I had no imagination" (5).

This "shortcoming" is again one which the narrator is not the least embarrassed to admit – there is even the suggestion in the narrator's assertions of his lack of imagination and his aversion to the words "create, creative, imagine and imaginary" that there is something virtuous in his inability to indulge in imaginative fancy. The narrator explains that in the works of those contemporary fiction writers who are most praised for their prodigious imaginations there was often little cause for envy to be found and much "faulty writing" in their publications. As Murnane the essayist dismissed the race for high culture consumption by way of Kermode's ignorance of the sentence, Murnane's narrator in *Barley Patch* dismisses the canon, the contemporary and in some sense the act of writing itself in the book's opening pages, coming back to the job only, perhaps, to answer why he bothered to begin in the first place.

The sheer permissiveness Murnane's narrator's discussion of his own authorial limitations presented to me as an apprentice writer was doubtless part of the passionate reaction I felt at first encountering *Barley Patch*. As a reflection of Murnane's own relationship to reading and writing, his narrator's assertions of his limitations offered me permission to feel unashamed of my inattentiveness to many a great work of literature, and more essentially, my wasteland of an imagination. Like Murnane's narrator, my own attempts at fiction had produced no plots, and I recognised none of the "personages" I'd sketched out in my own work as "characters" to be spoken about as though they were living beings with feelings and motives and intentions existing somewhere outside the facts assigned to them by the sentences on the pages I'd written. Reading Murnane's narrator's antipathies reminded me that I'd long ago come to see this kind of writing as a vain and unappealing waste of the relationship between readers and texts.

When I first began to read for myself, not long after I'd realised that there was some single intelligence behind the creation of books, and that this intelligence belonged to a person known as a writer, and that this act of creation was a job writers were paid to perform, novels served as a means of avoiding my immense fear of the night, and the nightmares inhabiting the dark. There were no smartphones or tablet devices to distract the mind back then, and so I turned to the tattered and worn titles of my stepfather's book collection. Fantasy, for the most part, made up the supply – with each novel more alike than the last: an elf, a dwarf, and a man with a sword and a romance subplot. One series, whose name I have long since forgotten, followed a band of wizard-folk who waged a guerrilla war to save their lands from an evil sorcerer. For the most part, they camped out in the forest and cooked skinned rabbits over an open fire, and made stews in pots with salted meats, while the bearded old wizard argued with his witch-wife, their bickering inevitably ending with the wizard sighing and saying "Yes, dear" while the companions smirked knowing smiles. For a child of a broken home, who had no reason to disbelieve the scripture teachers who said that we would not see our parents in heaven if they failed to uphold the sanctity of marriage, these fictional marital disputes were a torturous distraction.

On these endless nights with the strange square device of the paperback pressed into the pillow, body bent over it like some ascetic yogi frozen in meditative prayer, I traced the thin shapes of the letters on the page and felt the images of the novel's story running through my mind like a film, while I edited these images into a secondary story, on the fly; one in which I inserted myself into the narrative and changed its destiny. At the campsites, with the rabbits roasting on their ad hoc spits, I'd enter from the dark of the woods, a powerful wizard myself, and admonish the magical married couple for their petty bickering. "The world is at war!" I'd screech at them both with a booming voice, eyes glowering with a great wizard's obvious potency. "Can't you see your real enemy is out there – not here between each other!"

When the writer of this series of novels, the title of which I have long ago forgotten, eventually revealed that he had co-written the books with his wife, adding her name to the cover of all subsequent releases, I felt an enormous sense of betrayal. All this time, the marital tensions of these magical characters had been a surrogate for the supposedly real relationship of the author and his wife. It had all been a fake, a meaningless device! To discover such cheap self-insertions passed off as genuine fantasy disgusted this young reader, and I turned my back forever on the kind of fiction that Murnane calls "film-script" fiction, that vein of fiction that is solely aimed at creating in the mind of its readers a certain series of imaginary scenes. It was a kind of sin, I decided, to bear false witness, even in a world of pure imagination.

By the time I'd encountered *Barley Patch*'s narrator, two decades after having discovered the disingenuous nature of fantasy novelists, I'd finally managed to join the ranks of those who could be said to have been paid for the creation of a work of fiction. Having held to my childhood ideal about the distinction between "film-script" fiction and what I was yet to discover that Murnane sometimes describes as "meditative" or "true" fiction, I'd produced a work that was sometimes difficult to explain, and I often felt very insecure about describing it to people who might ask "What is your book about?" or "Is this a true story?". Murnane as author and his narrator seemed to be supplying, in the opening pages of *Barley Patch*, an authority for the approach I had taken, and articulated in the process what I had forgotten about my own origins as a writer of fiction. As significant as this offering from master to apprentice might have been, I suspect that this alone does not adequately account for the passionate intensity of revelatory force that overcame me when I first read those opening pages of *Barley Patch*, though I could not at the time have given any further explanation for the effect of this reading experience than to say, as I stood in my editor's office, that Murnane and I seemed to me to be related in some ineffable sense.

However I might have expected my editor to respond to this report of "reading myself" in the work of a master writer, I can see now that I should have anticipated how repulsive such a claim sounds. My editor rose from behind his desk, shaking his silver-haired head with a blushing incredulity, ushering me out the door, saying, "No, no, no! Murnane is nothing like you, nothing like you at all!" When we were out in the hall, my editor placed a hand on my shoulder and said with a tone of panic, "Murnane is what you might call a monastic writer! Nothing like your thing! You're more of a social type, more focused on … awkward encounters and strange interactions!" It took me some time to register this reading, and the hallway was very narrow, but my editor went on, guiding me away from his office, "Listen, I'll tell you the secret of Murnane's writing – so you understand what I mean. The secret is resonant recursions!" At this point, smooth as a magician, my editor reached down to snatch up a copy of *A Million Windows* (2014), which was by then the latest of Murnane's books to be published, copies of which happened to be stacked on a desk just beyond the hall. "Look here", the editor said, pointing to an image of a lit window inside a large house on the front cover of the book:

> In this work there is a section where the narrator describes "a house of two or three storeys, with the setting sun reflecting in a window like drops of golden oil", but the narrative itself is being written by the narrator in the fiction of the narrative, and the house is a work of fiction in the fictional world of the narrator's mind. Now, that image of golden drops in the window is presented in such a way by this narrator, by a narrator remembering an image of a window lit like hot oil, that by the time the reader has read it, the image is overlaid in their mind, refracted like an image bouncing between mirrors, and it is as if they have seen it again and again, a forced persistence of memory, and so they see it blaze in their mental landscape, that golden oil, like a dream lantern of their own inner life.

With that, my editor thrust the book into my hands and rushed back into his office and this time shut the door.

To begin with, I was deeply troubled by this irrefutable analysis of the technical distinctions between my own budding attempts at fiction and the resonant elegance my editor had identified in Murnane's work. There seemed to me to be some essential quality in the way Murnane worked, a kind of freedom to respond to the world on the author's terms, which I was desperate to acquire, and any apparent distinction between us threatened the likelihood of this acquisition. Exacerbating this fear was an understanding of Australian literature I'd recently acquired from an important Australian literary critic, who argued for the existence of two distinct traditions at the centre of Australian literature – the restrained, minimalist aesthetic exhibited by writers like Helen Garner, or Antigone Kefala, and the Baroque, ornate, ecstatistician's approach demonstrated most evidently in Patrick White – both traditions stemming from the deterritorialised loss at the heart of Australia's colonial culture. Whether or not this was true I had no means of determining, having, at the time, only a rudimentary knowledge of Australian literature. In hindsight, this theory was something I followed more by instinct than by examination. But believe in it I did, and so was faced with a series of demoralising data points. First, there were two distinct schools of Australian literature. Second, Murnane belonged to the camp of austerity. Third, I was myself a social ecstatitician. Therefore, this syllogistic thinking brought me to conclude, Murnane's path along the yellow road of fiction was not one I could take and remain a singular, coherent entity.

It was only a chance discovery, much later in my writing life, which showed me how utterly faulty was the mental processing described above. Uncovering a pile of books beneath the bed, many years after first encountering Murnane's work, I located a collection with a drawing of a racehorse on the cover, set against a map of towns with names that seemed to be the product of a kind of dream-sense: Kecskemet, Nagykoros, Jaszkaeajeno, etc.[5] Curious, I opened the book and discovered in the contents section that the second essay in the collection was on the subject of Jack Kerouac. I turned the book back to its cover, having neglected to read the author on first inspection, and cringed to discover this book was written by Gerald Murnane. Surely, one of our nation's most austere, monastic writers would show little mercy to the excesses of style which Kerouac had committed in his careening career of spontaneous bop-prosody. Unsurprisingly to those in the know, the reality of the essay could not have been further from the savaging I'd expected – but the effect upon me was no less intense: Murnane, in reading Kerouac, had experienced an apparently equal mental emancipation as a writer as I had felt in first reading the opening pages of *Barley Patch*. Murnane, I read in this collection, described reading *On the Road* in these terms:

> The book was like a blow to the head that wipes out all memory of the recent past. For six months after I first read it I could hardly remember the person I had been beforehand. For six months I believed I had all the space I needed. My own personal space, a fit setting for whatever I wanted to do, was all around me wherever I looked … my space coincided at last with the place that was called the real world. But the world was much wider than most people suspected. I saw this because I saw as the author of *On the Road* saw. Other people saw the same streets of the same Melbourne that had always surrounded them. I saw the surfaces of those streets cracking open and broad avenues rising to view. Other people saw the same maps of Australia or America. I saw the coloured pages swelling like flower buds and new, blank maps unfolding like petals. (19)

I read this passage and felt as though a sheet of ice falling by my feet had revealed a glacier the size of Gippsland to have me surrounded. The passage I've quoted above revealed not only an affinity between Murnane and a declared writer of the ecstatic, but the writing itself, the means in which this affinity was declared, was so obviously

---

5   Gerald Murnane, *Invisible Yet Enduring Lilacs* (Artarmon, NSW: Giramondo, 2005). All subsequent references are to this edition and appear in parentheses in the text.

in the style of someone who could see the shimmering potency lying latent in the apparently ordinary surfaces of the world.

In the light of this revelation, I flung the book down on my bed, and marched out into the hall, pacing back and forth, slowly rearranging the furniture of my mental space so Murnane would be seated on the other side of the room, with all the other ornate elaborators, as far from the rigid minimalists as I could place him. Had I continued reading the essay rather than succumb to my usual flaring of chemical imbalances, I may have been able to acquire a more interesting view of the distinctions between Murnane and certain literary traditions and expectations.

Towards the end of the essay on "Kerouac in Bendigo", not that I would bother to discover it until many years hence, Murnane recounts his readings of certain Kerouacian biographies, revealing "what mattered much more" to him about the American's life was the following: "I learned that Jack Kerouac, as a boy of twelve, and about ten years before I ran my first race on the lounge-room rug, rolled fields of marble-racehorses across the linoleum of his bedroom in Lowell, Massachusetts" (21). Proceeding from this detail is a discussion of the mutual "dream-racing" that Murnane and his American counterpart performed in their formative years. This information fascinated me, not merely because I found the focus of it to be typical of Murnane's faithful devotion to those details of the external world that most sing to the author's eye, but because my father, not many years younger than Murnane, would often talk of performing just such "dream-racing", and had likewise cultivated a substantial collection of marbles for just such a purpose – marbles which he had gifted to me many decades ago.

Had I read on, and encountered this aspect of Murnane's affinity for Kerouac rather than tossing the book aside to formulate and fulminate along the floorboards of the hall outside my room, I may have allowed the association between Murnane and my father's mutual predilection for dream-racing to percolate, and perhaps to conjure a particular memory. The memory I have in mind, as I sit and write this essay, is of my father calling me excitedly into the bathroom of our house in Granville, to observe some apparently incredible sight. The tiles of this bathroom, rose-pink squares about the size of slices of bread, had been steadily falling from the western-most wall for many years, and on each vacated square of the wall the tiles had left patterns and shapes where the evaporated glue had eaten into the asbestos. My father put his hand on my shoulder as I shuffled into the room and pointed to these strange vestigial shadow-shapes, and I looked at him from the corner of my eye, feeling a deep suspicion that I must quickly interpret what it was that he was hoping would be apparent. "Do you see it?" he asked. I looked quickly back at the stains on the wall. "That one, there!" he said, indicating one particular section. "Those pictures in the shapes!" he said. "Look – an Indian hunting a buffalo! You can see the spear raised above his head," he said of his favourite blot. Another looked somewhat like a seahorse wrapped in weed, while another was a vague flight of gulls coasting before the sunset.

Had I resisted the impulsive call to toss aside *Invisible Yet Enduring Lilacs* and go pacing around the hall in a fugue-like state of self-indulgence, I might have been able to connect this chain of associations leading from Murnane to Kerouac to my father, and thereby have discovered a means of contrasting my own familial predilection for passionate invention against Murnane's most recent injunction in *Border Districts* (2017) to maintain the purity of a guarded eye. Passion, I think, is an antithesis to this idea: I have read passion defined by a French poet as the perception of an infinitude inside a finite thing. That is, in some sense, to see what is not there. I suspect I know why we ought to fear the unbound eye, and why I might wish to exorcise it from my own practice.

As a child I was inflicted with what I have heard others call night terrors, dreams in which I lay paralysed in fright, as featureless shadow men pressed their ink-black faces against the bedroom window, their sucking lipless mouths threatening to steal me into an infernal plain so fearful, I would wake screaming and shuddering in shock and sweat, the flat, impassive eye-less glare of these devils still glowing ether-black inside my mind like bloodied vapour in the air. These nightmare beings so filled me with a horror of sleeping that I was forced to devise a kind of mystic ritual against the night. I'd lie in bed and picture one of these demon beings hovering in the air, then I would encase him in a makeshift prison: a golden orb the size of a coffin, or a concrete tomb without windows or doors. Around that I would place some other larger confinement, an immense silver dome, or some solid biosphere of forged iron. From here I would increase the scale: the planet that this original confinement was located on would need itself to be fully contained, and that planetary encasing would then need to be trapped in some colossal, intergalactic holding. Each prison would require another, greater prison, and this process would need to be endlessly repeated, prisons within prisons, interdimensional tombs inside the eyes of giants swallowed by solar-storms of unfathomable ice and stone within an atom of another dimension, caught in the solid yolk of a bronze egg frozen in a diamond case larger than an immeasurable sun, and on and on, until the sky outside, in the real world, would begin to lighten, and I could pass to sleep in the safe hours between dawn and breakfast, where demons have no foothold on our earth. Should I, at any time during this generative ritual of ever increasing imaginative feats, accidentally recall the original spectre of the demon creature in my mind's eye, then the exercise would fail, and I would scramble to place the escaped spirit back into a new and original restraint, or else face the villain's redoubled wrath.

I performed this complex ritual every night for many years, and I have long suspected that this activity is the reason I was drawn to the idea of writing, seduced by the promise of redemptive plains to be found in mental interiors. It was only once I was old enough to read unassisted that I was able to replace this tiresome practice of mental rapture with the act of training my eyes on the tight hermetic lines made by sentences in the pages of books.

If I were to have finished reading Murnane's essay on Kerouac, and from there made these simple connecting associations, I may have reached a position here, in these lines, from which it would be possible to interpret the pledge to explain a resolution with which the Goroke-based author begins his latest, and apparently final, work of fiction: "Two months ago, when I first arrived in this township just short of the border, I resolved to guard my eyes, and I could not think of going on with this piece of writing unless I were to explain how I came by that odd expression".[6] I may have suspected, had I only made the right connections, that in these opening lines, Murnane is offering us his first principles of fiction, at least fiction of a certain kind – what the author has elsewhere called "compound fiction". Such compounded fiction requires a certain ecstasy of limitation, an indulgence of faithful discipline – because that is what separates a commitment to the actual – a heralding intensity of "self-being" residing within things themselves – from the passionate failure of imagination which cannot distinguish the madness of simple fancy from the accumulative truth of a complex fiction.

Had I made this connection between Kerouac and Murnane and recognised this generative potential of an ecstatic limitation, I might have come to see that my original encounter with Murnane's narrator in *Barley Patch* had the intense effect of an existential awakening precisely because there is something existentially potent about the limitations the narrator deploys at the outset of the book. In asserting his own limitations as reader and writer, Murnane's narrator refuses the "bad faith" of the over-identified author of Australian letters and negates his way into a position of aesthetic and subjective freedom. The mythology of what an Australian author ought to be, what fiction itself ought to be, is refused in the opening paragraphs of that book by a narrator who will not allow the transcendent potential of his mind to be limited by the facticity of the cultural expectations which are associated with his role as author in a specific time and place. This freeing and generative potential of limitation is a recurring theme in much of Murnane's later work – with *Border Districts* a veritable manifesto for the limitations as the platonic first-cause of the author's entire body of work. The call to guard the eye a second seeing of the need to defend oneself from the intoxicating infinitude of being-in-the-world which threatens to devour the freedom of the observer in its overwhelming limitlessness.

---

6   Gerald Murnane, *Border Districts* (Artarmon, NSW: Giramondo, 2017), 1.

In a recent interview with ABC's *7.30*, Murnane-as-author looks directly into the camera and declares that "A person can reveal more about themselves by saying what they've never done, than by saying what they've done". Murnane then provides a brief catalogue of some of the things he has never done:

> I've never been in an aeroplane. I've never been in an ocean-going vessel. I've never voluntarily immersed myself in the ocean. I've never voluntarily gone into an art gallery. I can't remember watching television or listening to the radio for more than twenty minutes … I used to say I've never worn sunglasses, but I've developed cataracts and I had to wear sunglasses for a little while.[7]

There is a subtle delight on Murnane's face as he provides this list of negations, perhaps because the negative facts he asserts about himself in the persona of "serious fiction" writer are demonstrations of a determination to define oneself against an overwhelming cultural imperative to locate the meaning of life in our place and time with these very signs and symbols – *who is it that does not travel by plane? What madman will not wear sunglasses? What kind of Australian does not voluntarily immerse themselves in the sea?* These non-facts are presented as bold assertions of being-in-itself; they are indigestible facts for a larger cultural expectation about what one must be in this world, and Murnane's smile is his defiance of this consuming expectation.

Another interview appeared online in 2017. It was put together by my editor, the silver-haired man who first introduced me to Murnane's publications. It sees the author standing in a windy graveyard before a rusted barbwire fence, behind which stretches the pale gold of the level plains leading to a line of trees in the distance. Standing beside the author, to the left of the frame, is my editor, who looks strange with his silver hair enclosed in a black beanie, and he is nodding his head slightly as Murnane-as-author points to something off camera. The author eventually explains their surroundings in the following terms:

> We're standing at what was for most of my life the furthest horizon, the furthest distant place of my mental universe … I turned my back on the coast for most of my boyhood and looked inland towards the old original Western District, the home of the squatters, and even beyond that there was a mysterious land further west, and here I am now. It took me all of my life to get here.[8]

---

[7] *7.30*, "The Australian Writer Who Could Be the Next Nobel Prize Winner" (ABC TV, 7 May 2018).

[8] Gerald Murnane and Ivor Indyk, "Mental Places: A Conversation with Gerald Murnane", (Artarmon, NSW: Giramondo, 2016). https://www.youtube.com/watch?v=5PqzX4TC1BE.

For Murnane as author, the mental landscape is not some transcendental plain in which anything is possible, it is an image which at some demarcation in interior fact comes to an end, and goes no further. This is the discovery of Murnane's phenomenological examination of ontology in his body of work, and he has reached this distant goal through the sheer refusal of turning his back, guarding in this way his ever-sensitive eye against an endless expanse of the world.

The ethical and moral meaning of Murnane's body of work is also, in my reading, an existential one. There is often a suggestion of solipsism in Murnane's work, in his guarded interiors, but it is also the case that Murnane's many narrators all strive to be seen by some ideal other. Immutably locked out of the world of his ideal reader, Murnane's narrators constantly measure their worth as image-beings by how deserving they are of some other's contemplation. In the early pages of *Barley Patch*, Murnane's narrator describes his desire to be "daydreamed" about by some ideal female companion whose presence he feels about him whenever he is alone. This "image-companion" holds the one secret which the narrator cannot access for all his recursive meditation – in Sartre's terms this secret is "the secret of what I am".[9]

As the reader will know, a conference was held in Murnane's home town of Goroke in December 2017, and several scholars, critics and assorted other readers assembled to comment on the meaning of the master's body of work. When asked at the conference by a white-haired professor how it was that he had poured so much imagery into the plains and yet, as we might observe by looking out the window of the conference room, the plains remain largely empty, Murnane explained this "mere contradiction" with a conception of his inner-imaginary in terms not unlike these: "Within a house on the plains, there is a man downstairs in a large room reading a book that is part of a long series of books. A woman is there too, and she is reading the same series, but she is reading so intently that she has not noticed the man's arrival".[10]

"How's that for an answer?" Murnane asked the professor.

For Murnane-as-author, the immutable expanse of the real is no contradiction to a rich interior plain. The greater triumph of having written is not some measurable effect on the world outside the text – to change the world-in-itself is an operation outside the scope of fiction and its sublimating consolations. It is enough for the author to find himself in the same room, even unnoticed, by an ideal other to whom one has given faithfully of himself to be read. For this alone we should write, must write, have written. It is for this the writer, both apprentice and master, asks of themselves Rilke's fatal question in the stillness of their nights.

---

9   Jean-Paul Sartre, *Being and Nothingness* (1956; London: Routledge, 2003), 364.
10 See http://www.formsofworldliterature.com/another-world-one-gerald-murnanes-fiction/

References

Murnane, Gerald. *Border Districts*. Artarmon, NSW: Giramondo, 2017.
——. "In Praise of the Long Sentence". *Meanjin Quarterly* 75, no. 1 (2016): 56–65.
——. *A Million Windows*. Artarmon, NSW: Giramondo, 2014.
——. *Barley Patch*. Artarmon, NSW: Giramondo, 2009.
——. *Invisible Yet Enduring Lilacs*. Artarmon, NSW: Giramondo, 2005.
Murnane, Gerald and Ivor Indyk. "Mental Places: A Conversation with Gerald Murnane".
    Artarmon, NSW: Giramondo, 2016. https://www.youtube.com/watch?v=5PqzX4TC1BE.
Sartre, Jean-Paul. *Being and Nothingness*. (1956) London: Routledge, 2003.

3
Truth, Fiction and True Fiction

Shannon Burns

> Perhaps each of us is driven most urgently not by his wanting to be the subject of some or another biography and not even by his wanting to be the author of some or another memorable volume but by his wanting to grasp the paradox that has exercised him during much of his lifetime: by his wanting to understand how the so-called actual and the so-called possible – what he did and what he only dreamed of doing – come finally to be indistinguishable in the sort of text that we call true fiction.[1]

The novels and collections of fiction that represent Gerald Murnane's first major period of writing and publishing (1974-95) portray Murnane-like personages and narrators. Clement Killeaton's boyhood in *Tamarisk Row* (1974) mirrors Murnane's experiences in Bendigo as a child; Adrian Shard's inner life in *A Lifetime on Clouds* (1976) approximates Murnane's adolescent awkwardness and obsessive fantasies; the partial *Künstlerromane* of several Murnane-like writers in *Landscape with Landscape* (1985) are drawn from their author's experiences in his late teens, then as a bachelor in his twenties and as a husband and father; *Inland* (1988) draws from his epiphanic discovery of Hungarian writer Gyula Illyés' *Puszták népe* (*People of the Puszta*) – a book that had a deep and strange impact on Murnane, stimulating a literal and literary haunting – combined with childhood experiences (and, perhaps, a curious but chaste relationship with his female editor at Heinemann);[2] and the stories in *Velvet Waters* (1990) and *Emerald Blue* (1995) appear to be increasingly personal and revealing, despite the distancing devices that Murnane employs, which serve to deter readerly presumptuousness. Murnane has teased readers with a series of enduring images and motifs (two-storey buildings, blue and gold

---

1 Gerald Murnane, *A Million Windows* (Artarmon, NSW: Giramondo, 2014).
2 See Mark Byron's essay in this collection.

coloured reflections, flat grasslands, horseraces, nesting areas, etc.) and this tendency has only intensified since the later phase of his writing career began, with the publication of *Barley Patch* in 2009.

Throughout both of these periods, Murnane has given the impression in interviews, essays and the published work itself that his fiction is fundamentally "true" in partly aesthetic, partly autobiographical (and therefore subjective) and partly factual ways. Some critics have been reluctant to emphasise the autobiographical elements of Murnane's work, preferring, on the whole, to mark strong distinctions between the flesh-and-blood Murnane, his various narrators and protagonists, and the implied author of his works. In this, they take their cues from Murnane's own highly developed semanticism, which seems to privilege literal denotation over connotative or associative constructions of meaning or modes of interpretation. Other critics – mostly non-academic – have claimed that Murnane's fiction is fundamentally and essentially autobiographical, and treated it as such.

Murnane's narrators are always hesitant to call their reports "true" in the ordinary, mundane sense of the word, and the configuration of each narrative – how the chief narrator connects and sequences the images and personages in each story – represents the unique quality of each fiction more than their literal truth-status. But my work on a literary biography of Murnane has so far revealed that the fiction is far from superficially autobiographical; indeed, the boundary between Murnane's fiction and his life is extraordinarily fluid. After spending a great deal of time reading through materials in his archives and interviewing the author, I've come to believe that the distancing devices that Murnane uses (such as recursiveness, indirectness, and plain reportage stripped of emotive language), which function as cues and cautions against simplistic identification or careless attribution, obscure the vitally confessional and truthful nature of Murnane's fiction.

Those fictions are non-linear and idiosyncratically constructed. Murnane's archives show that he spends much time considering the pattern of his narratives, following affective and associative connections between each episode, and searching for a way to make the many parts resolve into a meaningful, and logical, narrative shape. He uses lists, diagrams, maps and other visual cues until he settles on a satisfying pattern, and then he adjusts that pattern again in the process of writing and redrafting (often by following an unexpected narrative thread, or while attempting to regather lost momentum). A literary biography of Murnane, by contrast, is more likely to be chronological, moving from A>B>C in a regular sequence, identifying resonant connections between the life and the fiction in a fairly uncomplicated fashion.

Tamarisk Row has often been characterised as a fictionalised autobiography, yet its faithfulness to Murnane's childhood experiences is difficult to assess, not least because it is often impossible to distinguish between events that occur inside the child-protagonist's mind and events that occur in the world of the novel. The line between reality and fantasy *within the text* is already unsettled. Given this disorienting complication, any attempt to then reliably parse "real life" autobiographical content seems hopeless. Yet, despite significant uncertainties around what is *really happening* in the fictional world of *Tamarisk Row*, the book remains autobiographical in deeper ways, because when *Tamarisk Row* diverges from historical truth it often, according to Murnane, reports an authentic internal truth or fantasy.

This balancing of material and factual experience against internal or imagined experience is a constant and, in my judgement, biographically noteworthy feature of Murnane's life – particularly his literary life. Importantly, Murnane insists that, to him, mental events are as significant as material events, and that they serve to comprise his true self. The autobiographical quality of his fiction is, therefore, twofold: instead of a hybrid of fact and fiction, it is a hybrid of material and inner – or ideal – truths. And the same goes for Murnane's "real" life. A biography, therefore, must attempt to take into account imagined and material experiences to an unusual degree.

As I questioned Murnane about his life in our first encounter in early November 2014, at his home in Goroke, he frequently pointed to episodes in his fiction, from *Tamarisk Row* onwards. I found this surprising at first, given his occasionally forceful reluctance to grant his fiction autobiographical status. When I asked him about the balance of fact and pure, plot-serving invention in his work, he said: "The invented parts are not the deepest parts of the stories. I invent a way of life, an occupation, even a domicile, for the purposes of the shape of the fiction. Quite often I made the narrator or protagonist single. I've written very little about married life".

If married, Murnane's fictional personages typically have fewer children than he; they often have fewer or no siblings (whereas Murnane had two younger brothers and a younger sister); and if they are writers they are almost always unpublished or little known. But some of the fiction is more inventive than the rest. According to Murnane, *Landscape with Landscape*'s "A Quieter Place than Clun" and the title pieces of *Velvet Waters* and *Emerald Blue* feature comparatively extensive inventions – the latter two partly due to formal necessity, in order to give the broader collection a meaningful shape or pattern. And, for the most part, the invented elements of those stories are obvious enough when compared to the basic facts of Murnane's life – which is helpful from a biographer's perspective.

In Philip Tyndall's documentary *Words and Silk* (1989), which explores Murnane's relationship with horseracing and his beliefs about writing, Murnane says, "[M]uch of my writing is about the lives I might have lived and the men I might have been". This holds for most of his fiction, but is complicated by Murnane's peculiar attitudes to reality and fantasy. In an interview with Ivor Indyk, he says, "I can say in all honesty and sincerity that I can't tell the difference between my fiction, my thinking about my fiction, and my life".[3] In my interviews with him Murnane extends this confession, or conceit, suggesting that the fictional personages who occupy his mind are almost as real to him as the flesh-and-blood people he engages with in his daily life. For Murnane, materiality plays second fiddle to presence, and corporeality is only one branch of reality.

In "The Breathing Author", Murnane writes: "I sometimes have the experience of seeing my fiction as an emblem of myself or an heraldic device representing myself or even as a large part of myself".[4] In that essay, Murnane insists that "he" is represented by and in his fiction to an uncommon extent and that he inhabits that fiction as readily and seriously as he inhabits the visible world – and I take it that Murnane is writing largely *as himself* in that essay.

"This is an interesting point", Murnane tells me: "I'm perfectly capable of writing 'as fictional fact' what for me was only a mental fiction, following on from a thought like, *What if I had asked so-and-so out? What would have happened?*" (It is revealing that Murnane uses a romantic example here; he seems to me to have an unusually intense romantic fantasy life.)

These speculative fictions are anchored in mental fantasies that are, in turn, connected to concrete experience. There are three layers of reality operating here, and they are as discrete as they are connected: the first is the real, as it seems to observers on the surface level of everyday, material experience and perception; the second is the real converted into fantasy in Murnane's mind, based on speculation; and the third is that fantasy transformed into so-called true fiction. The key seems to be that the fantasy undergoes a period of gestation in Murnane's mind – becoming a true inner experience before and while it's converted into fiction.

But perhaps this is an obscuring and convoluted way of considering the autobiographical dimensions of Murnane's fiction. A looser approach is possible, despite the author's cautions and contortions. When I asked Murnane's oldest friend, David Walton, his view of the connection between Murnane's real experiences and events reported in his books, he was surprised that readers might

---

3   Gerald Murnane and Ivor Indyk, "Mental Places: A Conversation with Gerald Murnane" (Artarmon, NSW: Giramondo, 2016). https://www.youtube.com/watch?v=5PqzX4TC1BE.
4   Gerald Murnane, "The Breathing Author", *Heat* no. 3 (new series) (2002), 24.

consider Murnane's books to be substantially fictional at all. "I don't know how you'd put a percentage on it", he said,

> but it seems mostly real to me. I mean he does create things in his mind. But no, no, no, most of it is real. I recognise a lot of events in the books. Life is strange enough that you don't have to make stuff up, really. He plays with it a bit and meshes a couple of events into one thing, but I'd say most of it is real.

Few scholars would be inclined to treat Walton's assessment as authoritative, but some readers might find it liberating.

According to Murnane, the essays collected in *Invisible Yet Enduring Lilacs* (2005) are factual for the most part, except for the title piece, which is substantially invented. This too offers some direction about how to distinguish between truth and invention in Murnane's work: his narrative method is to draw meaningful connections between seemingly unconnected events and images, and in "Invisible Yet Enduring Lilacs", in particular, the neatness of some of the connections stretches credulity.

In the later phase of Murnane's writing career he opts for subtler narrative ploys. From *Emerald Blue* onwards Murnane employs a literalist, reflective, recursive (and almost totally deadpan) narrative style. But Murnane's continuing conceit is his allegiance to what he calls true fiction, or a kind of fiction that draws its essence from an inner self. He signals the distinction between "true fiction" and a report of "mundane reality" in an important section of *Barley Patch*, which is worthy of close attention.

The events related by *Barley Patch*'s narrator occur in the early 1960s, when Murnane's fictional proxy is in his early twenties. He is having emotional difficulties, and decides to take part in a regular men's therapy group session. He tells the group that he spends all of his free time writing poetry or fiction and that his solitude may be preferable to acquiring a girlfriend or wife, given his literary ambitions. One of the members of the group seems to have read Freud and Jung and is familiar with modes of analysis common to psychology. As Murnane's narrator reports:

> The man used many technical terms. I understood him to be telling me that my trying to write poetry and prose fiction was no more than trying to find an imaginary girl-friend or wife. I understood from the demeanour of the other men in the group that they agreed with the man who used technical terms, even though most of them were unskilled in the use of such terms.[5]

---

5   Gerald Murnane, *Barley Patch* (Artarmon, NSW: Giramondo, 2009), 161. All subsequent references are to this edition and appear in parentheses in the text.

After this session, the young man decides to return to the group just once more, in order to "refute the claims of the man who used technical terms" and to "defend solitary males and bachelors against the wordy arguments of European theorists". But first the young man goes to visit his bachelor uncle, in the hope of gathering evidence for his refutation. According to the narrator:

> I told my uncle that he was fortunate to be a bachelor who could study bird books of an evening while his neighbours were dealing with their wives and children. My uncle then told me that he had for long feared he had been made sexually impotent by a kick that he had taken as a schoolboy. When he was ten years of age, so my uncle told me, he had been kicked viciously in the stones by a boy named Stanley Chambers. (164)

His uncle's confession is distressing, because it reduces what seemed to the narrator to be a principled and dignified life choice – bachelor solitude – to the status of sexual impotence or dysfunction, exactly as the members of the men's group had suggested.

The narrator then presents us with two possible subsequent events: in one the young man sticks to his guns and never goes back to the men's group; in the other, the young man goes back to the group and reports his uncle's confession, in the hope that "members of the group might repay my trust in them by suggesting how I might overcome some of my own fears" (163). The group disappoints him, however, with stock Freudian interpretations, and he never returns again.

The narrator clearly favours the first version, which is mediated, he says, by "a narrator of a work of fiction: a personage supposed by those readers to exist on the far side of their own minds for as long as they go on reading these pages" (162). The second version, we're informed, is provided for the benefit of lesser readers who confuse narrators with flesh-and-blood authors. The first truth is more consistent with Murnane's deeper values: trusting his own instincts and refusing to submit himself to the judgement of others or to fashionable ideas. The second passage is, I think, a more accurate version of events, yet it is the lesser truth, in Murnane's terms, because it conflicts with his ideal self.

Writing a biography of Murnane means grappling with these two core selves – the ideal and mundane – as well as their many splinter-selves: Murnane the child, student, seminarian, husband, father, teacher, epistolarian, public figure, racegoer and golfer, and all of the many distinct Murnane-like narrators and protagonists that occupy his fiction.

One of the joys of Murnane's work is the breadth of subjective responses it can produce. I often experience a strong emotional reaction, yet his literary archive shows that Murnane strips away emotive language as much as he strips away redundant adjectives. As a consequence, his fiction is ambiguously affecting, and that ambiguity is important. We might be cornered into reading Murnane's fiction in strictly literal ways, but the emotional response available to us is radically open-ended. This is because Murnane *never* tells us how to feel; and I think he gives us that freedom because he values it for himself. In Murnane's world, there is no such thing as wrong feeling.

I now have a reasonable sense of the intellectual, emotional, social and historical contexts that have influenced Murnane's writing; but, as far as *understanding* the fiction is concerned, it's vital to stress the *deliberateness* of Murnane's narrative strategies, not just because of their formal significance or aesthetic effects, but for how this deliberateness changes the meaning of the work and brings its autobiographical origins into doubt. Murnane's fiction consistently resists a direct connection with his life. The work of literary biography seeks to reveal significant information about the origin of the texts – how they were conceived and made – but, of course, it cannot reveal their meaning or serve to evaluate literary merit in an authoritative way.

A biographical focus *can* provide partial insights into the various impulses that have driven Murnane to write, however. As an example: much of Murnane's fiction is arranged around fantasies of intimacy with girls and women – erotic or otherwise – yet his narrators always encounter a blank spot, an explicit limit to knowledge and imagination, a blockage that separates *him* from *them*. The reason for this is partly biographical. Murnane rarely had the opportunity as a teenager to talk to girls who were not members of his family, and by his late teens he was, he says, too shy or terrified to approach them.

In his earliest unpublished attempt at a novel, "With Perished People", Murnane's stand-in, Eugene Brady – a nine-year-old boy who is tortured by curiosity about girls – recalls a powerful revelation, two or three years earlier, when he first paid conscious attention to a girl-cousin's exposed vagina as she urinated in front of him. His childish revelation is that girls and women appear to be "other" than him – their genitals are an outward sign of deeper difference – and they come to embody a mystery he desperately wants to encounter again. But, as Eugene sees it, a conspiracy of concealment – primarily directed by adults – thwarts his every effort to see a girl and compare himself with her. His sense of female otherness is thereby reinforced by strict controls and punishments that "grown-ups" employ against children's sexual curiosity, and in a Catholic child's case those controls and punishments extend into adulthood.

The thoughts or desires of girls and women typically elude Murnane's protagonists and narrators, and that inherent distance marks the production and reception of his fiction. Murnane's ideal reader is, in my view, feminine; in particular, she would embrace and reciprocate his peculiar methods of self-revelation. The narrator of *Barley Patch* is clear about the function of the feminine reader:

> The true account of my conception is simply told. Being no more than the conjectured author of this work of fiction, I can have come into existence only at the moment when a certain female personage who was reading these pages formed in her mind an image of the male personage who had written the pages with her in mind. (173)

The rest of us can only *mis*conceive the "conjectured author". (In biblical terms, the narrative seed is spilled and wasted on us.) Murnane's ideal correspondent is also female, as is the ideal biographer or Murnane-scholar. In practice, however, Murnane seems to have more male correspondents than female, his readership and the critical engagement with his work for now is tilted towards men, his current editors are men, and his biographer is a man (of sorts). We are all, no doubt, peculiarly feminine men, but that may be a poor substitute for the readerly engagement that Murnane covets.

References

Murnane, Gerald. *A Million Windows*. Artarmon, NSW: Giramondo, 2014.
——. *Barley Patch*. Artarmon, NSW: Giramondo, 2009.
——. *Invisible Yet Enduring Lilacs*. Artarmon, NSW: Giramondo, 2005.
——. "The Breathing Author", *Heat* no. 3 (new series) (2002): 9-31.
——. *Emerald Blue*. Ringwood, Vic.: McPhee Gribble, 1995.
——. *Velvet Waters*. 1990; Ringwood, Vic.: McPhee Gribble, 1992.
——. *Inland*. 1988; Artarmon, NSW: Giramondo, 2013.
——. *Landscape with Landscape*. 1985; Artarmon, NSW: Giramondo, 2016.
——. *A Lifetime on Clouds*. 1976; Melbourne, Vic.: Text Publishing, 2013.
——. *Tamarisk Row*. 1974; Artarmon, NSW: Giramondo, 2008.
Murnane, Gerald and Ivor Indyk. "Mental Places: A Conversation with Gerald Murnane". Artarmon, NSW: Giramondo, 2016. https://www.youtube.com/watch?v=5PqzX4TC1BE.
Tyndall, Philip and John Cruthers. *Words and Silk: The Real and Imaginary Worlds of Gerald Murnane*. Kangaroo Films, 1989.

4

"Images and Feelings in a Sort of Eternity": Gerald Murnane's Ideal Female Reader

Samantha Trayhurn

The blurb to Gerald Murnane's *A History of Books* (2012) states that the main body of work: "is accompanied by three shorter works, 'As It Were a Letter', 'The Boy's Name Was David' and 'Last Letter to a Niece', in which a writer searches for an ideal world, an ideal sentence, and an ideal reader".[1] Presuming that the three texts correspond in order to the three aims, "Last Letter to a Niece" presents an important insight into who Murnane writes for and, perhaps, some indications as to why he writes at all. In this essay, I posit that Murnane's quest for an ideal reader is no less than a quest for his own ideal existence. To validate these claims, I will draw on Murnane's 2017 address at the Goroke Golf Club, "The Still-Breathing Author",[2] as well as conduct a reading of "Last Letter to a Niece", and sections of his wider oeuvre.

First, it is important to clarify that this essay is concerned with Gerald Murnane, the author and man, not "Murnane" the "implied author",[3] or any of his personages. For this reason, I will relate my observations to "The Still-Breathing Author" address, because these words give a rare unobstructed insight into the thoughts and perceptions of Murnane. On this day, he did not declare otherwise,

---

1   Gerald Murnane, *A History of Books* (Artarmon, NSW: Giramondo, 2012), back cover. All subsequent references are to this edition and appear in parentheses in the text.
2   Gerald Murnane, "The Still-Breathing Author". First delivered at the symposium "A World Within This One: Gerald Murnane's Fiction", published in the *Sydney Review of Books*, 6 February 2018, https://sydneyreviewofbooks.com/the-still-breathing-author-gerald-murnane/, and republished in this collection. All subsequent quotations from "The Still-Breathing Author" in this chapter are from the version that appeared in the *Sydney Review of Books*.
3   A term which Murnane has occasionally borrowed from Wayne C. Booth to describe his narrators that, while they may appear to be synonymous with himself, are said to be distinct ontological entities. See Emmett Stinson, "Retrospective Intention: The Implied Author and the Coherence of the Oeuvre in Gerald Murnane's *Border Districts* and *The Plains*", in this collection; Wayne C. Booth, *The Rhetoric of Fiction* (Chicago: University of Chicago Press, 1961), 73.

so I conclude that he spoke for himself, and was not to be viewed under any of the other labels used to query the similarities between portions of his works and his lived life, without assigning him full accountability for the thoughts of his narrators.[4]

Here, I follow J.M. Coetzee in viewing Murnane as operating within a "dual-world system" where the "'real' (mundane) world and the real (ideal) world are suspended in reciprocal tension, each holding the other in existence". Coetzee goes so far as to say that Murnane is a "radical idealist", in that his images are rooted in a world "purer, simpler, and more real than the world from which they take their origin".[5] For Murnane, the physical world is less real than the unchangeable images that exist in another, often superior, world. In "The Still-Breathing Author", on the two occasions that Murnane mentions "the real world" he does so with the caveats "as we call it", or "as it's usually called", casting doubt on his own belief in such a title. While our visible world has traces of his churches, marbles, racecourses, and dark-haired women, there is also another world, a transcendental one, where there exist "image-objects" and "image-persons"[6] that correspond to all of these people and things.

Outlined in *A History of Books*, the associations for Murnane go something like this: a woman in the visible world may be distilled into an image of "a corner of a somewhat pale forehead with a strand of dark hair trailing across it" (198). This image might then go on to be connected with "a chief female personage" (198) from the book of an author born in the previous century, and further on to proliferate a detail in Murnane's writing that continues to trouble him, perhaps decades after the original observation. Evidently, the transcendental world is one composed of images that Murnane has spent his writing career trying to organise into a network, best illustrated by a series of diagrams made up of lines and polygons.[7] Embedded in these enduring images is Murnane's search for meaning. Regarding meaning, I concur with Anthony Uhlmann, who states that "meaning, or the feeling that we have when we do not feel that things are empty, is generated by this fraught and unstable exchange of differences between what seems to be and what is".[8] For Murnane, meaning is connection: "a thing has meaning … when it has a connection

---

4   For an in-depth discussion of the potential paradoxes that arise when looking at the concept of "implied-authorship" and Murnane's various personas (including those who appear in the flesh at events such as the one in Goroke), see Emmett Stinson's and Brigid Rooney's essays in this collection.
5   J.M. Coetzee, "The Quest for the Girl on Bendigo Street", *New York Review of Books*, 20 December 2012. https://www.nybooks.com/articles/2012/12/20/quest-girl-bendigo-street/
6   Coetzee, "The Quest for the Girl on Bendigo Street".
7   Murnane, "The Still-Breathing Author".
8   Anthony Uhlmann, "Signs for the Soul", *Sydney Review of Books*, 9 July 2013. https://sydneyreviewofbooks.com/signs-for-the-soul/

with another thing"⁹ – it is generated when his observations are translated into images that can be placed in his image network. While the living world is fleeting, in the imagined world things have, as Uhlmann states, "the potential at least, to persist".[10] However, it is a great source of anxiety for Murnane that he too does not occupy a place in this eternal image-world.

In *Inland* (2016), when Murnane's narrator quotes Paul Éluard, stating "there is another world but it is in this one",[11] he confesses to never having read Éluard, but implies that this ignorance opens up new possibilities of meaning. He concludes that the other world "is a place that can only be seen or dreamed of by those people known to us as narrators of books or characters within books" (149). So, while the other world is exceedingly attractive to Murnane, the only problem, it would seem, is that it is not yet accessible to him. It is in this conundrum that the role of Murnane's ideal reader becomes a very important one. She needs to bring Murnane into ideal existence, as in *Barley Patch* (2009), when the narrator states that an author comes into existence "only at the moment when a certain female personage who was reading these pages formed in her mind an image of the male personage who had written the pages with her in mind".[12] She must create his image-person.

For Murnane's ideal reader to be female provides extra complexity to the already difficult relationship that he and his narrators appear to have with the opposite sex. In "The Still-Breathing Author", Murnane openly declares that he has "never understood people, least of all females", and across all of his writing about female personages, a significant number of pages are dedicated to expressing dissatisfaction that real women can't be reconciled with his ideals. For example, in a lengthy scene from *A Million Windows* (2014), a young male spends two years observing a young girl who catches the same train to and from school. Before speaking a single word to her, he imagines their whole future together – marriage, a honeymoon, a large family. However, after the two young people have been conversing for two or three weeks, the narrator is so ill at ease that he can't recall the details of their conversations, and eventually decides that he wants "no more to do with the young woman".[13] He later recalls her only as "an image-person who might have been the chief character in a complicated daydream" (63). The real girl does not measure up to the ideal girl, and goes on only to exist as an image that must be filed away until it can be placed in his image network. Murnane's ideal female

---

9   Murnane, "The Still-Breathing Author".
10   Uhlmann, "Signs for the Soul".
11   Gerald Murnane, *Inland* (Sydney: Picador, 1989), 148. All subsequent references are to this edition and appear in parentheses in the text.
12   Gerald Murnane, *Barley Patch* (Artarmon, NSW: Giramondo, 2009), 173. All subsequent references are to this edition and appear in parentheses in the text.
13   Gerald Murnane, *A Million Windows* (Artarmon, NSW: Giramondo, 2014), 63. All subsequent references are to this edition and appear in parentheses in the text.

reader becomes an embodiment of all that Murnane cannot know or understand about the opposite sex. She exists in the interim plain between the visible and the invisible worlds, hovering on the periphery of both. In being unknowable, she stands at the head of the beguiling route by which Murnane can venture beyond the limits of his own mind.

At this point, however, readers, actual ones, need to remember not to confound the ideals about women in Murnane's writing and Murnane's ideal female reader, as I suspect these play two very different roles. While the former provide frequent catalysts to revisit a key concern across Murnane's body of work – how the "male gets into the female"[14] – the latter provides an endorsement for undertaking such an endeavour. For example, in *Barley Patch*, a young boy sneaks downstairs to look inside his cousin's doll's house, and while he intensely desires to reach inside, he resists the urge out of fear that he might leave some trace of his intrusion, encapsulating Murnane's sense that he is a voyeur in the world of women. He can look, but he can't touch – and what he sees can never truly be understood within the confines of his masculine mind. The ideal reader is symbolised by the figure of the Patroness: a woman the sole purpose of whose existence is "to remain aloof", and in doing so provide "a task worthy of a lifetime of effort: the simple but baffling task of gaining admission to her presence" (130). In remaining aloof, Murnane's ideal reader gives validation to a lifetime of writing. She provides the connections between what seems to be and what is, and in doing so generates a process that is meaningful.

In "The Still-Breathing Author", Murnane spoke directly about his ideal reader, telling the story of a young girl whose poetry he read in the newspaper when he was ten years old:

> She was the first version of the female who is my ideal reader. This personage has been never more than a blurred image in my mind and I have no wish for her to be otherwise. As I write these words, she may be a mere child or still unborn, but the desire to have her one day ponder my words in the hope of learning what gave rise to them – that sort of desire has sometimes kept me writing when no other motive would have done so.

The Patroness is recalled, and the fact that this ideal reader is Murnane's key inspiration is no small claim from an author who, at one point, gave up his craft for ten years. However, it seems that for Murnane, the attraction of his muse is embedded in her mystery. He does not wish to know her, and should he ever do so, his reason for writing might cease altogether. He desires her to "one day" ponder

---

14   Coetzee, "The Quest for the Girl on Bendigo Street".

his words, but not now. If he were to encounter her now, she would no longer be aloof, or blurred. She would be real, and would inevitably fall short of the ideal.

"Last Letter to a Niece" provides further insight into Murnane's desires about his ideal reader. The short text is written from the viewpoint of an uncle who is penning the last in a series of letters to his niece. The narrator reminds us in the opening paragraph that an ideal reader should not enter into a dialogue by stating, "you are not obliged to reply to me; and I add yet again that I almost prefer not to hear from you, since this allows me to imagine many possible replies" (191). Next, we are informed that this letter will differ from previous ones because, rather than concerning itself with the truth, it will "go in search of a higher truth" (192). We are not told what this truth is, but it appears to be associated with the fact that real women exist only to provide image fodder for the women of fiction, because as the uncle confesses in a long and guilt-ridden pronouncement, the women of books are the real objects of his affection, and he has never felt for real people what he feels for these characters.

The niece stands in place of the ideal reader because she is neither a woman of fiction nor a woman of the real world. She is the eternal image of the young girl. Unsurprisingly, the town where the uncle lives has a church, and the uncle goes to this church to find the last vestiges of demure young women who "dress modestly" with "eyes downcast" (196), so that he can "take home … a small store of remembered sights", because the true sources of his affections, the women in books, are "quite invisible" (196). We are again reminded of the frustrating gulf between the visible and the invisible worlds, and the inaccessibility of the latter to a man who, while he holds image fragments in his imagination, can't fashion them into a key that will allow him complete access. On expressing this frustration to his reader, he asks of her to "allow me to set you right, dear niece, and to make a true reader of you" (197). A true and ideal reader, then, must be made.

The remainder of the letter can be seen as a kind of instruction manual for how Murnane would like an ideal reader to engage with his work. First, she must know that all of the worlds and people of fiction are invisible, and can only be experienced by arranging a "poor stock of remembered sights" (198). Second, she should trust only "the findings of [her] own introspection" (197). Thus, when reading his work, an ideal reader must accept that the worlds of Murnane too are invisible, and will only be populated by images from her own stock. Third, she must know that he could only ever be drawn to a woman in the visible world if first he had "read about her" or he could be certain that she had "read about [him]" (200). On this point, I am not suggesting that Murnane has never had a meaningful relationship with a woman in the real world, but instead that this symbolically suggests that he will not be able to make a bridge between the real and ideal worlds without the aid of fiction. In the text, the only woman that the narrator is drawn to is one on an island surrounded by cliffs where no boats can moor. He holds out hope that she might write him a message, and that if thrown into the sea in a bottle, it might reach his own shore. Isolation and untouchability are again offset by hope.

Drawing to a close, the narrator explains to his reader that he first began to pen his letters when feeling cast down by these ideas, which have troubled him for a long time, and hopes that writing might be a "sort of miracle", which can make invisible entities "aware of each other through the medium of the visible" (203), and might bring about some "wholly unexpected outcome" (203). He asks the question: "But how can I believe this awareness is mutual?" It is something that cannot be answered, but there is a sense that the author wants desperately to believe that it is. These same ideas have concerned Murnane since the writing of *Inland*, which was first published in 1988, and are deftly summarised in the closing paragraphs when the narrator states:

> When I wrote the letter which was the first of all my pages, I was thinking of a young woman who was, I thought, dead while I was still alive. I thought the young woman was dead while I remained alive in order to go on writing what she could never read.
>
> Today while I write on this last page, I am still thinking of the young woman. Today, however, I am sure the young woman is still alive. I am sure the young woman is still alive while I am dead. Today I am dead but the young woman remains alive in order to go on reading what I could never write. (164)

If we conclude that the first paragraph is describing the "real" (mundane) world, the woman is representative of an ideal reader who does not currently exist. If the second paragraph represents the ideal (real) world, we are given an ideal reader who exists in wait of the words that, at the point of writing, still remained elusive. Whether they are as elusive now as they were thirty years ago is uncertain.

The conclusion to "Last Letter to a Niece" is equally cryptic. The final section jarringly jumps to a short excerpt by a seventeenth-century man who recounts his time following a Prince, while penning letters to a Countess P—. The final paragraph is addressed to the reader:

> Dear Reader …
>
> The Letters from Turkey were regarded by critics for a long time only as a source for the history of the exiles. Much futile research was done in an attempt to find traces of the mysterious Countess P— who proved never to have existed. Mikes never sent his letters to any 'aunt' but copied them into a letter-book, which was found after his death. (205)

It seems that part of what we should take from this statement is what we have already gleaned: there is no niece. The letters to Murnane's ideal reader exist in his own private works, but could "never be part of any book" (203). As the author very recently turned eighty, and last year said to the audience in Goroke, "I have been delivered of my books", perhaps further truths about his ideal reader await us in his legacy.

In closing "The Still-Breathing Author", Murnane read a poem from his then forthcoming collection *Green Shadows and Other Poems* (2018), concluding with the telling statement:

> I knew all along I could never avoid
> the truth I'd discovered when I first
> engaged with texts: the self-evident fact
> of there being no reader nor subject-matter
> only images and feelings in a sort of eternity.

At the end of his career, has Murnane given up hope of his ideal reader? Or is there comfort in knowing that there is no reader, only an image of her existing in a "sort of eternity"? Is this the higher truth that the narrator set out to explore in "Last Letter to a Niece"? The answers are not immediately apparent, but they demand pondering. Undoubtedly, many readers will go on to ponder these questions and many others in the work of an author who transforms experiences into images, and encourages his readers (ideal or otherwise) to do the same. Through this process, many images of Murnane will be conjured and – whether or not they are ideal – will persist in the rich other world that lies just beyond the outer regions of his mind.

References

Booth, Wayne C. *The Rhetoric of Fiction*. Chicago: University of Chicago Press, 1961.
Murnane, Gerald. *Green Shadows and Other Poems*. Artarmon, NSW: Giramondo, 2018.
——. "The Still-Breathing Author", *Sydney Review of Books*, 6 February 2018. https://sydneyreviewofbooks.com/the-still-breathing-author-gerald-murnane/.
——. *A Million Windows*. Artarmon, NSW: Giramondo, 2014.
——. *A History of Books*. Artarmon, NSW: Giramondo, 2012.
——. *Barley Patch*. Artarmon, NSW: Giramondo, 2009.
——. *Inland*. Artarmon, NSW: Giramondo, 1988.
Coetzee, J.M. "The Quest for the Girl on Bendigo Street". *New York Review of Books*, 20 December 2012. https://www.nybooks.com/articles/2012/12/20/quest-girl-bendigo-street.
Uhlmann, Anthony. "Signs for the Soul", *Sydney Review of Books*, 9 July 2013. https://sydneyreviewofbooks.com/signs-for-the-soul/.

5

Retrospective Intention: The Implied Author and the Coherence of the Oeuvre in *Border Districts* and *The Plains*

Emmett Stinson

This essay examines the dialogic relationship between Gerald Murnane's final novel, *Border Districts* (2017), and his third published novel, *The Plains* (1982), to argue that Murnane's late works enact a "retrospective intention" that revises the meaning of his earlier works. Murnane's writings depict a complex relationship between author, intention, text and reader through the notion of the "implied author", a figure that gives coherence to the total meaning of a work, while also being purely textual in nature. By comparing Wayne C. Booth's influential definition of the implied author and Murnane's use of the term, however, I argue that Murnane foregrounds and exploits its internal contradictions for generative purposes. The implied author functions similarly to what I will call retrospective intention.

Murnane has frequently discussed the disjointed and fragmentary manner in which his works were published, often out of chronological order and in a vastly different form than he intended. Nonetheless, I will argue that his late works, as exemplified by *Border Districts,* seek to present a fictitious continuity to his entire oeuvre. In particular, *Border Districts* intentionally echoes *The Plains* and extends a series of dialogic exchanges in the earlier novel through careful allusion. In so doing, *Border Districts* both extends and responds to themes and ideas from *The Plains*. But this literary intervention also effectively revises the earlier work's meaning in key ways. As I will argue, this process suggests a notion of intention in Murnane's work that is ramified and involuted with the result that new meanings can often be imbued in texts after the fact of their publication.

Intentionality and the Implied Author

Murnane's fiction and essays frequently discuss the relationship between the author and the work of art. In "The Breathing Author", the narrator states that "I cannot conceive of myself reading a text and being unmindful that the object before my eyes is a product of human effort".[1] The narrator of the essay (who certainly appears to resemble the real Gerald Murnane) discusses how reading inevitably leads him to pose a series of biographical questions about "the methods used by the writer in putting together the text", about "the feeling and beliefs that drove the writer to write the text", and "even about the life story of the writer". (157) These questions – which seem simple or even simplistic – resonate with claims made elsewhere in Murnane's fiction about being "an ignorant and gullible reader" who is less concerned with traditional aspects of the plot than he is with the kind of person the author is.[2]

But this biographical readerly interest is complicated by a concept from literary theory that Murnane has frequently invoked in his fiction: the implied author. He first discusses the concept in "In Far Fields", the first short story from *Emerald Blue* (1995): "I learned the term *implied author* from the book *The Rhetoric of Fiction*, by Wayne C. Booth, which was first published by the University of Chicago Press in 1961"; the narrator immediately appropriates this concept, arguing that the "writer of these words" who is the "I" within the fiction "is mostly aptly denoted by the words *the implied author of this piece of fiction*".[3] For Murnane, then, the narrator who appears to be speaking within the text and who also seems to be identical with the real author is actually an ontologically distinct entity.

In *A Million Windows* (2014), an even clearer articulation of the implied author is presented:

> The reader should think of me as a personage as being in some respects less than an actual person and in other respects more so. At the very least, I am a voice: the voice behind the text … or, rather, the implied author, by which I mean the personage of whom nothing is known except what can be inferred from this text. (33)

The implied author, according to this definition, is a textual effect: it is the implicit creation of an entity who seems to be real (but is not), and whose existence can only be meaningfully constructed from the process of reading a text. From this perspective, the biographical interests of Murnane's "gullible readers" seem not like

---

[1] Gerald Murnane, "The Breathing Author", in *Invisible Yet Enduring Lilacs* (2002; Artarmon, NSW: Giramondo, 2005), 157. All subsequent references are to this edition and appear in parentheses in the text.

[2] Gerald Murnane, *A Million Windows* (Artarmon, NSW: Giramondo, 2014), 71. All subsequent references are to this edition and appear in parentheses in the text.

[3] Gerald Murnane, *Emerald Blue* (Ringwood, Vic.: Penguin, 1995), 4.

strange obsessions, but rather the logical products of texts that necessarily generate fictitious, though implicit, representatives of the author.

Despite the importance of the implied author, there has been no systematic comparison between Murnane's discussion of the idea and Booth's own presentation of it. This matters because Booth's notion of the implied author is both complex and contested – and many subsequent critics have interpreted the notion in a broad range of ways. Murnane's appropriation of the term differs from Booth's usage in key respects, and understanding these differences helps to explain the role of authorial intention in Murnane's fiction. On the face of it, Booth's notion of the implied author resembles other concepts that were influenced by the rhetorical approach of the New Criticism, which was itself influenced by modernist notions of impersonality. For example, the implied author seems similar to Maynard Mack's concept of the "satiric persona", who resembles the author of a satire, but is nonetheless a distinct entity intentionally generated by complex rhetorical structures.[4] But Booth underscores that the implied author is more than just a "persona", "mask" or "narrator" generated within a literary work.[5] Instead, the implied author is the author's "second self" and incorporates "not only the extractable meanings" of a work but "that which is expressed by the total form", including "the moral and emotional content of each bit of action" and the "suffering of all of the characters".[6] In this sense, the notion of the implied author is not simply a matter of narrative structure or perspective, but is inextricably linked with the "intuitive apprehension of a completed artistic whole".[7] For Booth, the concept of the implied author is not simply about literary impersonality, but a means of conceptualising the relationship between author, text and reader from a textual perspective.

As Tom Kindt and Hans-Harald Muller argue, it may be best to understand the implied author as a solution to a very specific set of problems: Booth wanted to foreground the roles of authors and readers in literary criticism, but he also wanted to do this without running foul of Wimsatt and Beardsley's intentional fallacy,[8] in which any authorial intention not immanent to a text (that is, only those intentions, which can be derived through close analysis without reliance on external sources) must be discarded.[9] The implied author presented a solution to

---

4   Maynard Mack, *Collected in Himself: Essays Critical, Biographical, and Bibliographical on Pope and Some of His Contemporaries,* vol. 1 (Wilmington: University of Delaware Press, 1982), 60.
5   Wayne C. Booth, *The Rhetoric of Fiction* (Chicago: University of Chicago Press, 1961), 73.
6   Booth, *The Rhetoric of Fiction,* 73–74.
7   Booth, *The Rhetoric of Fiction,* 73.
8   William K. Wimsatt and Monroe Beardsley, "The Intentional Fallacy", *The Sewanee Review* 54, no. 3 (July–September 1946), 468-88.
9   Tom Kindt and Hans-Harald Muller, *The Implied Author: Concept and Controversy* (Berlin and New York: Walter de Gruyter, 2008), 50.

this conundrum by modelling the relationship between author and reader *within* the text and deriving authorial intention from the immanent rhetorical structure of the work, rather than the person of the author. In this sense, the concept serves as a means of navigating a logical bind generated by the New Criticism's methodology, which excluded anything external to a text.

But, as Kindt and Muller argue, the "solution" of the implied author also raises a new set of problems because the concept lacks a degree of terminological precision, and is certainly "not a technical term in the strict sense that, say, the heterodiegetic narrator is".[10] Within Booth's definition, there is a series of tensions and questions that he never definitively resolves. Is the implied author something intentionally created by real authors, or is it simply something that readers posit or infer? Is the implied author a reasonable facsimile of the real author or an essentially false presentation? Is it a guiding concept that sets the horizon of possible interpretations, or is it a necessary fiction generated by readers as they read across an author's oeuvre? As a result, the implied author might be thought of less as a coherent concept, and more as "a cover term for several concepts or variants of a single concept".[11]

Murnane's usage of the term "implied author" imports several aspects of Booth's concept while also modifying it. For both, the implied author presents a way of understanding how authorial intention can be discussed in relation to a text and the relationship between author, text and reader. Moreover, for both, the implied author suggests that knowledge about literary works is always inherently textual, rather than contextual. Moreover, the internal contradictions and unresolved questions raised by Booth's concept of the implied author are largely replicated in Murnane's own work. For example, what are we to make of the fact that the notion of the implied author in Murnane's work is itself discussed by the figure who is explicitly identified as the implied author? If we accept Murnane's argument, does this undermine the very status of the claim itself, which is no longer associated with the "real" author of the work, but instead with a rhetorically generated textual fiction? Are there multiple, different implied authors across Murnane's fiction or are they all more or less the same? Does it matter that many of these implied authors not only resemble each other but also seem to repeat more or less the same ideas? And, finally, is there a difference between the implied authors of Murnane's fictional works and those in his non-fictional works, especially given that, in the author's note at the beginning of *Invisible Yet Enduring Lilacs*, Murnane claims that he has never "tried to write fiction or non-fiction or anything in-between" and thus should have published "all my pieces of writing as essays"? (n.p.)

---

10 Kindt and Muller, *The Implied Author*, 2.
11 Kindt and Muller, *The Implied Author*, 7.

I would suggest that there are no "correct" answers to such questions, and as Nicholas Birns has pointed out, it remains unclear how seriously we should take such claims, both because of the ambiguous status of the claimants and the laconic irony that tinges virtually all of Murnane's work.[12] Regardless, the major difference between Murnane's and Booth's usages of the implied author is that Murnane delights in the ambiguities created by the concept. The paradoxes generated by the idea of the implied author are aesthetically generative for Murnane, as the discussion of it in "The Interior of Gaaldine" (1995) suggests.[13] In this story, the narrator, who again resembles Murnane, is given a briefcase full of writing whose contents describe the results of a complex imaginary horseracing game set in a fictitious country called New Arcadia (a set of details that corresponds to a horseracing game catalogued in Murnane's own "Antipodean Archive"):[14]

> I seemed to understand that the implied author of the pages – the person in my mind who had written these pages – had written the pages in order to cause to arise in the mind of one or another reader of the pages one or another image of a personage who would seem to the reader more likeable and more trustworthy than any person in the place where the reader was reading. (215)

According to this passage, the particular goal of this implied author is the creation of a "likeable" and "trustworthy" person that is, of course, the implied author himself. Here, Booth's concept of the implied author becomes a tautology: the intentional product of the implied author is the creation of the implied author. But this situation is even more convoluted, since the implied recipient or reader of the text in the story is also the implied author of the text we are reading, and *both* are, in some form, fictional personages who resemble, at least in part, the real Gerald Murnane. Murnane has even made this connection explicit in "The Still-Breathing Author", when he notes that the author of archives given to the chief character of the story (who appears to be Murnane) is someone "who devotes his life to an enterprise such as my Antipodean Archive would have become if I had devoted *my* life to it".[15] As he notes, this alternative version of himself exists "perhaps on another

---

12 Nicholas Birns, *Contemporary Australian Literature: A World Not Yet Dead* (Sydney: Sydney University Press, 2015), 173.
13 Gerald Murnane, "The Interior of Gaaldine", in *Emerald Blue* (Ringwood, Vic.: McPhee Gribble, 1995), 185-216. All subsequent references are to this edition and appear in parentheses in the text.
14 Murnane has discussed his Antipodean Archive in a variety of places. For a brief summary of the archive with pictures, see Gerald Murnane , "The Three Archives of Gerald Murnane", *Music and Literature*, 11 November 2013. http://www.musicandliterature.org/features/2013/11/11/the-three-archives-of-gerald-murnane
15 Gerald Murnane, "The Still-Breathing Author", *Sydney Review of Books*, 6 February 2018. https://sydneyreviewofbooks.com/the-still-breathing-author-gerald-murnane/. This essay is republished in this collection.

level of fictionality" – which seems to be the case insofar as he is the implied author (an inherently fictitious entity) of a text within Murnane's fictional text.[16] As this example suggests, the notion of the implied author in Murnane's work is not a solution to problems (as is the case for Booth), but a generative concept that creates nested levels of fictional ontologies that are elided in paradoxical or irresolvable formations. Moreover, the notion of the implied author does not become a way of revealing intent, but instead becomes the content and goal of authorial intent.

This constitutes the essential difference between Booth's and Murnane's usage. While the internal tensions and contradictions within Booth's concept could be viewed as a flaw, Murnane embraces and foregrounds the paradoxes generated by the notion. In this sense, Murnane's appropriation of the concept is wildly different to Booth's, and his aims do not resemble the goal that Booth (who, as Kindt and Mueller discuss, wanted to establish both ethical orders and readerly certainty through his rhetorical criticism) sought to establish. Moreover – and crucially for my argument here – the notion of the implied author presents a situation in which Murnane has sought to represent the relationship between text and author in ways that are simultaneously logical and inherently paradoxical. In other words, the deployment of the implied author concept in Murnane's work presents a set of logically contradictory goals that I will argue are characteristic of his late writing: on the one hand, there is a legitimate interest in or yearning for the fictitious creation of an authorial figure who will unite the work of art in an aesthetic totality, but, on the other hand, this very yearning creates a set of paradoxes that seem to undermine the first goal. Finally, these very paradoxes rely on a slippage between the textual manifestations of the implied author and what readers "know" about the "real" Gerald Murnane. Rather than wholly rejecting the context of the breathing author, Murnane's work sets the real against the fictitious in complex and often unexpected ways that alter a reader's understanding of both. In this sense, the purely textual implied author interacts obliquely with the material world.

Retrospective Intention in *Border Districts*

Murnane's use of the implied author concept helps to clarify what is at stake in *Border Districts*, a novel that, as I will argue, enacts a "retrospective intention" which revises Murnane's earlier writing after the fact. In so doing, it imposes a seeming coherence onto his work that enables his disparate body of work to constitute an aesthetic totality. This totality is essentially fictitious and retro-engineered, but such tendencies are already inherent in the notion of the

---

16   Murnane, "The Still-Breathing Author".

implied author, which as Booth argues, is a purely textual manifestation that nonetheless enables the "intuitive apprehension of a completed artistic whole".[17] The capacity of texts to generate a sense of completeness or to impose a sense of completeness on something incoherent is a key aspect of the concept of the implied author. Retrospective intention is simply another strategy by which a sense of aesthetic completion can be generated through textual means.

It is worth emphasising, however, that the very claim that there could be some larger coherence to Murnane's work is extremely suspect, if not straightforwardly foolish. Murnane has emphasised in interviews that the publication of his work has been marked by contingency and largely dictated by the vicissitudes of the market. In a 2015 interview with Tristan Foster for *3AM*, Murnane issues a strong warning to future critics who want to view his oeuvre as an orderly affair with a clear line of progression or evolution:

> You speculate that my body of work seems as though it was planned from the beginning. This is my opportunity to complain against another item of foolishness that occurs often in discussion about writers, especially those such as myself, whose books sell few copies. Often, the expression occurs 'He published his first book in …' Or, 'Fours [sic] years passed before he published his next book …' Such expressions bring to mind a powerful figure of the Great Writer choosing when and where and in what order he'll deign to bestow his books on the world. There may well be such authors, but I can assure anyone interested that I've never published any books. That task was performed by publishers, and until I was taken up by my present publisher, Giramondo, they had the upper hand [...] *A Lifetime on Clouds* was half a book – the publisher cut in half the long four-part work that I first submitted. *The Plains* was an expanded version of a section of a long work rejected by several publishers. I could go on. The first seven books of mine to be published, if they weren't mutilated versions of what I originally wrote, were, to a certain extent, compromises [...] So, let's forget the idea of Young Gerald seeing his life's work laid out in advance and progressing from book to book in an ever-so-orderly fashion.[18]

---

17   Booth, *Rhetoric*, 73.
18   Gerald Murnane, quoted in Tristan Foster, "Eight Questions for Gerald Murnane," *3AM Magazine*, 21 April 2015. https://www.3ammagazine.com/3am/eight-questions-for-gerald-murnane/. In the "Author's Foreword" to *Landscape with Landscape* (Artarmon, NSW: Giramondo, 2016), Murnane has restated this position: "I'm sometimes dismayed to hear my body of work described as some sort of orderly program that I devised early in my career and followed faithfully afterwards. The fourteen filing-cabinet drawers of my literary archive are filled with failed beginnings, wrong turnings and abandoned drafts, and elaborate plans that came to nothing" (2).

Among other things, these claims underscore the importance of publishing studies for literary history: Murnane notes the significant gap between creative intentions behind the works of individual authors, and the way that those works are transformed – often dramatically – and subsequently marketed and mediated by publishers. Not only do publishers act as gatekeepers, who decide which works get released, but they also make decisions about the marketing and framing of publications that have profound effects on the sales and thus the reception of texts. As John B. Thompson discusses, publishers' decisions to let certain books languish with little marketing support can have a huge effect on their reception.[19]

Murnane has repeatedly disputed any notion that his "published works comprise a sort of program" or "an orderly progression from one sort of writing to another"; while he does admit "that trends and developments can be found in my writing", he nonetheless has argued that, "for most of my writing life I could see no further than the book I was currently working on".[20] He has often given concrete examples of the failures and discontinuities between his authorial intent and the eventual publication (or not) of such works. In "The Breathing Author", for example, the narrator discusses his failure to complete a larger manuscript, entitled *O, Dem Golden Slippers*. This failure is not attributed to a creative inadequacy or problem, but rather to a set of contingent material circumstances:

> My drawing back from *O, Dem Golden Slippers* had something to do with my being a husband and a father of adult children. If I had been, as Marcel Proust was, neither a husband nor a father, or if I had been, as D.H. Lawrence was, a husband but not a father, I might not have drawn back. (183)

Although the meaning of this claim remains enigmatic, it serves as another exemplar of the fact that artistic intention can be thwarted, in various and complex ways, by material exigencies beyond the author's control. Indeed, Murnane has repeatedly emphasised that the act of authorial intention and creation has only the most tenuous link to eventual publication: "I wrote five of my first seven published books sitting at the kitchen bench … My mood while I wrote was usually a mild despair. I was many times ready to accept that what I was writing would never be published".[21] If we are to believe these claims, even after having published multiple books, Murnane still frequently suspected that his work would not be published.

In foregrounding the contingency of his published output, it would seem that any claim for the unity or coherence of Murnane's oeuvre must be dispatched. But

---

19   John B. Thompson, *Merchants of Culture: The Publishing Business in the Twenty-First Century* (Cambridge: Polity Press, 2010), 262-70.
20   Murnane, "The Still-Breathing Author".
21   Murnane, "The Still-Breathing Author".

Retrospective Intention: The Implied Author in *Border Districts* and *The Plains*

I want to argue that something more complex happens in Murnane's late writing, as exemplified in his final novel, *Border Districts*: Murnane's late works seek to turn contingency into necessity by reframing and recontextualising this work in such a way that gives it coherence. Indeed, this process actually constitutes, by some measures, a more impressive project than the enactment of an original authorial plan, since it manages to give coherence to a body of works after the fact through a process of creative intervention. In this sense, the coherence of the oeuvre is preserved, but – much like the concept of the implied author – it becomes a fictitious, textually generated coherence that is ontologically distinct from the "real" and contingent history of Murnane's publications.

Border Districts implicitly positions itself as both a response to and a revision of Murnane's own work in its opening lines: "Two months ago, when I first arrived in this township just short of the border, I resolved to guard my eyes, and I could not think of going on with this piece of writing unless I were to explain how I came by that odd expression".[22] This opening both mirrors and subverts the opening of what is usually regarded as Murnane's most important work of fiction, *The Plains* (1982), which opens with the lines: "Twenty years ago, when I first arrived on the plains, I kept my eyes open. I looked for anything in the landscape that seemed to hint at some elaborate meaning behind appearances".[23] The differences between the opening sentences are explicit but appear minor. The narrator of *The Plains* has his eyes open, while the narrator of *Border Districts* keeps his eyes guarded. This narrator has also arrived only two months ago, whereas the narrator of *The Plains* is looking back twenty years in an explicitly retrospective mode. This differentiates the narrators from the outset and also signals that – although both narrators, as implied authors, might resemble Murnane – they are ontologically distinct entities.

Both narrators may appear to be avatars of Murnane, but they are also different from him. *Border Districts* frequently plays with these slippages between the author's real identity and his fictional manifestations: for example, the narrator's move to a small town in regional Victoria seems to refer to Murnane's own real-life move to Goroke. But this seeming resemblance is also false, since there is a sharp distinction between the way the narrator of *Border Districts* describes the reasons behind this move and the motivations that Murnane has discussed. Murnane states that "One of the main reasons I came to Goroke was so that I could look after my son, at the age of seventy. I'm his father and I can't avoid helping him".[24] The

---

22 Gerald Murnane, *Border Districts* (Artarmon, NSW: Giramondo, 2017), 1. All subsequent references are to this edition and appear in parentheses in the text.
23 Gerald Murnane, *The Plains* (Ringwood, Vic.: McPhee Gribble, 1982), 3. All subsequent references are to this edition and appear in parentheses in the text.
24 Quoted in Shannon Burns, "The Scientist of His Own Experience: A Profile of Gerald Murnane", *Australian Book Review*, August 2015. https://bit.ly/38L4pyB.

resemblance between Murnane and the narrator of *Border Districts* also crucially inverts the usual mimetic relation in which the work of art mirrors the world. Here, both Murnane's real move to Goroke and the move of the narrator in *Border Districts* echo the fictional move in *The Plains*, which suggests that life is imitating art, rather than the other way around.

The opposed approaches to vision in the two works are arguably even more significant, however. In a "one-minute lecture" on *The Plains* that Murnane delivered at La Trobe University in 1988, he described the novel as being "the story of a man who tried to see properly".[25] *Border Districts* responds to this question of seeing, and it appears to directly contradict the earlier work: the wide-eyed openness of the youthful narrator is contrasted with an older narrator who has turned inward. But this relationship is more complex, since the narrator's desire to guard his eyes in *Border Districts* is not a rejection of vision, but a refocusing of attention away from direct perception and towards an indirect mode of observation:

> I mentioned earlier that I guard my eyes. I do this so that I might be more alert to what appears at the edges of my range of vision; so that I might notice at once any sight so much in need of my inspection that one or more of its details seems to quiver or be agitated until I have the illusion that I am being signalled to or winked at. (11)

The decision to guard one's eyes is not about rejecting perception, but about being open to what occurs at the limits of perception, described here as "the edges of my range of vision". Here, the "border districts" of perception become the privileged locus of more urgent truths so vibrant that they seem to "quiver or be agitated" in a way that makes the narrator think he is "being signalled to or winked at". The seemingly stoic gesture of guarding one's eyes is, in fact, only in the service of producing ecstatic visions – and is thus anything but dispassionate. This approach to seeing forgoes obvious visual pleasures in order to experience "deeper", and, indeed, more pleasurable experiences. The pleasure of these experiences is underscored by the sexual overtones of the language ("quivering" visions that resemble being "winked at") used to describe them. Moreover, the narrator's decision to "guard his eyes" ultimately ends in the illusion of being "winked at", which is, of course, a physical means of guarding one's eye – which suggests something tautological about the process in which guarded vision produces the ecstatic vision of a guarded eye.[26]

---

25 Quoted in Imre Salusinszky, *Gerald Murnane* (Melbourne: Oxford University Press, 1993), 43.

Although their methods differ, the narrators of both *Border Districts* and *The Plains* have similar goals: the narrator of *The Plains* keeps his eyes open for the reason that he is looking "for anything in the landscape that seemed to hint at some elaborate meaning behind appearances" (3). In both works, vision is important because it offers – or potentially offers – the means towards a sublime experience beyond everyday reality. When describing the goal of his proposed film, entitled *The Interior*, the narrator of *The Plains* states that "the hero of my film" will see "at the furthest limits of his awareness, unexplored plains" (51), a statement that comes very close to the philosophy of vision described in *Border Districts*. These correspondences go beyond mere allusion and instead constitute an extension of and engagement with the dialogic exchanges around the notion of vision already presented in *The Plains*. Establishing this claim, however, requires first coming to grips with the different concepts of vision articulated in *The Plains*.

Different notions of vision in *The Plains* are voiced dialogically through a series of different characters, including various landowners and several aspiring artists seeking patronage, among others. But perhaps the most significant discussions occur between the "chief character" of the novel (to use one of Murnane's favoured phrases) and his patron. In their first meeting the patron attacks the chief character's idea that he might create a "visible equivalent of the plains" before noting that he

> believed, nevertheless, that I might one day be capable of seeing what was worth seeing. If he could forget my young man's eagerness to look at simple coloured images of the plains, he might concede that at least I was trying to discover my own kind of landscape. (52)

Here, the narrator's attempt to view the hidden meanings of the plains directly is derided and explicitly attacked as a "blind" search (52). The patron's opposition to the narrator's desire to "keep his eyes open" is reinforced by the description of the patron who is lying on a "stretcher" with "his eyes covered": "I left him still lying with his eyes covered and recalled, the passage outside where the afternoon was tending towards evening, that he had not once met my own eyes" (51-52). This opposition between the narrator who has his eyes open, and the patron who keeps his eyes closed, establishes an apparent dichotomy between the sensible world that is empirically accessible, and an internal world of mentally generated imagery.

---

26 Occluded eyes are a recurring symbol throughout *Border Districts*, as in the case of the "young woman holding a glass marble firmly between upper and lower eyelid at the front of a normal eye" (53) or the narrator who looks "down the tube" of a kaleidoscope "into the afternoon sunlight" (58).

This opposition is rearticulated in what is perhaps one of the most famous and frequently discussed passages in *The Plains* – a long soliloquy from the patron that considers the plains, issues of perception, and the relation between the mental and sensible:

> Look. My eyes are closed. I am about to sleep. When you see me insensible, trepan me. Carve my skull neatly open ... Peer into the pale brain you find pulsating there. Prise apart its dull-coloured lobes. Examine them with powerful lenses. You'll see nothing to suggest plains. They disappeared long ago – the lands I claimed to see.
>
> The Great Darkness. Isn't that where all our plains lie? But they're safe, quite safe. And on their far side – too far away for you and me to visit – over there the weather is changing ... Another plain altogether is drifting towards our own. We're travelling somewhere in a world the shape of an eye. And we still haven't seen what other countries that eye looks out on. (102)

Some commentators have viewed this passage as a reflection on philosophical notions of phenomenology, which argue for the world being created by the mind rather than passively sensing it.[27] But this passage also engages with the thematic issues of vision and representation. Earlier, the patron appeared to articulate a claim that the plains could only be understood through internal mental imagery, but his point here seems to be that the connection between such mental processes and the physical biology of the brain cannot be scientifically reconstructed. Instead, the plains are posited as being in a realm of "great darkness", which appears to refer to mental or imaginative realms. But these claims are once again intentionally made even more convoluted to produce the generative paradoxes that are characteristic of Murnane's work. The world – which is meant to be sensible or visible – is then itself described as an eye that looks out onto other still unseen worlds. What is created here is an infinite regress of vision and observation: one looks at the world to discover its essence, only to find out that the world is another eye looking onto another world, and so forth. As Nicholas Birns argues, such moments in Murnane's work are "not seeking merely to divert or to elevate his reader from the material world, but to recognise its immanent fissures and contradictions".[28]

These complicated and self-referential notions of vision reach what appears to be their logical conclusion in the final scene of *The Plains*, where the narrator attempts to take a photo of his own eye:

---

27   See Salusinszky, *Gerald Murnane*, 45-47. For a Spinozan reading, see Patrick West, "The Ethical Vision of Gerald Murnane", *JASAL: Journal of the Association for the Study of Australian Literature* (1996), 221-27.
28   Birns, *Contemporary Australian Literature*, 176.

> I lifted my own camera to my face and stood with my eye pressed against the lens and my finger poised as if to expose to the film in its dark chamber the darkness that was the only visible sign of whatever I saw beyond myself. (113)

This image alone presents a series of complex paradoxes: the darkness of the film captures the darkness within the eye – an absence that is nonetheless the only material trace of the narrator's own visions. While it is tempting to read this final image, following Ihab Hassan, as the merging of "the observer and observed",[29] any such interpretation seems to be ironically undercut by further details. The image we get is not of the narrator's eye, but rather one generated by his patron, who has been asked "to record the moment" by taking a photo of the instant that the narrator takes a photo of his own eye (113). Moreover, the narrator is prompted to do this because he has seen his patron's photographs that depict him "as a man with my eyes fixed on something that mattered" who "recognised the meaning of what I saw" (112). The final image, then, seems to be an intentionally ironic undercutting of these other images, and the narrator's original desire to find "some elaborate meaning behind appearances" seems to have been dispatched by an acknowledgement of the inescapable subjectivity of both vision and meaning. In short, the narrator here seems finally to be convinced by his patron that the attempt to offer a visual representation of the plains is futile.

Border Districts places itself in explicit dialogue with this final scene and, in important ways, appears to reject the notion of vision articulated in its ending. Specifically, the imperative to guard one's eyes seems to be a direct reply to the invasive photograph that comprises the final image of *The Plains*. Not only does the narrator of *Border Districts* refuse to look directly at images, but also he seeks to keep his own eyes "guarded" from such invasive procedures. This becomes clear later in the novel when he imagines a woman holding a marble up to her eye, and notes that "I could never bear to have a glass marble, or any other object, resting against the surface of my eye" (53). The narrator of *Border Districts* thus literally guards his eyes, unlike the chief character of *The Plains*, who stands "with my eye pressed against the lens" (113).

Similarly, where the end of *The Plains* repeatedly discusses the "darkness" of the eye and internal mental spaces, *Border Districts* begins instead by focusing on a "white patch which appeared just now against a black ground at the edge of my mind which will not be easily dislodged", and represents the "white bib" or "*rabat*" of the priest who inspires the narrator to guard his eyes (1-2). *Border Districts* also ends with a quotation from Shelley that discusses "the white radiance

---

29   Ihab Hassan, "Realism, Truth, and Trust in Postmodern Perspective", *Third Text* 17, no. 1 (2003), 13.

of Eternity" (146). Here, again, the novel seems intentionally to select images that are the opposite of the darkness that appears at the end of *The Plains*. In many ways, the novels, although they discuss many similar themes, present notably different accounts of them. *The Plains* recounts the experiences of a young man who desires to present an idealised account of the plains, but ultimately lapses into a kind of solipsism that imprisons him in his own consciousness or perceptions. *Border Districts*, however, reaffirms this idealism by suggesting that more indirect means of vision than those used by the narrator of *The Plains* can provide transcendent kinds of experiences. Through these counterpoised claims and symbols, the two works constitute something like a diptych. Indeed, such opposed but complementary dichotomies already feature prominently in *The Plains* in the discussion of the rival Horizonites and the Haresman, who develop different approaches to understanding the plains.

In responding explicitly to various themes and ideas in the earlier novel, *Border Districts* inevitably changes the meaning and position of *The Plains* itself. First of all, *The Plains* – which has been viewed as a stand-alone novel during the three decades since its publication – now will inevitably be viewed as the first part of a novelistic diptych. Moreover, what had previously appeared to be a definitive conclusion to *The Plains* now becomes an intermediary or unfolding moment in a larger dialogic structure that occurs over two works. The result of this is that *The Plains'* meaning and relation to Murnane's work is changed after the fact, which is an example of what I have been calling retrospective intention. I do not think this is an accidental process for Murnane, and this retrospective mode of authorial intervention resembles in many ways what Borges describes in his essay "Kafka and His Precursors" (1962): "The fact is that every writer creates his own precursors. His work modifies our conception of the past, as it will modify the future".[30] Borges' argument, of course, draws on T.S. Eliot's well-known assertion in "Tradition and the Individual Talent" (1919) that "when a new work of art is created something ... happens simultaneously to all the works of art which preceded it" such that the "values of each work of art toward the whole are readjusted".[31] Murnane's late writing similarly works in two directions, modifying both the future as well as the understanding of his earlier works. The resemblance to Borges is significant here, since Murnane himself lists Borges as one of the eight authors whose "books I would like to read yet again during the years left to me".[32]

---

30 Jorge Luis Borges, "Kafka and His Precursors", in *Selected Non-Fictions*, trans. Eliot Weinberger (New York: Viking, 1999), 365.
31 T.S. Eliot, *Selected Essays 1917–1932* (New York: Harcourt, Brace & Co. Inc., 1932), 5.
32 Murnane, *Invisible Yet Enduring Lilacs*, 182.

Retrospective Intention: The Implied Author in *Border Districts* and *The Plains*

Retrospective intention is also important for Murnane's work insofar as it demonstrates the capacity of the fictional to overcome the contingencies of reality. The long quotation that I discussed earlier from the interview with Tristan Foster emphasises the contingent aspects of Murnane's career. But these later interventions, from my perspective, scan as an authorial attempt to convert contingency into necessity. Of course, "Young Gerald" did not see "his life's work laid out in advance and progressing from book to book in an ever-so-orderly fashion", but the later works of Murnane are able to give a seeming and, I would argue, real coherence to this work by imbuing a sense of connectedness after the fact. This is both a more ambitious project and, arguably, a more significant authorial achievement since this process effectively rewrites the past and "solves" the problem of the contingency of the market by retrospectively making coherent the incoherent. In a sense, the legacy here becomes one not of following an established plan of authorial development, but rather of being able to generate the sense of one where no such thing existed.

This is particularly significant in the case of *The Plains*, which began as a fragment of a longer novel, entitled *The Only Adam*. Originally, the sections about the plains bookended a longer narrative in the middle, standing "in relation to the setting of the rest of the book as a mirage stands in relationship to the landscape that gives rise to it".[33] In other words, *The Plains* originally was *not* meant to be a stand-alone novel, but a narrative that was in a discursive relationship with another, longer (and still unpublished) narrative:

> The fact is that I see my books from a standpoint wholly different from the reader's standpoint. Take my book *The Plains*. For the common reader and the scholar alike, the words of the title denote a text of about 35,000 words. The meaning of that text may be debated, but the text itself is a fixed entity. For me, the text of the published work is sometimes far from my attention when I respond to the sound or the sight of the title *The Plains*. Sometimes, I don't even think of my third published book as being called *The Plains*. Instead, I think of it as having the title that I first gave it and defended for several months until my publishers wore me down. That title was *Landscape with Darkness and Mirage*. Sometimes, the title of the published work brings to my mind some of the ninety thousand words of the unpublished work of fiction *The Only Adam*, of which the text of *The Plains* was once part. Sometimes the words *The Plains* bring to my mind my interview with one or another of the three publishers who rejected *The Only Adam*.[34]

---

33 Gerald Murnane quoted in Wayne Macauley, "Far Enough: The Peculiar World of the Plains", Introduction to *The Plains* by Gerald Murnane (Melbourne: Text Publishing, 2014), viii.
34 Murnane, "The Still-Breathing Author".

Murnane's focus on other possible versions of *The Plains* is consistent with his interest in other possible realities, and the various alternate versions of himself that appear as "implied authors" across his works. But this passage, which emphasises *The Plains*' original belonging to a larger text and a more complex context, also helps to clarify how *Border Districts* revises this older novel.

This information suggests that *Border Districts* re-engages or re-enacts the original intention of The Plains by once again making it part of a textual diptych. From this perspective, *Border Districts* becomes a late revision or rewriting of *The Only Adam*; while *Border Districts* and the unpublished novel might share little in common in terms of their content, both present a discursive engagement with the "mirage" that is described in *The Plains*. *Border Districts*, although it enacts a retrospective revision of intention that is both textual and fictitious, nonetheless functions as a material corrective to the contingencies of publishing by returning *The Plains* to something like the discursive relationship envisioned in its original conception. Here, intention simultaneously becomes original, delayed and retrospective all at once. Perhaps the key virtue of fiction in Murnane's work is its capacity to transcend the limitations of the material world.

References

Birns, Nicholas. *Contemporary Australian Literature: A World Not Yet Dead*. Sydney: Sydney University Press, 2015.
Booth, Wayne C. *The Rhetoric of Fiction*. Chicago: University of Chicago Press, 1961.
Borges, Jorge Luis. "Kafka and His Precursors". In *Selected Non-Fictions*, translated by Eliot Weinberger, 363–65. New York: Viking, 1999.
Burns, Shannon. "The Scientist of His Own Experience: A Profile of Gerald Murnane", *Australian Book Review*, August 2015. https://bit.ly/38L4pyB.
Eliot, T.S. *Selected Essays 1917-1932*. New York: Harcourt, Brace & Co. Inc., 1932.
Foster, Tristan. "Eight Questions for Gerald Murnane", *3AM Magazine*, 21 April 2015. https://www.3ammagazine.com/3am/eight-questions-for-gerald-murnane/.
Hassan, Ihab. "Realism, Truth, and Trust in Postmodern Perspective", *Third Text* 17, no. 1 (2003): 1–13.
Kindt, Tom and Hans-Harald Muller. *The Implied Author: Concept and Controversy*. Berlin and New York: Walter de Gruyter, 2008.
Macauley, Wayne. "Far Enough: The Peculiar World of the Plains". Introduction to *The Plains*, by Gerald Murnane, vii–xiv. Melbourne: Text Publishing, 2014.
Mack, Maynard. *Collected in Himself: Essays Critical, Biographical, and Bibliographical on Pope and Some of His Contemporaries*. Volume 1. Wilmington: University of Delaware Press, 1982.
Murnane, Gerald. "The Still Breathing Author". *Sydney Review of Books*, 6 February 2018. https://sydneyreviewofbooks.com/the-still-breathing-author-gerald-murnane/.
———. *Border Districts*. Artarmon, NSW: Giramondo, 2017.

——. *A Million Windows*. Artarmon, NSW: Giramondo, 2014.
——. "The Three Archives of Gerald Murnane", *Music and Literature*, 11 November 2013. http://www.musicandliterature.org/features/2013/11/11/the-three-archives-of-gerald-murnane.
——. "The Breathing Author". In *Invisible Yet Enduring Lilacs* (2002), Artarmon, NSW: Giramondo, 2005.
——. *Emerald Blue*. Ringwood, Vic.: Penguin, 1995.
——. *Landscape with Landscape* (1985). Artarmon, NSW: Giramondo, 2016.
——. *The Plains*. Introduced by Ben Lerner. 1982; Melbourne: Text Publishing, 2014.
——. *The Plains*. Ringwood, Vic.: McPhee Gribble, 1982.
Salusinszky, Imre. *Gerald Murnane*. Melbourne: Oxford University Press, 1993.
Thompson, John B. *Merchants of Culture: The Publishing Business in the Twenty-First Century*. Cambridge: Polity Press, 2010.
West, Patrick. "The Ethical Vision of Gerald Murnane", *JASAL: Journal of the Association for the Study of Australian Literature* (1996): 221-27.
Wimsatt, William, K. and Monroe Beardsley. "The Intentional Fallacy", *The Sewanee Review*, 54, no. 3 (1946): 468-88.

6

Stream System, Salient Image and Feeling: Between *Barley Patch* and *Inland*

Brigid Rooney

> At the level of the poetic image, the duality of subject and object is iridescent, shimmering, unceasingly active in its inversions.[1]

In 1988, the year that saw publication of *Inland*, Gerald Murnane gave a talk to an audience at La Trobe University that was subsequently published as "Stream System".[2] The talk opened with a seemingly factual account of its author's morning walk from his nearby suburban home to the Bundoora campus:

> This morning, in order to reach the place where I am now, I went a little out of my way. I took the shortest route from my house to the place that you people probably know as SOUTH ENTRY. That is to say, I walked from the front gate of my house due west and downhill to Salt Creek then uphill and still due west from Salt Creek to the watershed between Salt Creek and a nameless creek that runs into Darebin Creek. When I reached the high ground that drains into the nameless creek, I walked north-west until I was standing about thirty metres south-east of the place that is denoted on Page 66A of Edition 18 of the *Melway Street Directory of Greater Melbourne* by the words STREAM SYSTEM. (117)

The audience on campus no doubt drew pleasure from this fastidiously plotted itinerary across mundane ground. The narrator takes his bearings, detailing his progress with respect to topographical coordinates, drawing on toponyms (or noting their lack) with declarative precision. In its published form, "Stream System"

---

1 Gaston Bachelard, *The Poetics of Space* (1964; Boston, MA: Beacon Press, 1994), xix.
2 Gerald Murnane's talk was first presented at La Trobe University on 1 July 1988, with the edited version first published in the *Age Monthly Review* (December 1988/January 1989) and reprinted in *Invisible Yet Enduring Lilacs* (Artarmon, NSW: Giramondo, 2005), 117-47. All subsequent page references are to the latter edition and appear in parentheses in the text.

mimes this precision with uppercase typography for the eponymous coordinate as given in the cited source, a specified edition of Melbourne's Melway Directory. The narrator, furthermore, notes his travel in a north-westerly direction towards "the place" marked "stream system" only then to observe, unnecessarily, that he stands south-east of the aforementioned site. The north-westerly axis of movement is here crossed by a reverse optic – a looking back on the stated coordinate from the opposite direction. Such a manoeuvre, familiar to Murnane's readers, carries an inbuilt redundancy that not only calls attention to its narrator's fussy precision but also to his routine mappings of himself and his figures within definitive, verifiable locations, forming spatial geometries that seem to provide knowable, reassuring coordinates.[3] The minute plotting of the short walk from home to the south entry of the campus draws attention to the markings of a map that precedes the terrain, that organises, channels and regulates "streams" within its own elaborated, rule-bound, and internally consistent system.

What does it mean, as the narrator says towards the end of his talk, to "write fiction by following the stream system" (147)? And if one were provisionally to separate this stream system into its various parts, would it explain the feelings engendered in at least some of his readers by Murnane's fiction? Geographer Miriam Hill defines a "stream system" as an "entire network of channels, of all sizes, that drains an area"; observing how channels "are fed by the sheetwash flowing down the topography", Hill notes that the "total area that feeds water to a stream is called the 'watershed' or drainage basin."[4] The crucial point here is the function of landscape as watershed, as dynamic system, whether built, natural or both, fed by a network of channels or streams, their sources and their destinations somewhere out of sight. In Murnane's "Stream System" talk, the narrator marks his location with respect to Darebin Creek, Salt Creek and an unnamed creek. On arrival at the place marked "STREAM SYSTEM" on the map, he contemplates separate yet linked bodies of water fed by the three creeks. These bodies of water, however, do not appear to him, as on the map, as blue-coloured ovals, but rather as yellow brown in colour, and twisted like hearts. The prose flows on, proceeding metonymically from one image to the next rather than according to some underlying causal narrative logic, from the slightly twisted shape of these bodies of water to the twisted shape of a human heart, to the tapering shape of a remembered piece of gold jewellery glimpsed in a catalogue, to his father's five sisters, the narrator's aunts, to a cane chair in an aunt's room where he sat as a child facing north towards America, in

---

3   One of many examples of Murnane's geometric mapping of his preferred geography can be found in his fictional work *Barley Patch* (Artarmon, NSW: Giramondo Press, 2009), 89–90. All subsequent references are to this edition and appear in parentheses in the text.
4   M.H. Hill, "Stream Systems", Dr M.H. Hill's Homepage, Jackson State University, Alabama (2013). http://www.jsu.edu/dept/geography/mhill/phylabtwo/lab7/stsysf.html

which he recalls imagining looking to the north-east, beyond the stone walls of the aunt's house, towards pale-blue sky and yellow-brown grasslands – and so on.

The design of the "Stream System" talk makes its classification as a piece of non-fiction profoundly unstable. On the one hand, the narrator's precise account of his walk from home to campus positions his listeners in the actual, visible world, invoking in a verifiable way his bearings in space and time. While this mapping, together with the anecdotal, biographical-seeming information the narrator folds into his talk *seems* to invoke non-fiction, *seems* to be authenticated by the breathing author, "Stream System" unravels this status: in collapsing the fact-fiction divide it undermines the stability of the author-narrator relation. This happens through its repetition of a familiar performance, the voice and habitual gestures of the Murnanean narrator. This figure recurs in and unifies Murnane's writing, from *The Plains* (1982) onwards.[5] Whenever I refer, in what follows, to "the narrator", it is this Murnanean narrator that I mean, always a compound figure, hovering somewhere between fact and fiction – seeming to invoke the author and his sources yet systematically undoing the stability of any such authenticating source of meaning. Confirmation of instability arrives at the end of the "Stream System" talk when the narrator explains that all along he has been reading from the "draft of a piece of fiction", and that he had *not* that morning stood in front of a body of yellow-brown water; rather, he had composed his words in the preceding week. The word "fiction" thus emerges as another key term, one that Murnane prefers to "novel" or "short story". His preference for "fiction" foregrounds the word's derivation in Latin: "fingere" and "fictio", to make, fashion, fabricate or feign.[6] Fiction is a design, a contrivance, with the unstable shuttle between the real and the feigned, the inauthentic, its key feature. Instability and indeterminacy condition and render powerful the feelings at the same time as they make elusive the meanings to which Murnane's fiction gives rise.

The contrivances of Murnane's fiction, its steady disruption of mimesis, cohere with the understanding of fiction as fabrication, invention or feigning. Readers of Murnane's *The Plains* have tended to construe it as postmodernist in orientation, with its endless play of uncertainty, and its seeming avoidance of underlying truths or meanings. Others, critical of this apparent postmodernism, suggest there is little to Murnane's fictional enterprise other than narcissistic self-reproduction.[7] The

---

5   Gerald Murnane, *The Plains* (1982; Melbourne: Text, 2000).
6   *Oxford English Dictionary*, online, s.v. "fiction, n".
7   See, for example, Ken Gelder and Paul Salzman, *After the Celebration: Australian Fiction 1989–2007* (Carlton, Vic.: Melbourne University Press, 2009). In their survey, they remark that beyond its initial novelty, postmodernist fiction can strike readers as "self-indulgent and predictable"; they suggest this applies to Murnane: "Circling and re-circling a series of solipsistic reflections, his fictions can be seen as either hypnotic and evocative, or as monotonous and claustrophobic" (129).

view of Murnane's writing as merely self-indulgent seems tone deaf to its existential concerns, moral tenor and emotional freight. In my reading, the Murnanean narrator is indeed a paradoxical figure who inducts the reader through his own often self-defeating involutions, through the metafictional maze of his mental landscape, towards giddying moments charged with feeling. The design of Murnane's stream system, the way the reader navigates it, is predicated on both the imposition of distances and their occasional abeyance. In *A Million Windows* (2014), for example, the narrator explains how he "strives to keep between his actual self and his seeming self and his seeming reader such seeming-distances as will maintain between all three personages a lasting trust".[8] Relations of trust are not built on any easy traffic with an author figure who can settle or distil meanings once and for all. Rather, the "seeming distances" of the stream system spatialise time, regulate feeling and suggest meaning. Murnane's stream system is both his fiction's containing artifice and sourced in carefully distanced actual materials, in which bearings are taken from place, memory and life experience. Indeed, the greater the metafictional distances imposed, the closer the narrative draws to the most concentrated nexus of image, feeling and meaning. Yet the stream system ensures that meanings so produced resist any attempted paraphrase or closure.

I opened with "Stream System" and shall return to it briefly in my conclusion. I am far from the first to observe that this talk offers readers a key to Murnane's writing, a meta-language with which to describe both his preoccupations and the design that holds them. In this chapter, I seek to discern elements of the stream system in two of Murnane's longer works, starting with *Barley Patch* (2009), and then moving back in time to *Inland* (1988). In so doing I deliberately read across Murnane's fourteen-year hiatus, the break that now contours his whole body of work. This writing caesura amplifies silences within individual works as well as gaps between them. These eloquent silences marshal but do not finally pin down wider significance. What I hope to articulate is how the materially spatialised design of his narratives generates, regulates and releases feeling within and across Murnane's fiction. This happens through its sentence systems, through its metafictional and metaleptic crossings and through the orchestration of images. In particular, I seek to register those feelings summoned in and through the forms of Murnane's writing, his sentences and images, to observe how its geometries consort with its meandering flows and salient images, and how these patterns yield emotions, the sources and full significance of which, however, are caught only fleetingly or sidelong.

---

8   Gerald Murnane, *A Million Windows* (Artarmon, NSW: Giramondo, 2014), 125. All subsequent references are to this edition and appear in parentheses in the text.

First, however, taking "stream system" at the most literal, earthly, geographic level, it may be worth reflecting on Murnane's preoccupation with place, landscape and topography – the latter being most evident in his mappings of places, built and natural. Yet Murnane is less concerned with the vivid detailing of features than with shifting, dynamic interactions among elements, and here the concept of topology proves useful. Murnane's fiction exhibits a topological imagination. Topology is a mathematical and design concept. As distinct from geometry (the science of the measurement of abstracted shapes), topology is interested in the situation and placement of things, especially in the relations, the potential or thwarted connectivity, of forms, shapes and objects to each other. Topology concerns itself with shapes that are durable even as they undergo deformation. It prompts questions about both the pragmatic and aesthetic (design) consequences entailed in the siting and relative placing of things – that is, with the flow and interconnections that may be contrived or arranged among them. For Angus Fletcher, from whose book *The Topological Imagination* (2016) I borrow the term, topology is relevant for art and science alike. Both are concerned in different ways with perception, with apprehending in fuzzy yet grounded and three-dimensional terms the "terrestrial biosphere": "*living space*", suggests Fletcher, "is revealed by … *topology*,where the placement of our lives is an imagined quality of our existence".[9] Furthermore, he contends:

> to understand life we must be concerned with the way its local character coheres within a wider terrestrial location, as the Earth travels in the cosmos, by moving up and down varying scales of power and value. Eventually that concern allows us to think about just and equitable scales of life's resources on planet Earth – not elsewhere, but here on the planetary surface of our sphere.[10]

Murnane's stream system registers the interactive dynamism of otherwise fixed forms – where forms are epiphenomena represented in maps, constructs or designs, and always distinguishable from the terrain to which they refer. While system suggests an often human-engineered, durable order, stream suggests natural flux and elemental flow – something like time – that runs through things, bending, altering and transforming their shapes. The philosophical question Fletcher poses for the topological imagination is how it may help us address environmental change and its existential threat: "how", he asks, "shall we think of permanence in the midst of fundamental change?"[11]

---

9 Angus Fletcher, *The Topological Imagination: Spheres, Edges, and Islands* (Cambridge, MA: Harvard University Press, 2016), 2.
10 Fletcher, *The Topological Imagination*, 4.
11 Fletcher, *The Topological Imagination*, 3.

The existential challenge wrought by earthly impermanence and change imbues Murnane's fictional project, marking its preoccupation with memory systems and sites, and with archiving processes. Mid-century suburbia, that quintessential site of changeable modernity, is the living space that often houses Murnane's writing, including his narrator's writing room; in turn the suburbs are homely sites and shapes for Murnane's fictional archiving. Suburbs are unsettled, ephemeral and ubiquitous, and suburbia signifies marginal, monotonous and taken-for-granted spaces that are easily overlooked.[12] Viewed from a distance, suburban space is the systematic product of the cadastral survey. In close-up, however, it is rich in detail, with its private worlds and stratified social geographies. The scale shifting required for suburban terrain is also required for plains and prairies: in both cases, panoptic-level sameness camouflages micro-level diversity of life and scene. Suburbia in Murnane's writing serves as camouflage for the narrator, but also as platform for his dizzying glimpses of ever-receding plains.

In *Barley Patch*, we can observe patterns that recur within and across Murnane's fiction. Its narrative cycles through an intricate network of remembered suburban, outer suburban and regional locations in the roughly triangular space between Melbourne, Bendigo and Warrnambool, visiting the comfortable rural homes of the narrator's extended family, the more ramshackle homes provided by his debt-ridden, gambling father, and places inhabited by the young man during his fitful and lonely early career. The narrator details his indecisive dealings in worldly matters of dating, courtship, employment and sociability, his episodes of alcoholism and mental duress, his yearnings and frustrations. These behaviours are at one level the outward expression of a mid-century habitus formed by a parochial, socially conservative suburban milieu, and further amplified by that other socialising institution, a sexually repressive, pre-Vatican II Catholic Church. The Church – or rather the narrator's boyhood dealings with its figures, institutions and rituals – is the source of objects that stimulate contemplation (rosary beads, stained-glass windows, holy cards, female icons) and the dispositions of the narrator (his inhibitions, naivety and sublimation, and both his wariness and adoration of distant female figures). A formation both suburban and Catholic channels the narrator's elaborate fantasies, always absurd yet always sincere. In *Barley Patch*, for instance, the narrator reports that his chief character joins a seminary so he can freely meditate and write, access its upper storey, and glimpse far distant landscapes. This plan swiftly founders, and the Church itself, as elsewhere in Murnane's fiction, inherently disappoints chief character and narrator alike, failing to kindle belief or satisfaction in its dogmas.

---

12 I investigate the contradictions of suburbia in my book *Suburban Space, the Novel and Australian Modernity* (London: Anthem Press, 2018).

American eco-critic Lawrence Buell suggests that Murnane's metafictions are the means by which the curbing of desire is concomitant with its channelling into fantasy, generating his sublime vision of the plains:

> Murnane's deployment of his narrator's marginal position via a strategy of discursive metafiction allows him at once to de-realise through the filter of suburban fantasy and to reinstate through the magnifying lens of balked desire this particularly iconic subset of native hinterland, such that in *Inland* physical territory montages into dream, yet dream opens up into grand fantasy of an all-encompassing planetary grassland.[13]

Suburban Catholicism shapes the bodily comportment of Murnane's figures – the piously lowered eyes (looking from the sides of his eyes, "guarding his eyes") – as well as their exorbitant fantasies and yearnings directed towards ideal women.[14] While faith in Catholic dogma evaporates, as the narrator attests, its ritualised gestures, holy figures, divine personages and otherworldliness are transmuted in writing. Luke Carman takes the point further, identifying in Murnane's work and that of Jack Kerouac (deeply admired by Murnane) a similarly ornate aesthetic consistent with Catholicism, as seen in their mutual attempts "to express the experience of an infinite, divine creativity present in the material world".[15] The disciplined and the ecstatic are both manifest in the narrator's always deferred desire for communion with an ideal female personage.

What Catholicism arguably also furnishes is iconophilia, the love of images and what they yield. Iconophilia is no mere intellectual exercise for the narrator. The image is a thing of beauty, desire and enigma, glinting with feeling and stimulating the urge to write, as he explains in *A Million Windows*:

> Whatever sort of image the author has in mind, he feels a certain feeling seeming to emanate from the image. The feeling is persistent, intense, and sometimes troubling, and yet, at the same time, promising. When the author first becomes aware of this feeling, he might seem to receive the same sort of wordless message that sometimes reaches him from some or another image-person or image-object in some or another dream. He seems to receive wordlessly the message: *Write*

13　Lawrence Buell, "Antipodal Propinquities? Environmental (Mis)Perceptions in American and Australian Literary History", in *Reading Across the Pacific: Australia-United States Intellectual Histories*, ed. Robert Dixon and Nicholas Birns (Sydney: Sydney University Press, 2010), 16.
14　These locutions – guarding his eyes, looking from the sides of the eyes – recur, *inter alia*, in *Inland*, *Barley Patch* and *Border Districts*.
15　Luke Carman, "In the Room with Gerald Murnane", *Sydney Review of Books*, 24 April 2018. https://sydneyreviewofbooks.com/in-the-room-with-gerald-murnane/

about me in order to discover my secret and to learn what a throng of images, as yet invisible, lie around me. (181)

Each of Murnane's works, whatever its length or type (essay or book, fiction or non-fiction) obeys the above italicised dictum. Each work at first meanders but this meandering quality belies the careful placement and gathering of images until they throng together and reverberate. It is the task of the reader to pay attention, to discern and hold images in memory, to be receptive to their promise, to the feelings and meanings they engender. But what meanings, and what feelings? One approach is suggested by Anthony Uhlmann, who reads *A Million Windows* against recurring motifs and images, the clustering of sounds and silences, around a dark (hitherto suppressed) family secret. Uhlmann connects the revelation delivered in Murnane's fiction with images and details elsewhere in his archive that make for meaningful resonance in the spaces between visible and invisible worlds, between fiction and life.[16] The secret, however, is both unveiled and veiled. It is not possible to pin down the final truth. Instead we are afforded an oblique glimpse, through the sides of our eyes, as it were, and by means of metafictional systems and streaming images. Far from being something new, this design is the most consistent and recurrent feature, the central logic, of Murnane's writing.

We can observe the stream system design in fictions that span Murnane's writing hiatus. The fourteen-year caesura itself forms a kind of silence, and the narrator's metafictional returns across this gap increase the resonance among images. As Emmett Stinson suggests in his reading of *Border Districts* (2017), the fictions published after the writing break retrospectively revise elements of the earlier works, generatively reshaping meanings.[17] As the book that ends the break, *Barley Patch* does important rhetorical work, resuming transmission and restoring the interrupted flow of communication between narrator and reader, finally returning us in its title and the longer arc of its writing to the backyard setting in Bendigo of Murnane's earliest work, *Tamarisk Row* (1974).[18] Yet *Barley Patch* also poses unanswerable stream system questions about where a body of work begins or ends, or what the correct order of writing, and its provenance, might be. Crossing thence to Murnane's pre-break period, I observe the drifting and leaping images delivered via *Inland*'s stream system. My decision to work in reverse order of publication is in an effort to ward off the temptation to read the later work as

---

16 Anthony Uhlmann, "Silence and Sound in the Sentences of Gerald Murnane's *A Million Windows*", *JASAL: Journal of the Association for the Study of Australian Literature* 15, no. 1 (2015), 8. https://openjournals.library.sydney.edu.au/index.php/JASAL/article/view/9937.
17 See Emmett Stinson, "Retrospective Intention: The Implied Author and the Coherence of the Oeuvre in *Border Districts* and *The Plains*", this volume.
18 Gerald Murnane, *Tamarisk Row* (1974; North Ryde, NSW: Angus & Robertson/Sirius, 1988).

though it is more revelatory than the earlier fiction, though there is no doubt that to read Murnane's works in order of their publication is also illuminating. What reading against their chronology brings into focus is their spatialised, topological relations and interconnectivity. Each work forms its own internal micro-ecology; each is also tributary to Murnane's interconnecting literary landscape.

A Preposterous Reading of *Barley Patch*

Barley Patch is punctuated by questions, or rather musings, the first of which – "Must I write?" – produces different meanings depending where the emphasis is placed: is it "*Must* I write?" or "Must I *write*?"[19] In the first case, weariness is suggested: are we to suppose the break was a consequence of writerly exhaustion, or lack of inspiration? In the second case, did the break afford an opportunity for creative exploration by some other means than writing? There is no definitive answer. Both meanings are in play. As *Barley Patch* unfolds, the questions become more elaborate yet their division of the stream of thought and memory seems arbitrary. *Barley Patch* is comprised of two sections, the first being far longer than the second. Whatever organises this division of material is not obvious. Towards the end of Part 1 the narrator declares: "Some or another conception has been reported at last. This text is surely at an end" (174), and yet Part 2 rolls on. Even so, a logical structure can be identified, one that works to produce layers between visible and invisible worlds. The material in Part 1 mostly deals with its narrator's reported memories in and around the swampy, south-west coastal region of Victoria, whether scenes from childhood involving the narrator's parents and their siblings (uncles and aunts, married and unmarried) or the narrator's recollections of female personages met in fictions he encountered as a child. Part 2 reprises these patterns but via the doubly distancing metafictional frame of the narrator's reports on the doings of "the chief character" of a work of fiction he had abandoned fourteen years earlier. Each part develops its own internal network of phrases and images, and each achieves its own crescendo. Perhaps the most significant element, indeed the emotional core of this particular work, is what we learn of the narrator's relations with his youngest aunt and youngest uncle. The colours of black and gold ultimately preside, drawing together earliest memories and desired objects that resonate with what one might imagine to be the interior colours of the "barley patch".

---

19 Gerald Murnane, *Barley Patch* (Artarmon, NSW: Giramondo, 2009). All subsequent references are to this edition and appear in parentheses in the text.

In the narrative's present, the narrator sits at his writing desk in his room in a suburb of Melbourne. Confinement to this unremarkable room is the precondition for his expansions outwards, or rather inwards. The narrator's layered fictional scenarios take us inland to Bendigo but mostly south to the continental edge near Warrnambool. We learn of his interest in trans-oceanic grasslands in New Zealand or Tasmania, places he envisages at his back even as he gazes in a north-westerly direction. As always, entry to unrolling landscapes is ingeniously deferred, circumvented or sabotaged. At the same time, portals to landscapes proliferate in thwarted visits to the upper storeys of mansions, monasteries or convents, whether via Marcel Proust, Mandrake the Magician, lime green or emerald blue panes of stained glass in church windows, a calendar reproduction of Claude Lorrain's *Landscape with Samuel Anointing David*, or Irish horn rosary beads. Even these glimpses are only ever anticipated. No "visible" landscapes extend from the room in which the narrator sits or from the desk at which he writes. It is the blank enclosure of the writing room that engenders infinitely unfolding "invisible" landscapes.

Suburban spaces hosting childhood memories are filtered by Catholic habits of mind. Coalescing with the desire to glimpse landscapes is the narrator's desire to approach and commune with (female) fictional personages, such as Huldah in Sydney Courtier Hobson's *The Glass Spear*, a serialised story in *The Australian Journal*. Discarding all but those elements in any given work that may assist him in his endeavours, the narrator becomes a ghostly intruder in the remembered text. He envisages enacting the role of what Henry Jenkins, following Michel de Certeau, calls a textual poacher, operating autonomously within the margins and spaces afforded by his memory of a given text.[20] The logic of textual poaching extends well beyond remembered works of fiction, however, to all the systems and spaces through which the narrator navigates. In Part 2, the narrator reports how the chief character of his formerly abandoned work of fiction participates with a group of young men (though only speculatively) in a black mass, orgies and pornography. Even here, the movement of his speculations and desire carries the chief character swiftly beyond the tedium of obscenity towards the infinitely unfolding turf of the imagined model racecourse he plans to build.

The main system that guides the reader through *Barley Patch* is the rigorously crafted Murnanean sentence.[21] But insofar as each flows successively into the next, sentences also constitute the labyrinth through which the reader must travel.

---

20 See Henry Jenkins, *Textual Poachers: Television Fans and Participatory Culture* (New York: Routledge, 1992) and Michel de Certeau's discussion of reading as poaching in *The Practice of Everyday Life* (Berkeley: University of California Press, 1984), 169.

21 The care taken by Murnane over his sentences is regularly observed by Murnane himself and by his readers. See for instance Imre Salusinszky's discussion in *Gerald Murnane* (Melbourne: Oxford University Press, 1993), 10-12.

Stream System, Salient Image and Feeling: Between *Barley Patch* and *Inland*

Sentences form a spatial plane, both rigorously controlled and endlessly branching, a channelled yet flowing stream system. In each work, sentences carry a distinctive array of locutions. By locutions I mean ways of saying things – whether words that yield striking visual content or an array of prosaic yet ubiquitous phrases, like "so to call", "one or another" or "fictional personage". One effect of these locutions is topographical, or rather topological: they form the very fabric, texture and connectivity of Murnane's sentences. They provide comfort amid the branching, circuitous or looping tributaries of sentence-thought. The security afforded by the narrator's locutions is undermined, however, by the cumulative force of qualifying terms, his uses of the double negative or his ever-present conditional mood.

Just as any watershed or stream system differs from any other in its micro-ecology, so do variations in locution differentiate one Murnane text from another. The stream system that is *Barley Patch* features such phrases as "readers of goodwill", "hasty readers" and "readers of prowess". Two terms deserve particular note: "conception" and "preposterous". The word "preposterous" recurs five times in *Barley Patch*, in which the narrator's intricate scenarios are indeed "preposterous" in the everyday sense of absurd, ridiculous or outrageous. But the Murnanean project becomes "preposterous" in the original Latinate sense of *prae-posterous*, signifying inversion of an accepted order, when the last is put first. *Barley Patch* routinely inverts the order of given hierarchical domains – the high and the low, the morally pure and the pornographic, reality and fiction, cosmos and heterocosmos. An extended passage in Part 1 concerns the narrator's attempt to conceive of the period before his own conception by reporting on events around the courtship of his mother and father. The Tristram Shandy-like attempt to remember events leading to one's own conception is precisely "preposterous". The association of "preposterous" with "conception" results in a further twist towards the end of *Barley Patch*. In the relevant sequence the narrator reports what he might have said to a dream personage begging to become a character in his fiction, explaining how many a personage was the object of his continual curiosity, and how: "I longed to be on familiar terms with the personage, even if my only means of achieving this might have been the preposterous project of my becoming myself a personage in my own fiction" (254). The narrator's desire for a preposterous position is followed a few pages on by a preposterous manoeuvre. The narrator's detailing of the preoccupations of a "personage [sitting] among the filing cabinets" produces a *mise en abyme* in which the author-narrator impossibly becomes a personage in his own extended fictional system.

The proliferation of metafictional scenarios in *Barley Patch* preposterously inverts the categorical ordering of reality and fiction. Towards the end of *Barley Patch*, the narrator offers to explain what previous "readers of goodwill" seem to have missed in a previous fictional work, "The Interior of Gaaldine" – and this is indeed the title of the last piece in the last of Murnane's books to be published before his fourteen-year break.[22] Gaaldine, we are reminded by the narrator, is the fictional world imagined by the fictional inhabitants of the fictional world of Gondal invented by the Brontë children. In *Barley Patch*, the eponymous patch of barley, located on the perimeter of the narrator's childhood backyard in Bendigo, routes the narrator's metafictional regressions through the Brontës' Gaaldane: "If ever I had myself written a diary-entry comparable to the diary-entry mentioned above, I might have written that the people of the tamarisks were of a mind to discover the interior of the barley patch" (252–3). Any boundary separating the real from the fictional is here not just breached but utterly confounded. These preposterous manoeuvres, furthermore, mean that little clear distinction can be sustained between the Murnanean narrator who guides us within the fiction and any other Murnanean persona we might meet, whether in talks at universities, in filmed interviews online, or among steel filing cabinets. Murnane's preposterous project re-spatialises the seemingly divided topologies of reality and fiction, joining their separate territories into a continuous Mobius strip.

I have been suggesting that the branching tributaries of Murnane's sentence-system are conduits for his images. These words, with their little blazes of light, recur, disappear and re-emerge downstream, gradually gathering a rhapsodic intensity that, as Gaston Bachelard puts it, creates a "sudden salience on the surface of the psyche".[23] Bachelard's use of "salience" is especially resonant. The word comes from the Latin, *salientem*, the present participle of *salire*, to leap. Salience is used of pulses (beating strongly), of water (jetting forth, leaping upwards) and, in the context of heraldry, of animals (in heraldic images showing animals with hind legs on the ground and fore paws elevated, as if in the act of leaping).[24] Bachelard figures poetic images as surging, as resonating from without and reverberating within the psyche, so that "the duality of subject and object is iridescent, shimmering, unceasingly active in its inversions".[25]

In Part 1 of *Barley Patch*, the narrator reports how as a boy visiting his girl cousins he had sought to look inside their doll's house. He waits until night so he can peer inside undisturbed. He considers inserting a finger to touch objects in the upper room but is fearful of leaving a trace. The image of intrusion recurs, gathering a chain of associations: the image of a giant eye looking in, a hand ready to grope,

---

22 Gerald Murnane, "The Interior of Gaaldine", in *Emerald Blue* (Ringwood, Vic.: McPhee Gribble/Penguin, 1995). The subtitle of this piece reads: "A true account of certain events recalled on the evening when I decided to write no more fiction" (185).
23 Bachelard, *The Poetics of Space*, xv.
24 *Oxford English Dictionary*, online, "salient, adj. and n".
25 Bachelard, *The Poetics of Space*, xix.

the narrator as ghostly intruder in fictional places, an aunt using her finger to scrape food from behind her teeth, the finger of a priest inside the holy tabernacle. These images of intrusion seem to relay sexual anxiety, hinting at penetration or abuse. Intrusion is loaded with disturbing feelings. Yet later, surfacing in an entirely different context, the image seems to pivot in its associations:

> at a time when I supposed that I might begin to write a piece of fiction in which one of the central images was of a fern *protruding* through a wall of bluestone and another central image was of a strand of hair lying across the forehead of a female person, I began to understand that a further central image was of green bunches of fronds moving underwater at unpredictable intervals … (77, my emphasis)

Images gather resonance and salience by means of their distribution in the stream system. Collected from various half glimpsed sources, they are borne along on a flowing current, forming tributaries, networks and patterns, changing in value and character, so that what gradually takes hold are complex, unnameable feelings. Across *Barley Patch* beautiful images chime like bells sounding, or little shards of glowing glass. From the fernery to the fern frond protruding from a bluestone wall, to blue and green fronds waving in underwater currents or in an aquarium, to the image of a king-in-the-lake, to the forsaken merman, to strands of hair lying across a forehead, to little birds (pheasants, plovers or chats) nesting amid grasses, images become iridescent, shimmering and reverberating. Their perpetually altering distribution – their de- and re-contextualisation – garners tangible energy and emotional freight.

Emotion is charged by the dynamic between systematic retention and release, by the effort of containment and its sudden relaxation. In *Barley Patch* the narrator tells us that though he has read many books he now cannot recall many of their details. Concern with loss of memory correlates with the narrative drive towards systems that hold and contain. Near the end of *Barley Patch* the narrator refers us to Frances Yates' book *The Art of Memory*, fleetingly giving us to understand that grassy plains, racetracks, jockey colours, swampy wetlands, ferns, birds' nests, personages in books, and two-storeyed houses constitute a memory palace. These images, and the branches that bear them, become a mnemonic system securing the million threads of life, arresting time, decay and mortality:

> My memory-system might have seemed to occupy no more than an upper room in a building of two or three storeys but its figurative extent would have seemed to me no less than old Bruno's hermetical labyrinth would have seemed to him. Tract after tract of mostly level grassy countryside, each with trees on its farther side – this would have been universe enough for me. (263)

As is often the case in Murnane's fictions, *Barley Patch* takes shape as a memory palace, a system of memory retention capable of affording seemingly infinite expansion. Yet the apparatus is also provisional and tenuous. There comes a moment when the apparatus trembles, and the tenor of the prose shifts. Take, for example, the sequence that reports on relations between the narrator and his youngest uncle. This crucial sequence is prefaced by two alternative reading scenarios. The first scenario emphasises the absolute integrity of the fictive world, refusing the notion that reported images, personages or scenes could have any traffic with the so-called real world. The narrator advises that this first scenario, which strictly contains everything within the realm of fiction, is designed for readers of "prowess" (165). The second scenario, we are warned, is "for the sake of those readers whose prowess I could never admire" who imagine the narrator is no fictional personage but a "mere human person hardly different from themselves" (165). This untrustworthy scenario seems to relax metafictional distances and offer a glimpse of something real. What these two reading scenarios preface is an account of the narrator's long estrangement from his youngest uncle due to the latter's disgust at the former's first two published works of fiction.[26] Thereafter follows the narrator's report of his visit to the hospital bedside of this uncle, who is dying an early death from cancer. In the course of his account, the narrator's metafictional apparatus, maintained by such devices as qualifiers, double negatives and conditional tense, quietly vanishes. The prose acquires a graceful simplicity. For most of the visit the narrator and his uncle speak in their accustomed manner, referring only in coded terms to what had occasioned their rift:

> We were still outwardly cheerful as I prepared to leave, although we both surely knew that we would never meet again in the place that is sometimes called *this world*, as though to suggest that at least one other world may exist. When we came to shake hands, my youngest uncle thanked me for what he called my wonderful companionship during our earlier years together. I was so surprised that I was able to grasp his hand and to look him in the eye and then to stride to the door of his room and for some little distance along the corridor of the hospital before I began to weep. (170)

Notwithstanding the narrator's caveat, it would seem preposterous to suggest that this scene is meant only for readers who lack prowess. Its power derives from the way the realms of life and fiction resonate. Its relaxation of the narrator's vigilance,

---

26 These remarks of course conjure elements in Murnane's first two books, *Tamarisk Row* (1974) and *A Lifetime on Clouds* (1976), neither of which has the first-person narrator of his subsequent works, but both of which explore and exercise many of his chief preoccupations, sites and landscapes.

the lapse in his labyrinthine cogitations, the shift into something akin to *this* visible world produces tension with the reader's recognition that this can only be a temporary shift, that the usual mode of transmission will soon be resumed, that orders will reverse again.

In Murnane's writing, the feeling borne by the stream system remains hidden or latent within it, waiting for the moment of release. Emotion gathers around images and scenes that conjure earliest memories that deal in separation, mortality, grief and love. Camouflaged in the prose, emotion may suddenly break cover. These moments have their own objective correlative in *Barley Patch*, in its swampy wetlands. We see it in the image of striped quail chicks in ankle-high grass that the youngest uncle teaches his nephew how to see, just at the moment they run from cover towards the sound of the calling mother-bird.

Drifting or Leaping *Inland*

Stream system also characterises the design of Murnane's earlier work, *Inland*, though the latter is more melancholic than *Barley Patch*. *Inland* yields its own distinctive topology, its series of relations, connections and flows among figures, sites and landscapes. The narrator of *Inland* – as in the "Stream System" talk – always places himself *between* the topographical coordinates provided by streams, rivers or creeks. The condition of betweenness – between creeks, between distant places, between points in time, between girl-women, between the narrator's writing self and his dream landscapes – indicates the presence of stream system. We first meet the narrator in the Great Alföld, in Hungary's Szolnok County, between the Rivers Sio and Sarvis. He would seem to be a wealthy landowner, occupying a room in a manor house on a great estate. He writes, as he tells us in English, in his "heavy-hearted Magyar" language.[27] He says he is uncertain whether he will see, if he goes to his windows and looks out onto the landscape, a certain sweep-arm well with its long pole pointing to the sky, or whether he has only remembered or dreamed it. Later, without any clear rationale for the shift, the narrator tells of various locations in and around Melbourne and regional Victoria, recalling – or dreaming – scenes from his boyhood. The very first gesture of the narrator, as he summons each scene, is to place himself between streams – between Moonee and Merri Creeks, between Hopkins River and Russell Creek, between Scotchman's and Elster Creeks. This ritual forges a globally extensive, locally intensive network of memory places as the boy's family shifts from home to home, in micro-migrations

---

27 Gerald Murnane, *Inland* (1988; Sydney: Sydney University Press, 2003), 5. All subsequent references are to this edition and appear in parentheses in the text.

propelled by the father's predicament as a gambler in flight from his debtors. To be always between rivers might seem to suggest stability, but the effect of the series is to undermine any such stability, suggesting uprootedness, precarity and loss.

Murnane's topological imagination is evident in *Inland*, in its concern with relations among far-flung places, objects and figures, in its search for durability and connection amid change, ephemerality and loss. The narrator's Szolnok-Melbourne axis is triangulated by the location of his editor, translator and reader in the aptly named town of Ideal in South Dakota, in North America. Anne Kristaly Gunnarsen is married to the cold Swedish scientist Gunnar T. Gunnarsen; both are employed by the Calvin O. Dahlberg Institute, which is engaged in the scientific investigation of the world's plains and prairies. Anne Kristaly works on *Hinterland*, the journal of the Bureau for the Exchange of Data on Plains and Grasslands (BEDGAP). All these terms resonate curiously with the project of *Inland* itself – with its beds and its gaps, its (em)beddings within and gaps between multiple landscapes, between life and death. The Institute is a dark mirror, perhaps parody, of the narrator's enterprise in *Inland*, figuring encompassing yet potentially imprisoning desire. It is a system for classification and retention, the travesty of a memory palace in which sinister technocrats seem implicated in the abuse of women and servants. These things shadow other elements in the narrative.

It is unusual for an ideal female figure to be accorded a proper name in Murnane's fiction. That Anne Kristaly is so named distinguishes and isolates her, making her a counterpart of the isolated narrator. Yet her identification also makes her a reference point that facilitates her later inclusion within a coalescing network of unnamed female figures, including the girl from Bendigo Street, focus of the narrator's remembered boyhood desire. According to the narrator, Anne Kristaly thinks of him as dead, and consequently he must think of himself as dead. She does not receive his parcels full of pages because these, so thinks the narrator in terms that suggest depression and isolation, are intercepted by the sinister Gunnarsen or gangs of scientists. Vast distances – cultural, geographic, personal – are interposed between narrator and editor. These are crossed, however, by their parallel circumstances as migrants. For the birthplace of Anne Kristaly is the Transdanubian region of Hungary, while the birthplace, or "native district", of the narrator – located though he is in Hungary and writing though he is in heavy-hearted Magyar – is Melbourne. The plight of migrants, far from home, uprooted from their "native district", the displaced, the dislocated, the unhoused – forms the most significant emotional nexus of *Inland*, corresponding too with the narrator's memory of his encounter, in a 1950s school playground, with migrant girls from the Baltic region. The narrator's communications with ideal female figures – his writings and correspondence – are never direct but always involve tenuous mediation or go-betweens, whether with his editor in South Dakota, or with the girl from Bendigo Street via the girl from Bendigo. The similarity of the names of these latter girl-women connects their otherwise separate identities. Topologically speaking, their similarity promotes an interconnecting flow of meanings. The narrative's female figures mark and collapse distances between suburban and regional sites and between continents.

The sense of geographic expanse in *Inland* is counterpointed by the containment or confinement, in the implied present, of the writer in his room. The writer is functionally and thematically isolated, a figure out of time, whose role is to write, to thread together disparate places across vast distances in time and space. The word "drift" recurs regularly in *Inland*, developing significance: early on, the narrator observes "white or grey clouds drifting over my flat lands" and the "white or grey pages of books drifting across the space behind covers and spines" (7-8). The narrator also drifts in his room, his writing space, between Hungary and his "native district" within Melbourne. In his 1993 study of Murnane's fiction, Imre Salusinszky suggests that *Inland* has two narrators – or rather two "versions" of the narrator.[28] In the opening forty pages the narrator addresses his reader from inside the manor house in Hungary; beyond this point, he summons remembered locations in his "native district" in suburban Melbourne. Murnane, however, insists there is only one narrator.[29] Situated in his room, located in, dreaming about, or imagining himself dreaming about landscapes, the narrator is a unifying figure implicating multiple worlds simultaneously. Through the narrator's writing, disparate worlds become interconnected and networked. The narrator tends to avoid, for example, the proper names of locations – those, that is, at the scale of village or suburb – identifying these only with respect to surrounding rivers or creeks and preferring terms like "district" (233 mentions) or "county" (109 mentions) rather than "suburb" (only 3 mentions).[30] This common diction brings rhetorical unity to disparate landscapes of Hungary, North America and Australia. Places on three continents – Szolnok County in Hungary, Ideal in South Dakota and Moonee Ponds in Melbourne – drift apart and together, like the pages loosed from books, pages no longer held by the unifying form of the codex.

Words and pages from other texts – from Gyula Illyés' *People of the Puszta*, Emily Brontë's *Wuthering Heights*, Thomas Hardy's *Tess of the D'Urbervilles* and André Maurois' biography of Marcel Proust – drift into and interleave with the

---

28 Salusinszky nominally holds to a distinction by referring to the Melbourne narrator and the Hungarian narrator, yet he also recognises the spatial crossings and paradox involved, asserting that both narrators are "writing from the same library, but on opposite sides of the world". Salusinszky, *Gerald Murnane*, 76.
29 Gerald Murnane states this view in his "Foreword" to the 2013 edition of *Inland* (Artarmon, NSW: Giramondo, 2013), Kindle edition, Loc 36.
30 These figures are the result of the relevant word searches in the Kindle edition of *Inland*.

narrative. The image of interleaving narratives corresponds with the narrator's dictum that "each place has another place in it" (91), that "each person is more than one person" (83). These layerings cohere with the cited words, attributed to Paul Eluard, that "There is another world but it is in this one" (87). These words too have drifted into the narrative, having long ago become detached from their original context, and having reached the narrator via the preliminary pages of a book by Patrick White (unnamed but readily identifiable as *The Solid Mandala*). If we think of the narrator of *Inland*, as Murnane insists, as singular rather than split, then the drifting of pages and locations – that of his own and others – both towards and away from him, suggests the internalisation and immanence of multiple landscapes and texts within the writing, dreaming self. Each narrator is always more than one narrator, drifting or migrating away from, or towards, his multiple landscapes. He holds them together in his mind.

The drifting and layering of people, landscapes and pages, suggesting slow horizontal movement, is interrupted by a shocking image of vertical fall, in the image of a young woman who leaps into a well. This leap is the culmination of a series begun with the narrator's opening image, remembered or dreamed, of the sweep-arm well, with its great pole pointing up to the sky. The pole and the well bisect the lateral plains and prairies of *Inland*. The leap is that of a young woman in her desperate bid to escape, it would seem, the routine sexual abuse that is her lot as a girl of a *puszta* who lives in conditions of servitude. The image of the well and the girl's leap haunts the narrator, correlating with other hints of the abuse of women by violent men. The scene of the young girl's death is recounted by Illyés in *People of the Puszta*, in which he describes having witnessed, as a young boy, the moment when the young woman's body is pulled up from the well at dawn by cowherds. The page from his description drifts into Murnane's narrative. The cowherds place the young woman so she lies "on the thin ice formed by the water … spilt from the well", her eyes open to the sky. Illyés could not, as that young boy, have witnessed what he then reports, the terms of which must surely have been either surmised or rumoured: "She was barefooted, she had left her boots in the assistant farm-manager's room, by the bed from which she had suddenly leapt and dashed straight as an arrow to the well".[31] Illyés' text provides *Inland*'s most salient image. It is literally and figuratively salient, an image that leaps, impressing or engraving itself on the minds of its readers. The narrator is himself one such reader, having recalled the passage ten years after first reading it. The leap into the well reverberates with other images: that of the leaping of fingers across distances between keys on the typewriter, or the leap of a goldfish from a

---

31 Gyula Illyés, *People of the Puszta* (Budapest: Corvina Press, 1967), 188; the relevant passage is transcribed verbatim on pp. 140-41 of *Inland*.

tank to the floor in a backyard shed. These are patently incommensurate with, out of all proportion to, the grim scene of the young girl's leap. But these clustering images also interconnect with the scene of the narrator as a young boy carefully carrying his goldfish in a biscuit tin, while his father, fleeing his debtors, moves the family from one house to another. Impossible leaps and incommensurate crossings from one scene to another channel emotions and meanings, embedding memory in space and landscape, reverberating across visible and invisible realms, across times, places and continents.

The narrator's preposterous endeavour in *Barley Patch* to report on his own conception – both the events leading to his own birth and the conception of himself as an image-person among filing cabinets inside his own fiction – loops back into and reverses the endeavour of *Inland*'s narrator, who reckons with his reader as though he has already – as is the fate of any writer of books – died. The narrator believes himself to be thought of as dead by his reader. Conversely, his writing is an act of summoning the dead. He must animate and bring life to the (already dead, girl-women) figures in his fiction. For Salusinszky, *Inland* is a profoundly elegiac work that aims "to set up, through writing, an exchange of prisoners across the border between life and death" – in other words, through writing the narrator enters into death in order to set death's prisoners free.[32] "Inland" therefore refers not only to Murnane's familiar geographic tendencies, his constant movement away from the coast and towards hinterlands. Nor does it simply figure the metaphorical dimensions of his interior landscape. "Inland" encompasses all these meanings – but it is also a figure for extended prosopopoeia – for the narrator's address to and summoning of the dead, not least the prospect of his own death, as implied in his persistent orientation towards that which is "in land" – that is, his own future burial in earth.

A metaleptic series connects *Inland*'s impossible leap across continents with writing's leap across life and death, and vice versa – and these in turn mirror the leap between fiction and world, and between the several untranslated languages of the plains. In its concluding pages, the narrator of *Inland* visits a cemetery in the suburb of Fawkner in Melbourne, where he unaccountably weeps over the grave of a stranger, a migrant from distant Finland. Emotion is released through displacement and distance, through the image of the doubly distant, untranslated stranger whose story resonates with the narrator's own. Or else emotion runs its course through the texts of strangers that interleave with the narrator's pages. *Inland* closes with the words, in italics, of *Wuthering Heights*, words concerning "sleepers in that quiet earth" that have drifted into and merged with the narrator's voice, like pages or clouds. The narrator returns in the end to the heath and the

---

32   Salusinszky, *Gerald Murnane*, 90.

harebells, to the soil of his native district, to the deferred prospect of his own future burial. This is also a rhetorical return to the "constancy" of changeable things (11), to the elements of the watershed, to the soil and the rain that yields the "invisible yet enduring lilacs" of Proust's fictional Combray. These images in turn recall the many flowers in the narrative, including the folk names of plants from the dream-prairie of Anne Kristaly – names that induce "a queer mixture of feelings", and that evoke the heavy-hearted sounds of Magyar: "*Little bluestem; ironweed; fleabane; boneset; wolfberry; chokeberry*" (5).

Streaming System, Feeling Intensity

These observations about *Barley Patch* and *Inland* suggest the wide applicability of stream system to the dynamics of Murnane's writing generally, in which images are strung together in metonymic chains, and metaleptic crossings are effected between figures, states of mind, times and spaces, life and death. Feelings gather intensity through networked associations and the thronging of images: sweep-arm wells, drifting clouds and pages, little flowers on the prairie with their melancholic names, the name of a stranger inscribed on a grave, birds and blood in a forest clearing, little fronds of fern protruding or strands of hair waving underwater, a barley patch with its own Brontë-esque interior universe, yellow and gold colours pinned to a woman's breast. Images coalesce, forming memory places, and memory places conjure feelings and meaning in an infinite regress. These patterns are the invariable design of Murnane's fiction. Each work forms a watershed, its images gathering slowly and cumulatively, streaming in from different directions. An image courses through time, place and memory, disappearing from view and reappearing. With each reappearance, images multiply their associations, clustering and compounding with others, channelling feelings, hinting at meaning. Within this connective system, the self is a landscape sculpted by time's watery stream. The stream system spatialises time and writing, functioning as a holding pattern for the self's suppressed or longed-for connections, calling forth memory and its interlinked, always elusive emotional sources.

In Murnane's "Stream System" talk with which I began, the watershed of the Bundoora campus provides a series of anecdotes and images that fold personal and familial memory into local terrain. The narrator's memories of his father and aunt are implicated in the now forgotten past of the campus when it was a swampy, blackberry-overrun, rat-infested farmland on the grounds of the Mont Park Hospital for the Insane. The stream system elliptically yet inexorably connects the narrator's memory of a scene involving the inmates of the asylum in that precisely mapped spot, with other scenes in parallel that involve his difficult brother, said to be "a little backward" (138), whom the narrator remembers mostly avoiding. The narrative bears us obliquely on its current of images of blue and gold, of yellow-brown water, of oval and heart shapes, towards heartbreaking regret, never stated overtly but palpable, to do with the narrator's long turning away from his friendless brother.

This pattern – of divergently originating streams of thoughts and images that meander and drift through landscapes, but that ultimately coalesce in some half-hidden, suddenly recollected sense or feeling – recurs within and across Murnane's works. The design of Murnane's fiction is entirely consistent, its divergent meanderings delivering powerful feelings that conjure meaning but elude stable articulation. We encounter this design in "The Battle for Acosta Nu", a piece in *Landscape with Landscape* (1985), which has at its centre a seismic sense of loss, a grief barely held at bay by the narrator's obsessive plan to whisper of his ideal "Australian" landscape to his dying "Paraguayan" son.[33] In its seemingly more relaxed register of memoir, *Something for the Pain* likewise achieves closure through the simple image, observed at distance, of a trainer leaping onto the track to embrace his dying horse.[34] All are salient images that leap and jet forth, taking us by surprise, delivering their sudden release of pent-up feeling. All are borne along, distributed and generated by the stream system itself. These are the design elements that characterise Murnane's writing, with its veiling and unveiling of significance, its perpetual instability and emotional productivity – a stream system that comprises intricately layered and proliferating metafictional landscapes through which we navigate whenever we find ourselves inside Murnane's fictional worlds.

References

Bachelard, Gaston. *The Poetics of Space*. 1964; Boston, MA: Beacon Press, 1994.

Buell, Lawrence. "Antipodal Propinquities? Environmental (Mis)Perceptions in American and Australian Literary History". In *Reading Across the Pacific: Australia-United States Intellectual Histories*, edited by Robert Dixon and Nicholas Birns, 3-22. Sydney: Sydney University Press, 2010.

Carman, Luke. "In the Room with Gerald Murnane". *Sydney Review of Books*, 24 April 2018. https://sydneyreviewofbooks.com/in-the-room-with-gerald-murnane/

De Certeau, Michel. *The Practice of Everyday Life*. Berkeley: University of California Press, 1984.

---

[33] Gerald Murnane, *Landscape with Landscape* (1985; Sydney: Sydney University Press, 2003).

[34] Gerald Murnane, *Something for the Pain: A Memoir of the Turf* (Melbourne: Text Publishing, 2015).

Fletcher, Angus. *The Topological Imagination: Spheres, Edges, and Islands*. Cambridge, MA: Harvard University Press, 2016.

Gelder, Ken and Paul Salzman. *After the Celebration: Australian Fiction 1989–2007*. Carlton, Vic.: Melbourne University Press, 2009.

Hill, M.H. "Stream Systems". Dr M.H. Hill's Homepage, Jackson State University, Alabama (2013). http://www.jsu.edu/dept/geography/mhill/phylabtwo/lab7/stsysf.html.

Illyés, Gyula. *People of the Puszta*. Budapest: Corvina Press, 1967.

Jenkins, Henry. *Textual Poachers: Television Fans and Participatory Culture*. New York: Routledge, 1992.

Murnane, Gerald. *Border Districts*. Artarmon NSW: Giramondo Press, 2017.

——. *Something for the Pain: A Memoir of the Turf. Melbourne*. Text Publishing, 2015.

——. *A Million Windows*. Artarmon, NSW: Giramondo, 2014.

——. *Barley Patch*. Artarmon, NSW: Giramondo Press, 2009.

——. *Invisible Yet Enduring Lilacs*. Artarmon, NSW: Giramondo, 2005.

——. *Emerald Blue*. Ringwood, Vic.: McPhee Gribble/Penguin, 1995.

——. *Velvet Waters*. Melbourne: McPhee Gribble 1990.

——. *Inland*. 1988; Sydney: Sydney University Press, 2003.

——. *Landscape with Landscape*. 1985; Sydney: Sydney University Press, 2003.

——. *The Plains*. 1982; Melbourne: Text Publishing, 2000.

——. *A Lifetime on Clouds*. Melbourne: William Heinemann, 1976.

——. *Tamarisk Row*. 1974; North Ryde, NSW: Angus & Robertson/Sirius, 1988.

Rooney, Brigid. *Suburban Space, the Novel and Australian Modernity*. London: Anthem Press, 2018.

Salusinszky, Imre. *Gerald Murnane*, Oxford Australian Writers Series. Melbourne: Oxford University Press, 1993.

Uhlmann, Anthony. "Silence and Sound in the Sentences of Gerald Murnane's *A Million Windows*". *JASAL: Journal of the Association for the Study of Australian Literature* vol. 15, no. 1 (2015): https://openjournals.library.sydney.edu.au/index.php/JASAL/article/view/9937.

7
Gerald Murnane's Plain Style
Mark Byron

> I learned that no thing in the world is one thing; that each thing in the world is two things at least, and probably many more than two things. I learned to find a queer pleasure in staring at a thing and dreaming of how many things it might be.[1]

The role of grasslands in Gerald Murnane's fiction is as sustained and pronounced as his self-stated aversion to the coast and the ocean,[2] and his uneasy forbearance of mountain ranges. Murnane's narrative devotion to steppe-like ecologies provokes the question of style and how his narrative strategies might operate dialectically with his chosen geography. When thinking of how geography inflects prose style one might think of "oceanic" or "thalassan" style in Herman Melville's *Moby-Dick*, Virginia Woolf's *The Waves*, or John Banville's *The Sea*, or even the sea of sand in Michael Ondaatje's *The English Patient*. Alternately, the mountainous topography in Thomas Mann's *The Magic Mountain* or Cormac McCarthy's *Blood Meridian* mediates allegory and symbolism with the rhetoric of geographical representation. Absent such symbolic inducements, the steppe, plain, grassland – unvaried topography neither desert nor littoral, neither urban nor rural, yet a strangely replenishing source for agriculture, husbandry, and the history of human migrations – provide Murnane's fictions with a distinct ground from which to produce his complex narrative meditations.

This essay takes Murnane's 1988 novel *Inland* as the quintessential performance of this "plain style". Several major works engage directly with the grasslands of

---

[1] Gerald Murnane, *Inland* (1988; Champaign, IL: Dalkey Archive, 2012), 48. All subsequent references are to this edition and appear in parentheses in the text.
[2] For example, in the essay "The Breathing Author", Murnane reports his inability to swim, beginning with a visit to the sea with his mother aged six months: "I began to scream as soon as I saw and heard the sea", in *Invisible Yet Enduring Lilacs* (Artarmon, NSW: Giramondo, 2005), 162.

Victoria and further afield – *The Plains* (1982) foremost among them – but one also finds references to the Patagonian pampas scattered across *Invisible Yet Enduring Lilacs* (2005) and other works.³ *Inland* situates steppe ecology as a specific means by which to think through Murnane's familiar range of questions: what is it to write? For whom does the author write, and to whom does the narrator speak? How do the conditions of writing within narrative shape the effect of that narrative? By choosing three specific grassland zones – the Hungarian Great Alföld or Pannonian Plain, the Great Plains of South Dakota and northern Nebraska, and the vanishing grasslands of northern Melbourne County – *Inland* triangulates familiar narrative obsessions to create a generative poetics of the exclave. Each of these topographies is a kind of exclave, separated from a larger steppe formation but sharing its geomorphology: the Alföld or *Puszta* is a part of the Hungarian steppe exclave, itself an appendix to the great Eurasian steppe (the word *puszta*, a Slavic loan-word in Hungarian, is thus a member of a linguistic exclave); the replanted fields surrounding the South Dakotan Institute of Prairie Studies in *Inland* represent a manufactured exclave within the Great Plains of North America; and the northern grasslands of Melbourne County gesture towards a larger treeless space beyond Mount Macedon, and further afield, the Wimmera region beyond the Grampians. Each zone is a kind of subjunctive geography within which the narrator can productively engage in observing the world from the sides of his eyes, and indeed, in which the narrator himself is able to generate a provisional identity that spans the globe, at once in Szolnok County in the Hungarian *puszta* and in his "native district" in Melbourne County. By this careful calibration of geographic particularity with narrative method, *Inland* demonstrates how Murnane is not exactly a national writer, nor even a regional writer. Skirting specific forms of regionalism, the writing is not much concerned with vernacular, dialect, or local custom, but rather thought and modes of expression joining across vast distances, connected by a strange intimacy. This intimacy is literalised in "the girl from Bendigo Street", whose fate in the narrator's life becomes the embodiment of this exclave poetics.

---

3   One example is Murnane's remembered ambitions in turning away from poetry to write his first novel: "I had hoped to write a novel about a young man growing up in a large bluestone house on a grazing property on a place resembling the pampas of Argentina. The young man would spend much of his time in the library of his house, looking out from beyond walls of books at immense grasslands". See "The Cursing of Ivan Veliki", in *Invisible Yet Enduring Lilacs* (Artarmon, NSW: Giramondo, 2005), 49.

Inland Topography

The narrative contours of *Inland* resemble those of the *puszta*, steppe, grassland: apparently uniform on the surface, but often disguising a deep history and ecology, cultivated over time, and recorded in the strata beneath the text surface. The narrator occupies an estate house in Szolnok County in the Hungarian *puszta* for the first quarter of the novel, observing his book-lined room and taking surreptitious glances from the window to the fields and estate workers outside. He writes to his editor, Anne Kristaly Gunnarsen, a native of Szolnok County, but who is resident in the Calvin O. Dahlberg Institute of Prairie Studies in the town of Ideal in Tripp County, South Dakota. The narrative then shifts almost uniformly to Melbourne County,[4] where the narrator reflects upon his childhood and coming-of-age, recalling the influence of geography upon his rising amorous sensibilities, especially the proximity or otherwise of the Victorian grasslands in periods of transience. The central thematic focus of this larger portion of the narrative settles on the dawning affection he feels for "the girl from Bendigo Street". Following his move away from the school at which they meet he loses touch with her, and his attempts, closer to the narrative present, to track down this nascent adolescent love interest come to nothing. The narrative concludes in Fawkner cemetery in Pascoe Vale, bordering the forest, where the narrator reflects on the girl from Bendigo Street. Her young brother's grave acts as a kind of gnomon, orienting the narrator's reflections on his youth and his processes of mourning what might have been. The final paragraph is a direct, if unmarked, quotation of the final paragraph in *Wuthering Heights* in which Lockwood – the recipient of Catherine and Heathcliff's story in the frame narrative – contemplates the Yorkshire moors at the graveyard in which the novel's two major protagonists are ultimately reunited in burial.[5]

The narrative of *Inland* is conditioned upon the *negative event*. Things do happen to the narrator and are recorded and subject to reflection: his sequence of moving house during the formative years of adolescence certainly shapes the emotional contours of the novel, particularly its understated "plain style", and the move away from the girl from Bendigo Street turns out to be the foundational trauma that precipitates access to the larger reservoir or field of memory. Yet it is understatement, lack of disclosure, and missed declarations of affection and desire,

---

[4] Julian Murphy addresses the ambiguity of narration across the two parts of the novel: "it is never made entirely clear how the two narrators relate to each other; it remains possible that each may be a figment of the other's imagination". See Julian Murphy, "Being-in-Landscape: A Heideggerian Reading of Landscape in Gerald Murnane's *Inland*", *JASAL: Journal of the Association for the Study of Australian Literature* 14, no. 3 (2014), 1.

[5] The associations between Brontë's novel and the graveyard are established halfway through the novel when the narrator provides a history of his having read *Wuthering Heights* nine and nineteen years previously (118-19).

all captured figuratively in the way the narrator indulges in "looking askance" at the physical world, that delineate the depth of feeling in the novel and have it play out a minor event of adolescence into the life-shaping anguish generative of such profound, and profoundly reticent, passion. In this sense *Inland* shares a sense of scale of youthful non-events with the story "Araby" in James Joyce's *Dubliners*, where a young boy misses his chance to buy a trinket at the city bazaar for Mangan's sister who lives across the street, and who is likely unaware of his feelings for her. *Inland* achieves this combination of profundity and understatement by unifying the narrator's preferred topography of the grassland with the narrative preoccupation of the self-conscious act of writing.

The narrator's opening gambit sets the act of writing, and the first-person confession of the act, within the confines of the *puszta* on the Pannonian plains: "I am writing in the library of a manor-house, in a village I prefer not to name, near the town of Kunmadaras, in Szolnok County" (1). Situated in, but separated from, the grasslands of the Hungarian steppe, itself an exclave of the great Eurasian steppe, the narrator establishes a sense of displacement that provides visual perspective upon his surroundings, but equally in figurative terms on his own processes of memory and reportage. As Imre Salusinszky asserts: "More even than *The Plains*, *Inland* is a book written from and about the writer's room".[6] The brief opening section of the narrative concludes with a clue to the hidden complexities running beneath the surface of grasslands, recorded memory, and textual landscapes: "Sometimes I am aware of more fields behind the first field, and of grasslands behind everything – indistinct grasslands under grey, sagging clouds" (1). The tone of this sentence is typical of much of the novel: any overt sense of affect is diminished, but the subtle strength of the narrator's divinations (he nowhere questions the actuality of things hidden behind those things in plain sight) retains the potential for revelation, whether in a spiritual sense or in the ontological sense of Heidegger's notion of *aletheia* or "unconcealment".[7]

Murnane confesses to a technical understanding of writing rather than any conventional sense of poetics: "The task of this sort of writer is to report in the plainest language the images that most claim his attention from among the images in his mind and then to arrange his sentences and paragraphs (and, if applicable, his chapters) so as to suggest the connections between those images".[8] This reportage of an inner mindscape bears affinities with the strategies and tone of the *nouveau roman* – such as Alain Robbe-Grillet's novel *La jalousie*, or even Samuel Beckett's

---

6 Imre Salusinszky, *Gerald Murnane* (Melbourne: Oxford University Press, 1993), 75-76.
7 See Martin Heidegger, "The Origin of the Work of Art", in *Basic Writings*, ed. and trans. David Farrell Krell (London: Routledge, 1993), 143-212.
8 Murnane, "The Breathing Author", 169.

short prose piece *Le dépeupleur* or *The Lost Ones* – where affect is resisted at the text's surface only to emerge from its subterranean table at points of narrative stress. For Murnane this technical reportage elides the luxuries of psychoanalysis, casting the mind into a topography able to be read as landscape in all its hidden striations:

> In my view, the place we commonly call the real world is surrounded by vast and possibly infinite landscape which is invisible to these eyes (points to eyes) but which I am able to apprehend by other means. The more I tell you about this landscape, the more inclined you might be to call it my mind.[9]

This ontological vagueness fusing inner and outer worlds, textual landscapes and the mental images from which they spring, also finds expression in the ambiguous transition between narrative subjects. The Hungarian manor-house occupant and the resident of Melbourne County are figures within the same narrative consciousness, blending narrative action with exposition and reportage, and observable from a third-person viewpoint that permits identities to fold into each other. Here again Beckett provides an analogy or model in his postwar novel *Molloy*, especially the opening scene in which an observer notes two figures approaching on a road and who then, in the novel's two parts, becomes one of those figures and writes the report of another.[10]

Murnane's choice of the Hungarian Alföld as the setting for the first part of *Inland* folds this novel into an abiding theme recurring across several of his other works. The deep attraction of grasslands resides in the appearance of simplicity and the subtle indications of a hidden complexity beneath the uniformity of long grasses shaped by wind. He notes in the essay "Birds of the Puszta" that, as a youth, "I thought of plains whenever I wanted to think of something unremarkable at first sight but concealing much of meaning",[11] including "lost kingdoms" hidden from view. Taken literally, Murnane's childhood in Melbourne, Bendigo, and the Western Districts of Victoria was defined by the two rings of grassland around Melbourne, beyond which was "foreign territory". "Whenever I think of myself as being forced, for whatever reason, to flee from my native district, I think of myself as fleeing into the grasslands. In desperate circumstances I might flee as far as the outer grasslands, but I could never see myself as fleeing further" (57). Yet the security that comes with apparent topographic uniformity becomes more complex when matched with the inner landscapes of memory, and especially the memory

---

9 Murnane, "The Breathing Author", 177.
10 Samuel Beckett, *Molloy*, ed. Shane Weller (1951; London: Faber & Faber, 2009), 3-12.
11 Gerald Murnane, "Birds of the Puszta", in *Invisible Yet Enduring Lilacs* (Artarmon, NSW: Giramondo, 2005), 56. All subsequent references are to this edition and appear in parentheses in the text.

of books. When composing *Inland*, Murnane remembers most clearly "what I call spaces-within-spaces" in the books of fiction he has read, providing a narrative cognate to the exclave geographies he invokes in his own fiction (60), or what he calls elsewhere, after Rilke, "a world floating like an island in the ocean of the self".[12]

The narrator writes across actual and virtual distances separating the two grassland spaces in the first section of the novel – the Hungarian *puszta* and the South Dakotan Great Plains. This bridging act generates a series of anxieties and assertions, firstly in terms of the act and substance of writing.

The narrator reports that his editor, Anne Kristaly Gunnarsen, "was born where the River Sio, trickling from Lake Balaton, finds an unexpected partner in the River Sarviz from the north" (2). This geographical specificity, of a territory bounded by two waterways, deploys what Nicholas Birns calls "contrapuntal waves of alternate geographies to demonstrate the essential motility and transitivity of all landscapes, the association between sexual and geographical desire, the amorous and cartographic impulses".[13] It demarcates all the important places to appear in the novel as intermedial locations, and binds Anne to the narrator. He fears her disapproval in his writing: "I dislike what I have just written. I believe my editor too will dislike it when she reads it" (2). But his disapproval of her imagined husband animates him to a higher degree, calling into question the very integrity of the grassland in which the Institute is located. It is "not a real prairie" but rather a "wasteland" sown with seeds by the Institute's scientists to mimic the conditions of virgin prairie: "Each summer, when the plants have grown to their full height, Gunnar T. Gunnarsen and his fellow scientists step gently in among the plants to count them" (3-4). This unlikely activity (nothing short of fraud in the narrator's mind) is matched in Anne's husband's name: not only is it marked by a repetitive redundancy, its etymology also motivates the narrator to consider him an imagined figure of nemesis, from which an elaborate conspiracy is hatched. Gunnar attempts to sideline his wife from the editorial position attached to the Institute's journal *Hinterland*, and, the narrator affirms, "has always wanted me dead" (12). The reader is given a clue to this burlesque fantasy in the name: Gunnar ("brave and bold", warrior, fighter, from the Old Norse *gunnr* "war" and *arr* "warrior") already contains *war* and *warrior*, and thus Gunnar T. Gunnarsen is "the war-warrior, son of war-warrior".

12　Murnane, "The Cursing of Ivan Veliki", 50.
13　Nicholas Birns, "Infinite Desires: Love and the Search for Truth in the Fiction of Gerald Murnane", *Southerly* 55, no. 3 (1995), 48. Reflecting on the narratological influence of Marcel Proust upon *Inland*, Murnane notes the two paths of Guermantes and Méséglise in *Du côté de chez Swann*: "I remember the Narrator as a man made up mostly of landscapes and urged to study those landscapes until the impossible takes place in front of his eyes and the many landscapes and the two Ways merge to form the whole of a private country – his true homeland". See "Birds of the Puszta", 60.

Scholars often note the strong correlation between grasslands and the location of writing in Murnane's fiction and *Inland* in particular. On closer inspection, this relation is founded upon the specific topology of the exclave: the narrator is at liberty to write because, located at his desk in Szolnok County or in Melbourne County, he is able to view or imagine the grasslands that surround him; and the Calvin O. Dahlberg Institute of Prairie Studies produces the journal *Hinterland* as well as numerous reports in its steel and glass building set within, but separated from, the Great Plains of North Dakota. For the narrator, this poetics of the exclave allows him to imagine the confluence of writing and grasses:

> When Anne Kristaly Gunnarsen signs a letter, her name reaches far out towards the centre of the page. If I look at her name for long enough, all her ens and esses turn into grass-stems and all the grass-stems lean as though a wind is blowing over them. If I stare at a page from Anne Kristaly Gunnarsen I can see words turning into grass – long, silken Magyar grass that would touch my thighs if I walked among it; short and brittle American grass that I could trample; and down below the tangle of stems, boneset or chokeberry or tiny reds and blues with no names in her language or mine. (11)

The narrative introduces a visitor, a writer, into the room in Szolnok County. What follows is a merging and reversal of roles of narrator and interlocutor in a deft narratological game. But what is of significance in terms of narrative topography is the method by which the different locations in the narrative are triangulated with the reader's position, effected through the repetition of André Maurois' famous phrase (eventually given in full on p. 130) concerning the power of Proust's sensory imagination, "the scent of invisible yet enduring lilacs". The visitor has never and will never see America but wishes "to breathe with ecstasy, through the curtain of the falling rain, the scent of invisible yet enduring dream-prairies" (27); the narrator reflects on the visitor's wish "to breathe with ecstasy, through the curtain of the falling rain, the scent of invisible yet enduring ghosts of places" (28), conflating Tolna County, Tripp County and Melbourne County; he then addresses his adversary, Gunnar T. Gunnarsen, who writes of his wife never seeing the Great Alföld "but who breathes in ecstasy, through the curtain of the falling rain, the scent of invisible yet enduring lands sloping gently between the Sio and the Sarviz" (31). This rhetorical formula then makes the decisive shift in the novel, transporting the narrator from Szolnok County to Melbourne County: "I have never seen, nor will I ever see, Tolna County; I cannot even breathe, through the curtain of the falling rain, the scent of invisible yet enduring beds of streams" (43).

With the narrator's writing position shifting to Melbourne County for much of the remainder of *Inland* – aside from one or two brief interludes – a new mode of charting an inner landscape develops from recording the space between waterways at each significant location in the narrator's history. He writes in the present tense from a position between Russell Creek and the Hopkins River (somewhere near the Victorian coastal town of Warnambool), and, noting the waterways that define the region in which the Institute of Prairie Studies is located, turns the narrative to the recollection of his youth, bounded in his "native district" by the Merri River and the Moonee Ponds Creek (and thus taking in much of northern Melbourne including Brunswick, Coburg, and the grasslands of Craigieburn). Later the narrator provides a detailed account of his peripatetic youth, largely the result of his father's attempts to escape his gambling debts, by demarcating the waterways between which his family moved: starting in 1944 with a move to Bendigo – "My father and his wife and sons lived for four years in three different rented cottages between Bendigo Creek and Huntly Race" (131) – to the sale in 1960 of the house between Scotchman's Creek and Elster Creek and subsequent move to the Western Districts between Sutherland's Creek and Hovell's Creek, where his father was to die soon afterwards (136).

> All those empty spaces [in the map of one's life], reader, are our grasslands. In all those grassy places see and dream and remember and dream of themselves having seen and dreamed and remembered all the men you have dreamed you might have been and all the men you dream you may yet become. (64)

This ability to plumb the regions between hydrological landmarks, turning empty spaces on one's life map into fertile grasslands of memory and writing, has the narrator declare: "With all my notes, I might have become a scientist of the depths of language … I might have studied the soil and even the rock under the language of my homeland" (68-69). Language is a geological formation open to a chthonic hermeneutics, where innate knowledge of the dialect of one's "native district" becomes a central feature of all language. This becomes more widely significant when considering the looming presence, just out of view, of the Eurasian steppe as the home of Proto-Indo-European and thus the archaic progenitor of all Indo-European languages, including English – but, crucially, not Hungarian, thus allowing its deployment as a language of displacement.

This geomorphology shapes the central focus of the narrative: the narrator's youthful relationship with the girl from Bendigo Street. As they begin to spend time together in his "native district", the narrator gently attempts to understand her: "every few days she rewarded me by telling me quietly something that was unimportant in itself but seemed a message from beneath the surface of her" (96). Matters of surface (words) and depth (feeling) complicate the mutual implication of grasslands and written language. The pivotal moment in their relationship comes when the girl from Bendigo Street relays a message to the narrator via the girl from Bendigo: "*She says she likes you very much*". The narrator reacts in the register of surfaces and depths, using these indices as ways of navigating his own words and his understanding of those of his beloved:

> When I hear the silence that comes between my own words sometimes, I think of prairies or plains – as though all my words are being spoken from grasslands. But whenever I hear the silence that comes between the first five and the last two of the seven words spoken to me by the girl from Bendigo, I think of depths. (107)

This sense of undiscovered depths governs the relationship through to its final moments, when the narrator makes it known that his family will be leaving his "native district" for "the district between the Ovens and Reedy Creek" (167) and the girl from Bendigo Street asks the distance involved. As the narrator reflects on this moment in a nearby cemetery many years later, he understands that the depth of unstated words carries as much significance as the grassland topography of written words: "The girl has asked me her question as though it was a small matter to her, but I had read in her face that it was not a small matter to her, and I have not forgotten today what I read in her face" (167). The narrative becomes an understated elegy, based on subtle exchanges between two solitary adolescents, borne upon a substrate of deep feeling: the rock and soil that give the grassland its topographical distinction.

Understanding Plain Style

The operations of plain style in *Inland* have given rise to a variety of interpretations of the novel and its author's motivations for writing it. Sue Gillett has identified the way *Inland* privileges its male figures at the expense of the female figures – although this reading risks missing the genuine loss mourned towards the novel's end, and disregards the import of extended quotations from Gyula Illyés' *People of the Puszta* (1936) that sets up an affinity with female characters and their limited choices.[14] Ken Gelder sees in Murnane's prose evidence of a kind of "monomania", rarefied in style and content, and abetted by the support of such conservative critics as Imre Salusinszky and Peter Craven.[15] In his groundbreaking monograph, Salusinszky identifies the aesthetic of "the plains" that has directed Murnane's

---

14 Sue Gillett, "Loving and Hating the *Inland* Reader: Postmodern Ploys or Romantic Reaction", in *A Sense of Audience: Essays in Postcolonial Literatures*, ed. William McGaw, special edition of *Span* 30 (1990), 59-68.
15 Ken Gelder, "Politics and Monomania: The Rarefied World of Contemporary Australian Literary Culture", *Overland* 184 (2006), 48-56.

vision, "an imaginary space that describes what he sees both at the furthest edges of his external awareness and when he looks deepest into himself", likening this consistency of vision to that of William Blake.[16] This psychological depth opens Murnane's work to phenomenological interpretations, and for Salusinszky corrals a particular intellectual lineage – Fyodor Dostoevsky, Franz Kafka, Jean-Paul Sartre, Alain Robbe-Grillet and Samuel Beckett through to Thomas Bernhard and Paul Auster, as well as a disposition towards philosophical writing reminiscent of Thomas Carlyle, Arthur Schopenhauer, Friedrich Nietzsche, Ralph Waldo Emerson, Ludwig Wittgenstein, and especially Jacques Derrida.[17]

Murnane's writing invites psychological readings, although Salusinszky chooses not to draw upon the theories of Freud, Lacan, Klein, or indeed any other mode of psychoanalysis. Instead, following the literary phenomenological tradition stemming from Dostoevsky's *Notes from the Underground*, emphasis is placed upon the way the mind (presumably the narrator's mind) confronts reality: "Murnane's books are about the adventure of consciousness, finding itself in a world but never quite knowing the extent to which that world is real".[18] In this sense, place, and Melbourne in particular, becomes a kind of allegorical function. Given the etymological origins of the term allegory – the Greek ἀλληγορία combines ἄλλος (other) ἀγορεύω (to speak) to mean "other voicing" – Murnane's allegories, and *Inland* in particular, are then acts of ventriloquism in relation to their "actual" geographical settings:

> The point is really that in this, by now, habitual opening gesture of an exact physical placing, there is hidden something much more important than Hungary anyway: the words, "I am writing". This is where *Inland* comes from: not from Hungary or – other sites in the book – America or Melbourne, but from a writing-table in a library.[19]

This view leads Salusinszky to consider the narrative of *Inland* to be split between two writing subjects, giving "a phenomenological account of what it is to write, as both narrators remind us of the physical activity of writing as an inscriptive process, and of writing as the process of constructing one sentence after another".[20] The mental experiences of these subjects such as dream, fantasy and imagination, are thus subordinated to memory, where the mind is a theatre of memory. This view of narration installs a kind of crypto-author or ur-narrator whose memory

---

16 Salusinszky, *Gerald Murnane*, 1.
17 Salusinszky, *Gerald Murnane*, 2-3.
18 Salusinszky, *Gerald Murnane*, 2.
19 Salusinszky, *Gerald Murnane*, 75-76.
20 Salusinszky, *Gerald Murnane*, 76.

coordinates the elegiac fabric of the novel. In the act of writing, the personae within *Inland* absent themselves and leave behind "inscriptions upon the tiny tombstones that are the pages and spines of books".[21]

For Salusinszky, the framing of the act of writing is self-referentially elegiac, where writing is a kind of dying for the reader, and loving someone is to hold them in loving memory, drawing upon Derrida's work on the mutually generative nature of mourning and love.[22] Other aspects of Derrida's work are invoked to structure an understanding of *Inland*: the novel as a postcard destined never to reach its recipient; inversions of depth (grasslands) and surface (ponds) in a chiastic logic; the boundaries of death culminating in the Gospel of Matthew recited on the last Sunday in the Church year after Pentecost, suggesting an ontological apocalypse; and the translation of words across languages, and back (such as the case of American terms "translated" into Hungarian in the first section, but presented to us in English) as a system of *différance*, supplementarity, or even an economy of substitution embodied in the *pharmakon*. Salusinszky's focus on mourning, elegy and eschatology as the abiding themes of *Inland* leads him to consider the novel's terrain as a psychogeography, "the native district of consciousness" enabled by a phenomenological reduction in the narrator's act of writing.[23] The reader is able to make sense of the bifurcated narrative at the pivot point where the narrator burns the letter from the girl from Bendigo:

> Out of a funeral – a burning and interring and casting upon waters of remains – begins a writing, a writing that will produce the further remains called *Inland* ... a love-letter from the second narrator to his childhood girlfriend, which he begins by writing as if he were a mid-century Hungarian landowner who has participated in the exploitation of a girl in a book. In a reversal of the Landscape sequence the second narrator has written the first.[24]

This is an elegant and plausible reading of the novel, although by seeking to sublimate the material conditions of the narrative, its navigation between bodies of moving water in several locales across the globe, and its gravitational pull towards grassland ecologies, this kind of interpretive structure risks missing the force of Murnane's exclave poetics.

---

21 Salusinszky, *Gerald Murnane*, 77.
22 Specific works of relevance include: *The Politics of Friendship*, trans. George Collins (1994; London: Verso, 1997), and *The Work of Mourning*, trans. Pascale-Anne Brault and Michael Naas (Chicago: University of Chicago Press, 2001), among others.
23 Salusinszky, *Gerald Murnane*, 79.
24 Salusinszky, *Gerald Murnane*, 80.

Characters are situated in landscape in the novel, even as they are mediated by memory, desire, mourning and mystification. This immersion in the world is sublimated by Salusinszky into a textual system and the condition of writing, and by Julian Murphy into an "ontological world" whereby a Heideggerian Being-in-the-world may take effect.[25] Murphy gives these two "worlds" equal weight, distinguishing Murnane's use of landscape from any conventional metaphorical usage, and following Harald Fawkner, identifies how the narrator's reported perception shapes the construction of the self. This process is most prominent for Murphy in the novel's "second beginning" in Melbourne County, the narrator's native district and location for his Being-in-the-world. The wind throughout *Inland* permits reflection on its "ancestral path" and to its indication of an extended geographic zone beyond the narrator's ken. Wind erases boundaries, including that between the human body and its environment.

Murphy's Heideggerian analysis of *Inland* tends to foreground Murnane's "two worlds" – here the physical and the ontological worlds:

> The narrator's awareness that his physical body is within the physical world is accompanied by an awareness that his Self is also enmeshed in the world of Being. Such a conceptualisation of the Self-within-world aligns with Heidegger's notion of Being-in-the-world, in which the individual comes into existence already in the world.[26]

This analysis is restrictive in that it implies a body in the world that bears some kind of coherence or continuity, where the narrator of *Inland* takes the liberty of moving between scenes of writing in Melbourne and Hungary, in order to conduct the work of memory and commemoration. In a cognate sense, Salusinszky's refraction of Murnane's writing strategies by way of Derrida also invokes a separation of perception and its inscription in the supplemental logic of the text. Despite this, there has been a sustained interest in how Murnane's fiction squares with more classical positions in phenomenology. Harald Fawkner's incisive analysis of *Inland*, among Murnane's other novels, engages with a sense of the world in a state of "givenness" – an underlying ontological condition not dissimilar to Heidegger's notion of "worlding", but with a sharper sense of the modes of perception in navigating and understanding that world.[27] Lena Sundin has also shown how the

---

25 Julian Murphy, "Being-in-Landscape: A Heideggerian Reading of Landscape in Gerald Murnane's *Inland*", *JASAL: Journal of the Association for the Study of Australian Literature* 14, no. 3 (2014), 2.
26 Murphy, "Being-in-Landscape", 9.
27 Harald Fawkner, *Grasses That Have No Fields: From Gerald Murnane's* Inland *to a Phenomenology of Isogonic Constitution* (Stockholm: Stockholm University, 2006).

narrative threads of *Inland* bear affinities with bodily processes of respiration and its mingling of body with elements of world.²⁸

Lastly, Paul Genoni identifies the reception of Murnane's writing in recent years within the framework of global literature. Despite the challenges of Australian literary production shifting the burden to popular genres and a rising "international" style, dispersed niche audiences can arise, "to whom access to global culture is a means of both self-identifying and associating with others who share similar tastes or interests irrespective of their national affiliations".²⁹ Genoni claims Murnane to be Australia's first "postnational" writer, "to whom that landscape serves as a gateway to the images that reside deep within his own consciousness rather than as a component of the processes of geo-political annexation and social enculturation by which the nation was formed".³⁰ Murnane may be able to claim Australian credentials by virtue of his lack of international travel, yet his work tempers any entrenched notion of Australia in its refractory view and allegorical inducements, such as the "Inner Australia" in *The Plains*. Genoni's evaluation is framed by the question of postcoloniality: "As used by Murnane these images – primarily those associated with landscape, exploration, space, emptiness, home – cohere to produce a remarkable examination of an individual suffering the trauma of exile, with all that term implies for a postcolonial nation".³¹ This view also aligns neatly with the notion of Murnane's writing as exclave fiction, separated from a larger body (the nation, the Eurasian steppe, "Australian literature") but sharing its expansive tectonics.

Exclave Poetics

Inland's gnomic text surface and narrative profile therefore invoke inventive modes of reading: deploying philosophical frameworks from the Heideggerian, to phenomenology and deconstruction; and refracting the novel through the lens of World Literature, as well as regional and post-national literary formations. The structure of the novel in two mostly separate sections of dissimilar size, narrated by non-identical writing subjectivities, mimics the geography of *Inland*'s first section:

---

28 Lena Sundin, *Iconicity in the Writing Process: Virginia Woolf's* To the Lighthouse *and Gerald Murnane's* Inland (Göteborg: Göteborg University, 2004), 118; quoted in Murphy, "Being-in-Landscape", 9.
29 Paul Genoni, "The Global Reception of Post-national Literary Fiction: The Case of Gerald Murnane", *JASAL: Journal of the Association for the Study of Australia Literature* 9, Special Issue (2009), 2.
30 Genoni, "Global Reception", 6.
31 Paul Genoni, "Gerald Murnane", in *A Companion to Australian Literature since 1900* (Rochester, NY: Camden House, 2007), 302.

the Alföld or Pannonian Plain as an exclave of the Eurasian steppe. This morphological and symbolic affinity between narrative and geography resonates as a method by which to understand the narrative of youthful desire, prevarication, loss, and profound mourning that emerges from the plain style of the narrative's surface to become its most identifiable feature. How this exclave poetics functions depends on understanding the properties and significance of the exclave itself, and its relation to the larger topographic body to which it is appended and from which it is separated. The word *exclave* derives from the Latin *clavis* or "key", suggesting in the context of *Inland* not only a term of geographical separation but also an index or guide to unlocking certain kinds of knowledge, perception and experience.

The Eurasian steppe is comprised almost entirely of grassland, giving it a particular ecological profile: "Natural grassland occurs in situations too arid for the development of closed forest, but not so adverse as to prevent the development of a closed perennial herbaceous layer that is lacking in desert".[32] This common vision of the steppe is of undifferentiated marginal land, not rich enough for sustained agriculture, and although often treeless, insufficiently arid to be classed as desert. The vast Eurasian steppe, home to Turkic, Mongol, Altaic and other groups, has long cast a shadow over the civilisations of Europe, Persia and China. Its essential mystery arises in its sheer size: the word itself derives from the Russian word степь and the Ukrainian word степ ("grassy plain"), applied to the vast Siberian territories far beyond the Ural Mountains and the western Russian cultural centres. As an ecological region of temperate grasslands and savannas, the Eurasian steppe includes parts of Romania and an exclave portion (the Pannonian Steppe or *puszta*) in Hungary, but is most commonly associated with the territories of Ukraine, Russia, Kazakhstan and Mongolia, as well as Xinjiang and parts of Manchuria in China. The climate is semi-arid: hot summers and cold winters, and the poor soil supports grazing animals such as goats, sheep, camels and occasionally yaks. Steppe geography also occurs in southern Africa (veld) and North America (prairie, great plains), although these regions are rarely referred to by this term. Perhaps the most striking characteristic across geography, culture and climate is the unexpected diversity and richness lurking within an otherwise unprepossessing ecology. This is equally rich material for verbal and visual representation, and clearly a vital resource for Murnane's fiction, by which to suggest hidden depths to apparently uniform surfaces, whether of memory, affect, mourning, testimony, or the representation of these in written narrative.

Removed from both coast and mountains, the steppe has marked the location of a threat to urban civilisation since at least Roman times, where its seemingly

---

32   R.T. Coupland, "The Nature of Grassland", in *Grassland Ecosystems of the World*, ed. R.T. Coupland (Cambridge: Cambridge University Press, 1979), 23.

autochthonous inhabitants emerge from its vast spaces to visit chaos upon the centres of culture. These marauders – on horseback, by caravan or on foot – appear without warning with the promise of an ever-replenishing force. They came to represent a counterpoint to settled civilisation, and often projected an image of potential collapse lurking within the cultures they were deemed to threaten. The abject twinning of the steppe peoples with the citizens of Rome, Byzantium, Baghdad and Vienna sends an echo across history back to the origins of language itself. The widely accepted Kurgan Hypothesis – the Russian word курга́н (*kurgan*) refers to the *tumuli* or burial mounds characteristic of this culture – states that the family of Indo-European languages originated in the migrations from the Eurasian steppe in the fourth millennium BCE, from which Proto-Indo-Europeans flourished and dispersed west and south. The Kurgan people of the Pontic steppe, north of the Black Sea, are also believed to have brought the domesticated horse to Europe,[33] and coupled with some of the earliest known uses of the wheel, developed the warrior's chariot.[34] Later migrations from this area include the Celtic tribes that were to settle Western Europe and the British Isles from the eighth century BCE. Unfairly depicted as *barbaroi* by the Romans, such groups were instrumental in advancing matters of astronomy, and gold and silver smithing.

This topography, of vast wilderness that disguises many of the foundational technologies of civilisation, provides Murnane with a fertile store of images and historical resonances by which to develop his own narrative preoccupations in *Inland*. Yet his focus centres upon the Pannonian exclave rather than the Eurasian steppe itself, and on the Hungarian people and language (which of course does not belong to the Indo-European family of languages but to the Finno-Ugric family). The early establishment of Gunnar T. Gunnarsen as a potential rival and hostile presence in the narrative of *Inland* can be understood very clearly in the context of steppe grasslands: his name confers a Norwegian (and thus Indo-European)

---

33 Murnane's affinity with horses and the racing industry is a prominent aspect of his persona that needs little elaboration. However, his reflections on the origins of horse husbandry in the Eurasian grasslands combine with the racing industry in his first attempts at literary composition: an epic poem with the title "Ivan Veliki", set on the steppes of Central Asia. Murnane reports finding the word "Veliki" in a racebook: "My hero's surname was actually the name of a mare, but the word brought to my mind an image of a young man striding through tall grass". The grass itself produces a kind of exclave poetics, linking the Hungarian *puszta* with Melbourne County: "I saw that the grass of the steppes was the same grass that I had often seen on the vacant blocks of land along the Houghton Road, East Oakleigh". "The Cursing of Ivan Veliki", 45 and 48.

34 There is an enormous specialist literature on these topics of horse husbandry, the emergence of the wheel, and the development of Proto-Indo-European, spanning several scholarly fields such as anthropology, linguistics and archaeology, among others. For a comprehensive overview of these topics and how they illustrate the convergence of technical mastery in multiple fields, see David W. Anthony, *The Horse, the Wheel, and Language: How Bronze-Age Riders from the Eurasian Steppes Shaped the Modern World* (Princeton, NJ: Princeton University Press, 2007).

heritage as well as a direct reference to a warrior ancestry in its meaning, thus combining two kinds of historical marauding forces: the Norse Vikings and the nomadic steppe peoples. Murnane's fascination with the Hungarian language, and his legendary acquisition of it later in life, thus serves specific purposes in the novel. In his essay "The Angel's Son: Why I Learned Hungarian Late in Life", he expands on the range of the language as a source of thinking about topography, the history of migrations, and the history of languages:

> I understand that scholars have for long debated the precise origins of the language – and of the Hungarian people themselves. It can be safely said that the language is a very old language. The main body of the Hungarian people brought the language through the Carpathians and into Central Europe in the ninth century of the modern era, but language and people had travelled before then an immense distance during many centuries from their place of origin somewhere in Asia. I like sometimes to look at my atlas and to read aloud the name of the city of Alma Ata in Kazakhstan. What I hear are two Hungarian words meaning 'Father of Apples'. Likewise the 'Bator' in the name of the capital city of Mongolia is the Hungarian word for 'brave'. Many Hungarian words and expressions set me wondering about the mysterious centuries before the people and their language arrived in Europe. I mention here only a Hungarian name for the Milky Way: hadak útja, the soldiers' road.[35]

This long quotation demonstrates Murnane's thinking across space and time, taking in vast narratives of human migrations and the melding of cultures and languages. Yet in keeping with his exclave poetics, the major source looming beneath the narrative surface is the poet Gyula Illyés' study of local Hungarian culture, *Puszták Népe* (1936) or *People of the Puszta* (1967). Murnane refers to the first photographs of Hungarians he saw as a boy, presumably in a newspaper, which provoked his interest in the Hungarian *puszta*, as well as a photograph of a wedding party of ethnic Hungarians in Transylvania containing an outsized effigy of the bridegroom lodged in the trees above.[36] Murnane reports that "most of the details" in this latter photograph "are important items in *Inland* … The white farm buildings, the poplar-shaped trees, the American girl behind the camera". He also claims that the effigy, rather than the bridegroom, "is the narrator of my book" (63). But it is *People of the Puszta* in which the grasslands of Eurasia and the Hungarian national identity converge for Murnane: "The book had such an effect on me that I later

---

35 Gerald Murnane, "The Angel's Son: Why I Learned Hungarian Late in Life", in *Invisible Yet Enduring Lilacs*, 219-20.
36 Murnane, "Birds of the Puszta", 62-63.

wrote a book of my own in order to relieve my feelings. Any reader interested in this matter is referred to *Inland*, 1988".[37] The Magyar migrations from Central Asia retain the ancestral memory of origins for a people hemmed in by mountains: "The trampled *puszta*, the actual grassland of Hungary, was not for the Hungarians their grassland of last recourse. When the Hungarians stared at the *puszta* they might have been dreaming of another grassland far away – a grassland of grasslands" (64). This essentialist or mythical mode of thinking about the Eurasian steppe captures the exclave poetics Murnane deploys in the Hungarian aspects of *Inland*.

This geomorphology, itself based on hidden continuities across physical barriers – namely the Carpathian Mountains separating the Pannonian Plain from the Eurasian steppe – is generative of the entire narrative. Once the narrator shifts to a different visage in the larger section of the novel set in Melbourne County, the focus shifts from one female figure to another: from the farm worker courted by her co-worker, exploited by her supervisor, and observed by the narrator from his manor-house window, to the girl from Bendigo Street. These two figures are separated in geographic and narrative terms, but are also bound together by virtue of the narrator's inner landscape expressed in his writing on loose pages:

> Two details from *People of the Puszta* stayed with me afterwards until I was driven to turn them into a book of fiction … an account of the drowning of a young woman in a well and the author's penetrating as a man the libraries and drawing rooms of the same manor houses that had seemed awesome fastnesses when he had been the son of oppressed farm labourers. (65)

Crossing between Murnane's source text, his reading of it, and its deployment in the first section of *Inland*, is a carefully constructed event Nicholas Birns calls the library epiphany: "rendered through the medium of books or language, but its ultimate significance is emotional; books are vehicles of cognition, passports to a variety of rich experience located beyond their covers, if in practice unrealizable outside them".[38] *Inland* goes further than this: the initial narrator rehearses the elements of the epiphany, but gives way to the Melburnian narrator, whose epiphany moves along like the waterways in his story, parallel to the reading position, and ultimately outside the covers of a book in the grounds of the Fawkner cemetery. This is the novel's major formal breakthrough, where landscape, configured as an exclave, supersedes the library as a site of revelation. This final scene also obliquely absorbs the first section of the novel. As the narrator wanders the graveyard looking for the right words, he comes across the grave of a Finnish

---

37   Murnane, "The Angel's Son", 218.
38   Birns, "Infinite Desires", 54.

immigrant. This site, memorial to a native speaker of another branch of the Finno-Ugric family of languages, elicits the most visceral expression of emotion in the novel, and in the narrator's adult life:

> I wept in a way that I have never wept for any person I have met during my life. I wept for only a few minutes but violently, in the way that I weep sometimes for a man or a woman in a book that I have just read to its end. (169)

That this moment and its record should capture the reading experience – we too have just read to the end of *Inland* – absorbs the reader into the same exclave poetics.

In his ethnographic study of the region's inhabitants, Illyés describes the setting of the manor house, "in the middle of an extensive and delightful park, with its tennis-court, artificial lake, orchard and majestic avenue of trees".[39] This cultivated zone is further separated from the surrounding Alföld by virtue of a high wrought-iron fence and a remnant moat or ditch. What attracts Illyés' attention is the construction of the farm quarters occupied by the peasants: "According to the ethnographers, these outhouses are still constructed on the architectural principles once common in the original Central Asian homeland, out of a few bits of wood plastered with mud and straw".[40] The obscure ethnic origins of the *puszta* people are matched by their marginal status, living "in utter isolation, more hidden away and cut off than any villagers",[41] and showing a pronounced suspicion of outsiders. Illyés admits to a longstanding prejudice against this minority – much like that endured by the Roma throughout Europe or the *an lucht siúil* or Travellers in Ireland. This is set against the more esteemed origins of the Magyars:

> Of the various theories concerning the origin of the Hungarians, none has struck me with greater force and certainty of revelation than the latest one, which states that the Hungarians came here not with Árpád, but as the mute baggage-carriers of Attila, if not even before him. At all events it was due to their unwarlike nature that they were neither driven out nor slain with the Huns or the Avars … They yielded all they had to their noble conquerors, even their exquisite Ugric language – a normal historical process in the relationship between conqueror and conquered.[42]

---

39 Gyula Illyés, *People of the Puszta*, trans. G.F. Cushing (1936; Budapest: Corvina, 1967), 7.
40 Illyés, *People of the Puszta*, 8–9.
41 Illyés, *People of the Puszta*, 9.
42 Illyés, *People of the Puszta*, 12. Notably, the proper name Árpád derives from *árpa*, the Hungarian word for barley, itself of Turkic origin – providing a neat link with Murnane's novel *Barley Patch* (Artarmon, NSW: Giramondo, 2009).

Illyés alters his view of the peasant population in a series of homecomings to the *puszta*, overcome by the bleakness and emptiness of the sunsets: "Only then, freed from a fanatical enthusiasm for peasants and from that passion for home found in great reformers, could I survey the landscape and take a dispassionate view of its all".[43]

This dilatory excursus helps situate the *puszta*'s inhabitants in relation to the Eurasian steppe, but it is the account of a female farmhand's suicide in Chapter 12 that arrests Murnane's attention and forms the basis for the understated sequences of observations in and beyond the manor house in *Inland*. Having been forced into sex with a farm official in the manor house, the young woman's body is found in the well – a common method of female suicide. The official chases off the labourers there to offer help: "The official – and I cannot help it if all this sounds rather like a medieval horror-story filtered through the imagination of [József] Eötvös – circled round and round the dead body, white as a sheet and utterly unable to do anything".[44] The peasants are without the power to defy authority, thus the act of suicide is the most radical transgression of the social order:

> Yet the girl by dying suddenly developed a personality and stood apart from the community … Later in my imagination this girl became the angel of defiance and revolt for me, with her pale, dead face and the raw flesh showing through it. I envisaged her character, the powerful spirit in the "simple peasant girl"; the spirit which revealed itself in the fire of suffering to me was like that of Joan of Arc.[45]

Illyés meditates on the unfortunate culture of exploitation, where according to a village proverb, "Only bread is not shared", and notes that any tut-tutting extended only to the actions of the "old swine" and not so far as the welfare of the young girls being sexually harassed or abused. Illyés resents the girl for having had access – compelled as it was and subject to violence – to the inner sanctum of the manor house, a privilege he was only to enjoy much later on his return to the *puszta*: "However well I knew its inhabitants, the manor-house was still a feudal castle and a witches' den, and in its unpretentious way it did indeed swallow up young maidens".[46] This is the context of the window scene at the outset of *Inland*, where the narrator occupies the manor house, and peering periodically from one of the windows, views the overseer who views the labourers. Illyés discovers that, navigating between the choices of "submission or death", some girls attempt to evade the advances to which they are subject, and when successful they then stage

---

43 Illyés, *People of the Puszta*, 19.
44 Illyés, *People of the Puszta*, 189.
45 Illyés, *People of the Puszta*, 189–90.
46 Illyés, *People of the Puszta*, 192.

these events in comedies that would last for weeks.[47] Similarly, the narrator turns the potential drama outside to literary ends by constructing the narrative we read, and by reflecting on the act of writing as he does so. The serial gazes in the scene – the narrator watching the foreman who watches the "sullen young man" whose attentions fall upon the female labourer – conjures an atmosphere of conspiracy out of writing and grasses:

> Now, having written this, I see that the husband of Anne Kristaly Gunnarsen has always wanted me dead. I see him crouched above the wolfberry on the dream-prairie of Anne Kristaly and hating me because I see him and he cannot see me. (12)

The function of grassland is to camouflage, just as the surface of writing can hide specific meanings, motivations and plotlines beneath its unvaried surface. This is what ultimately unites the novel's two narrative scenarios: the economy of desire for the female farmhand in Illyés' book, and her defiant suicide, is given a second iteration in the consciousness of the first narrator. Yet it is also translated into the lost love of the second narrator in his youth, and the lifetime attempting to reconcile the melancholia that comes of unrequited loss. These narrative exclaves all belong to the larger geomorphological structure of the novel, as Murnane has gone to some effort to elucidate:

> I've never been able to explain how the different narrators of *Inland* take over from one another – give way to one another. Now, I'll try again. Imagine that a certain man fell in love with a young woman who was both dead and written about in a book. Now, if that man wanted to meet that young woman, he could either die, or become part of a book. He probably can't become part of the book that was already written, but perhaps he and the young woman can meet in some other book. So there you have the key to *Inland*. And I should add that the young woman lived and died in a country where the man who read about her had never been. He only knew the country from books. This man tries first to be a narrator of a book. At one time, he tries to be a character. And he tries to write the young woman into the book. But I can't go on. The book is too complicated to sum up like this.[48]

Gerald Murnane – or better, perhaps, his author function – falls in love with the defiant farmhand who suicides in Illyés' text. He can never meet her, or become part of the book in which she is discovered, but he has the ability to create a new

---

47 Illyés, *People of the Puszta*, 202–3.
48 Quoted in Susanne Braun-Bau, "A Conversation with Gerald Murnane", *Antipodes* 10, no. 1 (1996), 47.

terrain in which they meet: not the Hungarian Alföld of the first section of *Inland*, as the narrator never steps away from his book-lined room, but translated into his meeting with the girl from Bendigo Street in the second section of the novel. The girl from Bendigo Street does not die, but her young brother's grave marks out the topography of the narrator's loss. These slippages, deferrals and separations are precise expressions of an exclave poetics.

Conclusion

The exclave permits a shared identity with a larger formation, but a qualified identity all the same. While the Alföld or Pannonian Plain is geomorphologically a part of the larger Eurasian steppe it is separated from it by the Carpathian Mountains. Similarly, the rich material of the narrator's memory obeys distinct boundaries, dwelling on the geographic and hydrological location of the narrator's youth as he orbits the central moment of his emotional life – his interactions with the girl from Bendigo Street that quickly suffer incidental but final separation. This imposition of distance in the course of potential, and potentially profound, emotional intimacy, has the novel's geographic, emotional, narratological and intertextual concerns converge in a poetics of the exclave. The final scene in the graveyard captures this sense of deeply grounded displacement. As the narrator ponders the words whispered between the two girls decades before, the narrative hinges on the proximity of the key to his emotional life and the insuperable border or ring-fence that time and memory places in the intermedial zone:

> There is no final resolution here; but neither is there a literalizing end-point, a restrictive telos, a goal that can serve to dominate and subordinate everything that leads up to it. The untranslatability of the whispered words aspires toward a liberation as exhilarating as the endless horizons of any imagined prairies. Both in landscape and in love, Murnane celebrates the indefinite beauty of unconsummated desire.[49]

Endlessness – whether geographically, emotionally, or in the workings of the imagination – may be understood but not directly experienced. Yet the reader and narrator may occupy a position that affords a view of the endless plains, grounded sympathetically in relation to that promised unreachable zone. The poetics of the exclave require precisely this kind of strange intimacy, engineering a surface division that belies a subterranean commonality. Here is the real mystery of the girl

---

49   Birns, "Infinite Desires", 62.

from Bendigo Street: she is unattainable, lost, a figment of memory, but in working through his meditation on his loose sheets, the narrator's marginal experience of deferred intimacy taps into a common ground, absorbing each of his narrative subjects as well as the reader open to the hidden complexities of the steppe.

References

Anthony, David W. *The Horse, the Wheel, and Language: How Bronze-Age Riders from the Russian Steppes Shaped the Modern World*. Princeton, NJ: Princeton University Press, 2007.

Birns, Nicholas. "Infinite Desires: Love and the Search for Truth in the Fiction of Gerald Murnane", *Southerly* 55, no. 3 (1995): 48-62.

Braun-Bau, Susanne. "A Conversation with Gerald Murnane", *Antipodes* 10, no. 1 (1996): 43-48.

Coupland, R.T. "The Nature of Grassland". In *Grassland Ecosystems of the World*, edited by R.T. Coupland. Cambridge: Cambridge University Press, 1979, 23-29.

Derrida, Jacques. *The Work of Mourning*, translated by Pascale-Anne Brault and Michael Naas. Chicago: University of Chicago Press, 2001.

———. *The Politics of Friendship*, translated by George Collins. 1994; London: Verso, 1997.

Fawkner, Harald. *Grasses That Have No Fields: From Gerald Murnane's* Inland *to a Phenomenology of Isogonic Constitution*. Stockholm: Stockholm University, 2006.

Gelder, Ken. "Politics and Monomania: The Rarefied World of Contemporary Australian Literary Culture", *Overland* no. 184 (2006): 48-56.

Genoni, Paul. "Gerald Murnane". In *A Companion to Australian Literature Since 1900*. Rochester, NY: Camden House, 2007, 293-306.

———. "The Global Reception of Post-national Literary Fiction: The Case of Gerald Murnane", *JASAL: Journal of the Association for the Study of Australian Literature* 9, Special Issue (2009): 1-13.

Gillett, Sue. "Loving and Hating the *Inland* Reader: Postmodern Ploys or Romantic Reaction". In *A Sense of Audience: Essays in Postcolonial Literatures*, edited by William McGaw, special edition of *Span* 30 (1990): 59-68.

Illyés, Gyula. *People of the Puszta*. Translated by G.F. Cushing. 1936; Budapest, Corvina, 1967.

Murnane, Gerald. "Birds of the Puszta". In *Invisible Yet Enduring Lilacs*. Artarmon, NSW: Giramondo, 2005, 45-50.

———. "The Angel's Son: Why I Learned Hungarian Late in Life". In *Invisible Yet Enduring Lilacs*. Artarmon, NSW: Giramondo, 2005, 191-225.

———. "The Cursing of Ivan Veliki". In *Invisible Yet Enduring Lilacs*. Artarmon, NSW: Giramondo, 2005, 45-50.

———. "The Breathing Author". In *Invisible Yet Enduring Lilacs*. Artarmon, NSW: Giramondo, 2005, 149-90.

———. *Inland*. 1988; Champaign, IL: Dalkey Archive, 2012.

Murphy, Julian. "Being-in-Landscape: A Heideggerian Reading of Landscape in Gerald Murnane's *Inland*", *JASAL: Journal of the Association for the Study of Australian Literature* 14, no. 3 (2014): 1-11.

Salusinszky, Imre. *Gerald Murnane*. Melbourne: Oxford University Press, 1993.

Sundin, Lena. *Iconicity in the Writing Process: Virginia Woolf's* To the Lighthouse *and Gerald Murnane's* Inland. Göteborg: Göteborg University, 2004.

8
Landscape within Landscape: The Intertwining of the Visible and the Invisible in Gerald Murnane and Henry James

Suzie Gibson

At the 2017 "Another World in This One" symposium – held at Gerald Murnane's beloved Goroke Golf Club – I could not pass up the opportunity of asking this Australian writer about Henry James, especially as his book *A Million Windows* (2014) pays homage to the preface of *The Portrait of a Lady*.[1] I was keen to know what Murnane thought about such an influential Victorian novelist. To my surprise, he said that James' novels "have no landscape". This comment, presumably meant as a criticism, seemed logical at the time, uttered as it was in the rural context where Murnane was most at home. My immediate response was to agree, since Murnane's writing contemplates sweeping vistas that contrast sharply with James' crowded metropolitan spheres. But the more I thought about this comment the more I came to the conclusion that James' novels do have landscape – just not the kind of terrain that Murnane prefers.

James' landscapes are not rural spaces of freedom and abandon; rather, they tend to be enclosing environments that often undercut a character's autonomy. There is, however, a deep interiority, a secret domain within James' worlds that offers the promise of liberty. This secret hidden sphere, another world in this one, is closer to Murnane's literary imagination than he perhaps realises. Murnane's own paper from the symposium – "The Still-Breathing Author", later published in the *Sydney Review of Books*[2] – articulates this secret invisible realm as his

---

1 In James' 1908 preface to the New York edition of *The Portrait of a Lady* he imagines the complexity of perception as a "house of fiction" with a "million windows" where behind each aperture is a pair of eyes. The multifaceted nature of perception is conveyed through the idea that each pair of eyes looking through windows is watching the same human scene except that one sees "more" while another sees "less". This analogy reveals James' interest in how the point of view is a deeply subjective and complex experience. Henry James, *The Portrait of a Lady* (1881; Hertfordshire: Wordsworth Classics, 1999), 7.
2 Gerald Murnane, "The Still-Breathing Author", *Sydney Review of Books*, 6 February, 2018. https://sydneyreviewofbooks.com/the-still-breathing-author-gerald-murnane/

mind's vast interior. Moreover, he emphasises his mind's interiority as a boundless "place" that he has "barely begun to explore". Whilst it seems that rural landscape is central to Murnane's writing and imagination, it is but an external expression of his mind's geography. This concept of an invisible "mindscape" is extremely Jamesian, as the American writer explores the obscure, interior worlds of thinking and feeling. Furthermore, James' interest in the terrain of the mind is perhaps best demonstrated in his difficult later works, *The Ambassadors* (1903) and *The Golden Bowl* (1904), where most of the drama occurs within the thoughts and sensations of characters.

It may seem that James invents his successor, Murnane. And even more provocative than this idea is that, in a very Borgesian sense, there would be no Henry James if it were not for Gerald Murnane. As Borges puts it in his famous essay, "Kafka and his Precursors": "The fact is that each writer *creates* his precursors. His work modifies our conception of the past, and it will modify the future".[3] Unmoored from a linear concept of influence, James and Murnane reflect one another in a dynamic exchange of precedence and consequence. As such, Murnane creates James inasmuch as James predates Murnane. Their interlocking is also expressed through a shared pictorial imagination that renders captivating landscapes: *The Plains* (1982) evokes a photographic, twentieth-century sensibility, whilst James' ornamental style conjures a nineteenth-century painterly aesthetic.

In fact, there are many notable, even uncanny resemblances between Murnane and James that deserve elaboration, in spite of the still-breathing author's insistence that he is not necessarily dependent upon any literary influence: "I assure you that for most of my writing life I could see no further than the book I was currently working on".[4] Despite this claim, Murnane cannot be partitioned off from literary tradition and history. He would on some level surely agree: *A Million Windows* recognises that like James he too draws upon a "few ingredients" in developing his works.[5] However, such a recognition is soon followed up by Murnane's assertion that unlike James he was never fully cognisant of the very "ingredients" that inform his writings. Never being quite aware of the elements that make up one's work conjures a mystical nether-world that is yet to be charted. Indeed, there is a unique mysticism to Murnane's literary sensibility that is different from James' highly material, money-centred and class-obsessed worlds. There are also discernible differences between these two men who have both been described as "writers' writers".[6] What this all suggests is a dynamic interplay of similarity and difference

---

3   Jorge Luis Borges, "Kafka and His Precursors", in *Selected Non-Fictions*, ed. Eliot Weinberger (New York: Penguin, 1999), 363-65.
4   Murnane, "The Still-Breathing Author".
5   Gerald Murnane, *A Million Windows* (Artarmon, NSW: Giramondo, 2014), 3. All subsequent references are to this edition and appear in parentheses in the text.

where a paradox comes to fore: James and Murnane are similar in their difference just as they are also different in their similarity.

Through undertaking a close reading of Murnane's *The Plains* and one of James' most admired novels, *The Ambassadors*, I explore this paradox as well as the idea that each book utilises landscape as a means of revealing the complex interior lives of their respective male protagonists. In the considerable oeuvres of both authors, these most celebrated works best convey each writer's unique representation of landscape and how it enraptures their journeying protagonists. Murnane's much later book *Border Districts* (2017) will also be touched upon here, addressing a significant shift in consciousness from his earlier work, *The Plains*. Touted as his final book, *Border Districts* arguably brings us closer to this "still-breathing" author's contemporary thoughts and feelings.

Beginning with *The Ambassadors*, James strikingly foregrounds his lead character's thoughts and sensations once he becomes immersed within a dazzling Paris:

> Many things came over him here, and one of them was that he should doubtless presently know whether he had been shallow or sharp … Poor Strether had at this very moment to recognise the truth that wherever one paused in Paris the imagination reacted before one could stop.[7]

The Ambassadors chronicles Lambert Strether's intricate thought processes, ignited by leaving his provincial American home town of Woollett, Massachusetts, in order to sojourn in the capital of the nineteenth century, Paris. One of the many things that come to Strether while in Paris is the idea that he has missed out on life. The cultural, architectural and aesthetic delights of the city awaken in James' sensitive hero a painful sense that he has not quite lived. Travelling in the capacity of being his fiancée's ambassador – where it is his mission to persuade her wayward son, Chad Newsome, to abandon his romance with a sophisticated older woman – Strether's imaginative life expands to the point that he renounces this objective. However, while *The Ambassadors* keenly records the minutiae of its hero's Parisian adventure, much remains unrevealed. The main reason Chad must break off his romance and leave Paris is that he is charged with running the family business; yet we are never informed about the exact nature of this "business". Strether's resistance to identifying the manufactured object suggests its likely vulgarity. Such an omission is also generally indicative of James' later writings, which have a

---

6 Harriet L. McInerney, "Apprehending Landscapes: The Uncanny and Gerald Murnane's *The Plains*", *Antipodes*, 31, no. 1 (2017), 133.
7 Henry James, *The Ambassadors* (1903; Oxford: Oxford University Press, 1985), 68. All subsequent references are to this edition and appear in parentheses in the text.

tendency towards concealment, even abstraction, fostering our imagination and also readerly speculation.

This kind of abstraction contrasts sharply with the style of a later American author such as Philip Roth. His Pulitzer Prize-winning 1997 novel *American Pastoral*, for example, chronicles in minute detail the day-to-day running of his family's glove-making business, as recalled through protagonist "Swede" Levov. The loving manner in which Roth's narrative embraces the rich texture of real things celebrates what Catherine Morley has called "the strange beauty of the banal":[8] glove making itself becomes a crucial extension of Levov's character. Roth's intricate and affectionate descriptions of glove making also disrupt the idea of factory work being dehumanising. By contrast, our very lack of knowledge concerning the Newsome business in *The Ambassadors* produces the opposite effect: one is inclined to suspect that their enterprise is too brutalising to describe.

Like James, Murnane's tendency towards abstraction, which could be seen as identifying with the former's proto-modernism, omits what could be thought of as "banal" particulars that are so fundamental to character development in a novel like *American Pastoral*. For example, we never even know the name of *The Plains'* narrator, who journeys to the middle of Australia in order to imaginatively "leave" the continent. We also never know the name of the large town that he decides to settle in. All we know is that Murnane's protagonist ceases his journey once he comes across locals with a particular "way of speech and style of dress" that convinces him that he had travelled far enough into the plains.[9]

Comparable to Strether's pleasurable sensory impressions, Murnane's protagonist is also enriched by his new-found environment:

> Late that night I stood at a three-storey window of the largest hotel in the town. I looked past the regular pattern of streetlights towards the dark country beyond. A breeze came in warm gusts from the nearest miles of grassland. I composed my face to register a variety of powerful emotions. And I whispered words that might have served a character in a film at the moment that he realised he had found where he belonged. (4-5)

Murnane's narrator records his experiences much like a camera, the point of view being refracted through his perspective. The constant repetition of the first-person pronoun – "I stood at a three-storey window"; "I looked past the regular pattern of streetlights"; "I whispered words that might have served a character in a film" –

---

8   Quoted in Debra Shostak, *Philip Roth: American Pastoral, The Human Stain and The Plot Against America* (New York: Continuum Publishing, 2011), 12.
9   Gerald Murnane, *The Plains* (1982; Melbourne: Text Publishing, 2000), 4-5. All subsequent references are to this edition and appear in parentheses in the text.

emphasises the power of place upon one's senses. This excerpt also moves subtly from the first to the third person, the narrator imagining being like "a character in a film". This near-imperceptible movement from an "I" to a "he" also has a distancing and doubling effect where Murnane's authorial presence is subtly evoked. This layering of vision conveys a complexity of perception that is very much a Jamesian concern.

This idea of complex, double vision is also articulated in *The Ambassadors*, such as when James asserts that Strether was "burdened by a double consciousness" (2). Indeed, much of the novel's conflict is enacted through Strether's competing sense impressions; these seek to understand a new world that is in reality the old world of European art and society. As with Murnane and his narrator in *The Plains*, there is an affinity between James and his lead character. Like Strether, James embraced Europe over the American frontier. Strether also possesses the kind of literary sensibility intrinsic to James. Strether identifies himself as a writer, albeit of modest success, whose publishing is limited to the green-covered volumes of the provincial *Woollett Review* that is owned by his fiancée (44-45).

In *The Plains*, Murnane's narrator is also immersed in art and aesthetics: he intends to make a film about the grand vistas of interior Australia. *The Plains*' filmmaker and *The Ambassadors*' fledgling writer are both introspective and intellectual protagonists whose understanding of the world is filtered through complicated interiorities that might overthink, even aestheticise, everyday experience. This predilection is especially brought to the fore when encountering attractive female characters. In *The Ambassadors*, this is best revealed when Strether is confronted with the sexual appeal of Miss Gostrey:

> His impression of the noticed state of his companion, whose dress was "cut-down", as he believed the term to be, in respect to shoulders and bosom ... and who wore around her throat a broad red velvet band ... It would have been absurd of him to trace into ramifications the effect of the ribbon from which Miss Gostrey's trinket depended, had he not for the hour, at the best, been given over to uncontrollable perceptions. (34)

Strether's uncontrollable perception involves distinguishing his new-found female friend from his prudish fiancée, Mrs Newsome; he thinks that his American betrothed would never dare expose her bosom or seductively exhibit her throat through a velvet choker. In an effort to distance himself from Miss Gostrey's physical charm, he also compares her to notable historical figures such as the virgin Queen and later Mary Stuart, that all lead back to the thought of his imposing future wife. These series of associations involve powerful female figures that regulate the sexual dimension of his perception. Likewise, the narrator of *The Plains* shyly skirts around the question of female sexuality:

> I met her at dinner on my first evening in the great house. As the only daughter she was seated opposite me, but we said little to each other. She seemed not much younger than I, and therefore not as young as I wanted her to be. And her face was not quite so untroubled as I had hoped, so that I had to visualise anew some of the compelling close-ups in the final scenes of my film. (90)

The reticence of the narrator's impressions concerning the landowner's only daughter takes the form of a series of qualifications: for instance, she is young but not youthful enough; her face is reasonably peaceful but not sufficiently "untroubled" enough. Dwelling within this series of qualifications is an invisible realm of desire that later becomes more apparent, as when he imagines her gazing over an iridescent landscape:

> I want to bring to light the plain that only she remembers – that shimmering land under a sky that she has never quite lost sight of ... those plains she recognises when she gazes out from her verandah and sees anything but a familiar land.
> Last I want to venture into the plain that even she is not sure of – the places she dreams of in the landscape after her own heart. (93-94)

Murnane's filmmaker comes across here as a romantic who seeks to know the invisible terrain of a daughter's heart. The repetitious focus upon her delicate series of movements – "she remembers"; "she recognises"; "she gazes" and "she dreams" – conjures a wistful picture of a young woman whose subtle actions suggest her deep inner consciousness. However, this idealised image of femininity perhaps reveals more than anything the invisible landscape of the filmmaker's heart. Such an overtly romanticised vision of a young woman also suggests that Murnane's narrator might not be very knowledgeable when it comes to women. Tellingly in his speech at the symposium Murnane admitted to never understanding females and here in *The Plains* it appears that his narrator might also find this difficult. The filmmaker's glorious, even resplendent vision of the landowner's daughter parallels Strether's tendency to elevate the women he encounters, and this is very much brought to the fore when he naively believes in Chad and Madame de Vionnet's "virtuous attachment" (128).

Similar to Murnane's filmmaker, who constructs a very idealistic vision of the landowner's daughter through her connection to landscape, Strether too develops a picturesque image of Chad's French mistress through the lens of her shimmering Paris. And just as the filmmaker comprehends the landowner's daughter through her shining terrain, so too does Strether try to fathom Madame de Vionnet through the rich topography of her belonging and belongings:

> He seemed at the very outset to see her, in the midst of possessions not vulgarly numerous, but hereditary, cherishe, charming … he found himself making out, as a background of the occupant, some glory, some prosperity of the First Empire, some Napoleonic glamour, some dim lustre of the great legend; elements clinging still to all the consular chairs and mythological brasses and sphinxes' heads and faded surfaces of satin striped with alternate silk. (171-72)

Strether's particularly nostalgic sensibility is displayed through his assessment of Madame de Vionnet's beloved objects and furnishings, which reveal an "ancient Paris … he was always looking for" (171). The woman and the city come to represent all that Strether never knew he desired. Once more his mind turns to the realm of history: he idealises Madame de Vionnet as a figure that echoes the glory of the French Empire and its Napoleonic years. Like *The Plains*' unnamed filmmaker, *The Ambassadors*' male lead has a boundless imagination. He strives to understand the mysterious plain of femininity through the landscape of her dwelling. However, very different from the sparse imagery of *The Plains*, James' novel is full of objects and historical curios. It is only when Strether travels to the country that he comes to learn of the true nature of Chad's "attachment" to Madame de Vionnet. Here the wide-open spaces of a pastoral terrain make it possible for Strether to see more clearly. Such a rural scene is rare in James, where characters are usually in enclosed social settings such as drawing rooms, galleries and salons.

James' painterly aesthetic is channelled through Strether, whose appreciation of nineteenth-century landscape art inspires him to temporarily leave metropolitan Paris in search of Émile Lambinet's rural green vistas:

> such days, whatever should happen, were numbered, and he had gone forth under the impulse – artless enough, no doubt – to give the whole one of them to that French ruralism, with its cool green, into which he had hitherto looked only through the little oblong window of the picture frame. It had been as yet for the most part but a land of fancy … the background of fiction, the medium of art … He could thrill a little at the chance of seeing something somewhere that would remind him of a certain small Lambinet that had charmed him, long years before, at a Boston dealer's and that he had quite absurdly never forgotten … (380)

The charming Lambinet of Strether's memory is transformed into a lush reality when he lies down and naps within the grasslands of country France. His intoxicatingly rustic experience, however, is soon disrupted by a vision not uncharacteristic of a Lambinet landscape, except that the two boating lovers he perceives in the distance are not an anonymous pair but Chad and Madame de Vionnet. This climactic moment in the novel provides James' protagonist with a second epiphany – the first being his earlier realisation that one must "live all you can" (153) – and he comes to see the true carnality of Chad and Madame de Vionnet's relationship. In this scene, James' prose famously enacts this realisation through a stream-of-consciousness reverie that connects Strether's inner life with the external world of perception:

> For the two very happy persons he found himself straightaway taking them – a young man in shirt sleeves, a young woman easy and fair … The air quite quickened, at their approach, with further intimations; the intimation that they were expert, familiar, frequent – that this wouldn't, at all, be the first time. They knew how to do it … it made them but the more idyllic, though at the very moment of the impression, as happened, their boat seemed to have begun to drift wide … It had by this time none the less come much nearer – near enough for Strether to dream the lady in the stern had for some reason taken account of his being there to watch them. (418-19)

Strether's series of thoughts concerning the idyllic pair – "this wouldn't be the first time" and "they knew how to do it" – emphasises the sexual dimension of their coupling. His impression of their "expert, familiar, frequent" boating also implies that they are experienced, regular lovers. Once more Strether cannot help aestheticising the scene by imagining the couple "or something like them" in a painting (418). However, once Madame de Vionnet recognises Strether – while he too is realising that the "easy and fair" young woman is in fact Chad's mistress – then the shining splendour of his idyllic landscape vanishes:

> It was a sharp, fantastic crisis that had popped up as if in a dream, and it had had only to last a few seconds to make him feel it as quite horrible. They were thus, on either side, *trying* the other side, and all for some reason that broke the stillness like some harsh note. It seemed to him again, within the limit, that he had but one thing to do – to settle their common question by some sign of surprise or joy. (420)

Strether's "sharp, fantastic crisis" is the shocking knowledge that he has been duped. Witnessing the panic of his deceivers further intensifies his disappointment. Notably, in this penultimate section of the novel the word "dream" appears frequently, and this is in part about Strether's movement from enchantment to disenchantment. *The Ambassadors* is a meticulous chronicle of Strether's rite of passage from the sphere of dreams into the realm of knowledge. It is also important that such knowledge is attained when he ventures beyond the city of dreams. It is as if the sparkling lights and glamour of Paris have enabled Chad and Madame de Vionnet to pull off their ruse. A tranquil, verdant rural landscape exposes the deep intimacy of their relationship.

The Ambassadors is about awakening; about Strether undergoing a movement from innocence to experience. This form of interior travel is made possible by his departure from his place of belonging – Woollett, Massachusetts – where he is challenged and charmed by an unfamiliar shimmering Paris. James' "Preface" describes Strether's development as a "revolution" of consciousness enabled through "the influence of the most interesting of cities" (xxxviii). By contrast, *The Plains'* unnamed filmmaker travels to a country where he finds that he belongs, and it is experienced as a series of recollections in which the interior landscape of the mind coheres with exterior topography. There is a deep consonance between Murnane's narrator and his rural setting, and so there is no environmental conflict enabling or forcing transformation.

If there is any character development in Murnane's fictions, then it takes place across an expanse of thirty-five years and between two books, *The Plains* (1982) and *Border Districts* (2017). In the earlier work, the narrator keeps "his eyes open" (3) when he travels to rural Australia, whereas in the later text, the narrator is "resolved to guard" his eyes.[10] This movement from openness to wariness traces a shift in consciousness. By the time of *Border Districts*, such a transition is explained by an older writer who reflects upon his Catholic upbringing and the extraordinary amount of respect given to priests during his childhood. The narrator of this later work contemplates his youthful belief in Catholicism and how in one day it miraculously vanishes. This movement away from religion is linked to a story about a "lifelong" believer who loses her faith when she recalls the trauma of being sexually abused by priests (21-23).

In contrast to *The Plains*, *Border Districts* seems to be more of a direct chronicle of Murnane's memories and preoccupations, including the power of the invisible upon his imagination. Recounting his early embrace of Catholicism and his adult awareness of ecclesiastical sexual crimes certainly conveys a deep psychical wound that has likely led to the later guardedness of his vision. Unlike the expansive imagery of *The Plains*, *Border Districts* is a telescoped account of an author's memories that have come to shape him both as a man and writer.

There is then development in Murnane's writing, just not the kind enacted in *The Ambassadors*, where it is concentrated through a character and takes place within the sphere of one book. Despite there being no character transformation in

---

10   Gerald Murnane, *Border Districts* (Artarmon, NSW: Giramondo, 2017), 1. All subsequent references are to this edition and appear in parentheses in the text.

The Plains, Murnane and his filmmaker appear to be more idealistic than James and even his philosophical character Strether, and this is evoked through a constant yearning that oscillates around the fabled figure of the landowner's daughter:

> [W]hen I hurried to the window and looked for her in the shady park, her figure was never quite distinct from the shadowy after-images of whatever I had been reading. Alone in the distance she might have been the woman of three generations before who had been addressed each day for fifteen years in a long letter that was never delivered ... Or creeping towards the hesitant, timid bustards, she might have been her imagined self – the girl I had read of in her earliest diaries, who went to live among the tribes of ground-dwelling birds to learn their secrets. (95-96)

The narrator's series of speculations concerning the young woman invokes a rich interiority. The repetition of the words "shady" and "shadowy" evokes a darkening realm of dreams and hallucinations. The elusive figure of the woman enables the narrator to imagine her life through a number of scenarios. If there is any plot in *The Plains*, then it comes across as a filmmaker's series of fantasies suggesting that he might love the young woman he never knows. Echoing Strether, Murnane's filmmaker possesses an extraordinary imagination and literary sensibility; yet very different to James' lead, who is described as a slim man of fifty-five with a "thick dark moustache" and abundant hair (34), we never know Murnane's narrator's age or physical features. Also, not knowing anything specific about the narrator's personal life renders him as an abstract figure. This all creates a sense of remoteness that is further intensified by Murnane's manipulation of time.

Readers access *The Plains* as a narrator's recollection of his youthful voyage to the interior of Australia. We are never directly informed about the purpose of the narrator's travel. Instead we are left to surmise, based upon the contents of his suitcase, which include a film script, that he intends to cinematically record the landscape. We also have no knowledge of the young traveller's past life that might explain his journey. By contrast, in *The Ambassadors* we learn very early on that Strether has a "crowded past" (58), since he was once married and had a boy-child only to lose both his wife and son to illness. In *The Plains*, all that we know is that Murnane's unnamed narrator struggles to fulfil his mission of making a film about the plains because experience is not reducible to a series of images. Murnane's narrator is an unfathomable figure whose series of perceptions might reveal an ethereal poet but who in truth resembles no one except perhaps the author himself.

The number of other figures who move across the landscape of the narrator's vision – landowners, plainsmen, painters, philosophers, freckled dark-haired women and brooding patrons (116) – also appear as outlines, even abstractions. There is a deep irony in all of this, for while Murnane's young filmmaker has travelled to the place of his belonging, readers cannot forge an emotional or psychological bond to him or with anyone else. And this is because, unlike *The Ambassadors*, *The Plains* is not a novel in the nineteenth-century sense of the word. Character does not operate as a vehicle through which readers identify in forging an understanding of themselves and their place in the world. No such affinity is fostered in *The Plains* and, as such, Murnane's work moves more extremely towards the realm of abstraction – a plain that James certainly experimented with but whose proto-modernism does not quite go so far. Such obscurity is suggested through Murnane's contemplative narrator, whose sensory enjoyment of landscape ignites abstract thoughts concerning unseen territories:

> I stare at this land now, and every glowing acre of it sinks into my same old private darkness. But others may be looking at the plains too. That weather – it's only a sign of all the invisible territory around us all at this very moment … I fancy an expedition into the unseen world … (155-56)

The Plains' filmmaker recollects all that he sees and imagines, including a "glowing acre", "private darkness", "invisible territory" and "unseen world" that resemble a series of chiaroscuro images. The play of black-and-white imagery parallels a moving picture, where the shining light of the narrator's vision evokes a film director's "private darkness". In *Border Districts* and "The Still-Breathing Author", Murnane emphasises that his writings report upon experience – they do not fabricate or contrive. Murnane also does not quite accept that he is a writer of fiction and this is why he is insistent that his books are "works" instead of "novels". This again marks a significant departure from nineteenth-century literature, and even aspects of twentieth-century writing. And once more this is redolent, perhaps strangely so, of Murnane's romantic sensibility, where he is desirous of chronicling the truth. In Murnane's writing there is a strange consonance between romanticism and modernism in that the spirit of his writerly abstraction is driven by the desire to be authentic, yet simultaneously the very obscurity of his prose can be alienating. Connected to these competing tendencies is the idea that Murnane also sees himself as a "technical writer" who strives to render the most authentic account of his "mental imagery".[11]

As a technical writer, Murnane once more conjures James' meticulous style. However, unlike James, Murnane does not seek to render identifiable characters whose personalities are revealed through their past lives, the perceptions of other characters, or, particularly, in conversation. In fact, there is no conversation in *The*

---

11   Murnane, "The Still-Breathing Author".

Plains. When landowners speak, they do not interact with one another, but rather run their own verbal race like horses in Murnane's beloved Melbourne Cup:

> 1st Landowner: ... our own generation too extreme when they define the ideal complexion for a woman. No one wants his wife or daughter brown from the sun ... All my life I've dreamed of a certain arrangement of ... I refuse to use that banal word "freckles". Their colour must be a delicate gold ...
>
> 2nd Landowner: ... bustards of course, and plains-wanderers, and painted quail and stubble quail, and the brown songlark with that odd call it makes. And I ask myself ... (61-62)

This series of unconnected, even stream-of-consciousness, statements, continues between the seven landowners, whose utterings fail to foster interpersonal communication. These "personages" – Murnane and James are both fond of this term, which also creates a sense of remoteness – speak of the world they inhabit, a sphere that the narrator hopes to one day capture on celluloid. Eventually this series of assertions about the ideal complexion of women and the various birds of the region turns to the narrator's particular reason for being among proprietors and plainsmen when landowner "seven" declares that out of all the "forms of art" cinema is the most capable of showing "the remote horizons of dreams" (78). And so, with these words we are reminded that Murnane's journeying narrator has a mission to cinematically record life on the plains. However, his quest to capture the interior of Australia is frustrated by a doubt that a camera can reveal "plains within plains" (83). Murnane's narrator may be a filmmaker but he is more concerned with the invisible world of the heart and the imagination. This is perhaps most excruciatingly revealed in a scene where he and the landowner's daughter find themselves in a library:

> But as the months passed and she came almost every afternoon to sit between me and the shelves labelled TIME, I was more compelled to declare something to her. I sensed between us the mass of all the words we might have spoken as a stack of unopened volumes as daunting as any of the actual shelves that stood above each of us. (132)

Murnane's narrator-filmmaker evokes a Jay Gatsby-like yearning – someone who idealises a woman whom he does not know. The image of a mass of unspoken words as daunting as "unopened volumes" also captures a deep melancholy that is again redolent of Fitzgerald's Gatsby. Murnane's journeying narrator moves both towards and away from the daughter of his dreams as he imagines writing a book that only she will read, only to then immediately abandon this idea as if such intimacy is too much. In a very Jamesian way, nothing sexual happens between the filmmaker and the patron's daughter because in the narrator's words, it would somehow violate the "poise of the world" (136). I have never imagined the world as having "poise" and yet Murnane's romantic consciousness conjures this idea. The timorous manner in which his narrator encircles and admires the landowner's daughter parallels Strether's resistance to embrace the reality of a relationship with Maria Gostrey, who in the final scene of *The Ambassadors* proclaims that she would do anything for him:

> "There's nothing, you know, I wouldn't do for you."
> "Oh yes – I know."
> "There's nothing,' she repeated, 'in all the world."
> "I know. I know. But all the same I must go." (438)

Strether chooses not to live in Paris, even though it teaches him how to live. His Parisian adventure also teaches him that he has nothing in common with his puritan betrothed, Mrs Newsome, and yet this does not mean that he belongs to another whom he understands better, namely Maria Gostrey. Strether's emotional leave-taking of Mrs Newsome and his intended departure from Paris also do not mean that he belongs to his stultifying home town of Wollett, Massachusetts. In fact, it is unclear where and to whom Strether belongs. This question of belonging is central to Murnane's literary imagination. In *The Plains*, the narrator's journey to the interior of Australia leads to discovering his place of belonging. In Murnane's writing, physical landscape operates as a comforting sphere that provides aesthetic pleasure. By contrast, James' proto-modernism comes to the fore through Strether's lack of belonging. *The Ambassadors* leaves both Strether and readers poised between the past and the future. In the end, James' protagonist is without a physical landscape as his mind becomes his one true home. This idea of one's mind being an ultimate place of belonging anticipates Murnane, whose concept of the eternal plain is a boundless mindscape.

A notable analogy between *The Plains* and *The Ambassadors* is that James' lead fails as Mrs Newsome's ambassador, just as *The Plains*' narrator fails to complete his film. Failure in James and Murnane is not necessarily unfortunate since it acknowledges the true complexity of experience:

> My failing was that I could never arrange my subject matter – the arguments and narratives and expositions that kept me talking for never less than half a day – so that it culminated in a revelation that somehow emphasised or contrasted with or prefigured or even seemed to deny all likelihood of the lesser revelation of the land … (166)

Once more the narrator's series of qualifications, "somehow emphasised or contrasted with", "or prefigured", enacts James' cautionary literary style. The filmmaker's daunting ambition to capture every particle of his experience on the plains cannot but fail because cinematography is about telescoping, even narrowing vision. There is then also a lack of neatness in *The Plains* that acknowledges how sensory perception is just too vast to capture on film, or perhaps in any other medium. Realising that he cannot make his film, Murnane's narrator considers other aesthetic possibilities: "I had almost decided to call myself a poet or novelist or landscaper or memorialist or scene-setter or some other of the many sorts of literary practitioner flourishing on the plains" (170). Here the narrator speculates upon alternative forms of representation that might best reveal the plains and his abilities. He also comes to think that writing might be his true vocation since the camera merely multiplies and doubles vision (171). For *The Plains*' narrator, the camera's mirror image of the world is just too simplistic. But neither can an alternative form of representation be settled upon. His copious notes about the plains cannot be disciplined into a coherent narrative. While searching for another medium in which to represent the plains, the question of belonging comes to the fore once again as the narrator tries to locate himself through his aesthetic calling. In light of this, if there is any development in *The Plains* then it appears here as a series of thought progressions that oscillate around the question of the narrator's identity and artistic skills. Gradually, Murnane's narrator becomes more emphatic about the idea of being a writer, and as such the voice of *The Plains* moves even more closely towards the literary identity of its creator.

The final page of *The Plains* travels back to the realm of desire, where the narrator imagines that "some young woman" might perceive him "as a man who saw further than others" (174). Interestingly, the writer-filmmaker is keen to have his ability to see further recorded by his patron, who lifts his camera in order to capture the moment when he too raises his camera to the exterior world of the plains. This doubling of vision is also a doubling of technology. Like James, who was fascinated by the nature of perception, Murnane is captivated by the multifaceted and often complex process through which one perceives the world. In Murnane's many works, including *The Plains*, perception is mediated through eyes, cameras, windows, coloured glass and shadows. The narrator's and the patron's two cameras add layers to this rich field of perception, in which they enact an intertwining of vision. This overlapping is very evocative of Maurice Merleau-Ponty's phenomenology, where he imagines the seer and the seen being enveloped within the world of vision.[12] In *The Plains*, this intersection and interaction between perceiver and perceived leads to a great darkness where being too close exposes one to a profound obscurity:

> I would always ask my patron at last to record the moment when I lifted my own camera to my face and stood with my eye pressed against the lens and my finger poised as if to expose to the film in its dark chamber the darkness that was the only visible sign of whatever I saw beyond myself. (174)

This moment of recording perception, enacted through an eye/I that presses itself against another eye, the camera lens, exposes a darkness that reaches beyond the self. Paradoxically, such darkness is articulated as the "only visible sign" of what the narrator sees. This final scene in *The Plains* is also a meditation upon the contradictory nature of perception that involves an intertwining of darkness and light. Once more this is redolent of black-and-white cinematography. In *A Million Windows*, Murnane mentions the influence of a "Swede's films during the 1960s" (4). This Australian writer's oblique reference to Ingmar Bergman's extraordinary cinematic landscapes reveals the director's aesthetic influence upon his literary imagination that also conjures a grand interplay of shadow and radiance.

In "The Still-Breathing Author", Murnane touches upon another kind of darkness that illuminates *The Plains*. He reveals that while the text of approximately 35,000 words is a fixed publishing object, it is for him but a fragment carved out of a much larger work of 90,000 words.[13] We are also informed that its original title – *Landscape with Darkness and Mirage* – was something that he fought over with publishers only to be worn down. The hidden territory of the plains then also encompasses this idea of an as-yet inaccessible larger body of writing. This encourages one to contemplate another mysterious plain that exists for the time being as a submerged text. A larger body of work hidden from the world of vision is redolent of a profound secrecy. Knowing that *The Plains* is excised from a much weightier body of writing may perhaps go towards explaining its stylistic obscurity.

The Plains arguably pushes the limits of representation even further than *The Ambassadors*: writing itself becomes a plain, even a topographical mark. Despite the fact that James' later novels are famed for their difficulty and near-abstraction, they do not go as far as Murnane in this regard. And this is because the American novelist still writes and thinks within the realm of identifiable characters and discernible narratives. While plotline may not be obvious in *The Ambassadors* and James' later works in general, there is nonetheless a narrative hidden beneath all of his linguistic qualifications and peripatetic movements. In *The Plains*, Murnane moves more fully towards the realm of abstraction, where personages are bereft of proper names and are instead generally identified through what they do or

---

12　See Maurice Merleau-Ponty's last, incomplete work, *The Visible and The Invisible* (1964; Evanston, IL: Northwestern University Press, 1968), where he writes about the embeddedness of perception, 76-80.
13　Murnane, "The Still-Breathing Author".

own. The march of landowners, filmmakers, patrons and writers traversing the narrator's field of vision comes across like flickering screen images. This has a powerful distancing effect. If there is a vividness of character in *The Plains* then it is conveyed as a formless, mystical yearning. Such mysticism is also evocative of a great darkness beyond.

Both *The Plains* and *The Ambassadors* are literary and intellectual triumphs that explore the interior landscapes of the mind. James' Strether and Murnane's unnamed narrator are bewitched by landscapes, women, and women within landscapes. Both shy away from the question of sex and the idea of forging intimate relationships with the women they admire. In this respect, Strether carries a whiff of American puritanism, while Murnane's lead bears the markings of his author's Catholicism. Furthermore, in these works, external, physical territory is crucial to revealing the aesthetic and intellectual power of their lead characters. Their respective environments – nineteenth-century Paris and the robust terrain of rural twentieth-century Australia – shimmer through the consciousness of James' and Murnane's protagonists. And although James' urban landscapes are more generally drawing rooms, mansions and country retreats, they are also deeply sensory spheres of thinking and feeling. By contrast, *The Plains* and other Murnane novels – *Landscape with Landscape*, *Inland*, and finally *Border Districts* – suggest a persistent fascination with the wide-open spaces of a uniquely Australian rural setting. In all of these texts, landscape figures as a powerful force that contextualises and enfolds.

Upon experiencing the environment of Goroke and its surrounding plains, Murnane's preoccupation with landscape began to make sense to me. The undulating plains of rural Victoria provided me with a feeling of being embraced. Being enveloped, even protected by landscape, does mark a significant departure from James' worlds that dramatise over and over again the perils of urban, intensely social terrains that especially undermine young marriageable female characters. *The Ambassadors* is not exempt from this disturbing pattern, with Chad abandoning his lover Madame de Vionnet for a life back in America, where he plans to make a significant industrial contribution to the world of consumerism.

In light of this, there is an unmistakeable materiality in James' novels that repeatedly chronicle a ruthless will to power tied to an obsession to procure immense monetary wealth. By contrast, Murnane's world is a far more "dreamy" sphere, unmoored from material and economic concerns. Arguably this is what makes Murnane an idealist, even a romantic, whose epic grasslands and grandiose plains ponder the natural beauty of a sphere far removed from urban ambition and capitalism. In the final stages of *The Plains*, the material world features less and less as the narrator's field of dreams takes over. This is evocative of a grand mysticism at the heart of Murnane's writing that ushers us towards the horizonless plain of eternity. Yet despite these differences, landscape in both Murnane and James operates as a great source of literary inspiration. Without the allure of expansive plains and lush grasslands in the former, and burgeoning international cities in the latter, their respective protagonists would be bereft of the sensory pleasure that is so important to their boundless imaginations.

References

Borges, Jorge Luis. "Kafka and His Precursors". In *Selected Non-Fictions*, edited by Eliot Weinberger. New York: Penguin, 1999, 363-65.
James, Henry. *The Golden Bowl*. 1904; New York: Penguin, 1985.
——. *The Ambassadors*. 1903; Oxford: Oxford University Press, 1985.
——. *The Portrait of a Lady*. 1881; Hertfordshire: Wordsworth Classics, 1999.
McInerney, Harriet L. "Apprehending Landscapes: The Uncanny and Gerald Murnane's *The Plains*", *Antipodes* 31, no. 1 (2017): 133-44.
Merleau-Ponty, Maurice. *The Visible and the Invisible*. 1964; Evanston, IL: Northwestern University Press, 1968.
Murnane, Gerald. "The Still-Breathing Author". *Sydney Review of Books*, 6 February 2018: https://sydneyreviewofbooks.com/the-still-breathing-author-gerald-murnane/.
——. *Border Districts*. Artarmon, NSW: Giramondo Publishing, 2017.
——. *A Million Windows*. Artarmon, NSW: Giramondo Publishing, 2014.
——. *Inland*. Richmond Vic.: William Heinemann Australia, 1988.
——. *Landscape with Landscape*. Carlton, Vic.: Norstrilia Press, 1985.
——. *The Plains*. 1982; Melbourne, Vic.: Text Publishing, 2000.
Roth, Philip. *American Pastoral*. 1997; London: Vintage Books, 1998.
Shostak, Debra, ed. *Philip Roth: American Pastoral, The Human Stain and The Plot Against America*. New York: Continuum Publishing, 2011.

9
Memory, Image and Reading Traces of the Infinite: *A History of Books*

Arka Chattopadhyay

The experience of reading books is integral to the registration of consciousness and memory. The mnemonic traces of a lifetime of reading offer an imaginative reservoir. It can also work as experimental material for fiction writing. From the oral to the written and from reading out loud to silent articulation, reading has always influenced the mode and style of writing. When we read and process the material in a conscious way in order to make sense of the reading, a cognitive collusion takes place between word and image. Writing is yet another engagement of thinking through this word-image complex. As a literary writer, Gerald Murnane is interested in thinking through cognitive images and his fiction presents a dialogue of image and memory, mediated through the experience of reading. As Anthony Uhlmann reflects: "The reader of *A History of Books* wants books to leave him with images that will persist, that will outlive the books themselves".[1] What are the images that remain and what resonance urges them to live on long after the reading? These are Murnane's zones of fascination. In this chapter, I trace the contours of specular thinking in Murnane's novella *A History of Books* (2012) in terms of the interaction between the memory of reading traces and the imagery of thought. From Murnane's network of interconnected reading traces and their images, we will see if thinking in fiction can approach an infinite structure of thought by tapping on the interplay of book as a container and life as a material that is difficult to be contained.

---

1 Anthony Uhlmann, "Signs for the Soul", *Sydney Review of Books,* July 2013. https://sydneyreviewofbooks.com/signs-for-the-soul/

Gerald Murnane

From Language to Image

It is interesting to note Ferdinand de Saussure's use of the expression "word-image" in his foundational theory of linguistics. To zoom in on language as a collective and inter-subjective phenomenon where words and images work together to produce meaning, Saussure reflects:

> If we could embrace the sum of word-images stored in the minds of all individuals, we could identify the social bond that constitutes language. It is a storehouse filled by the members of a given community through their active use of speaking, a grammatical system that has a potential existence in each brain, or, more specifically, in the brains of a group of individuals. For language is not complete in any speaker; it exists perfectly only within a collectivity.[2]

In Saussure's linguistic structure of the "signifier" and the "signified", the former is qualified as a "sound-image" while the latter evokes a concept. As he observes, "language is a storehouse of sound-images, and writing is the tangible form of those images".[3] When we hear and understand a conversation, we are approaching the words as auditory images that generate concepts and produce meanings. As we read a piece of writing, we read by way of seeing, which is an intensely visual process. The words themselves are registered first as images on the page and as we process them, the image is linked with the concept.

The point that we make sense of things through images finds a different kind of support in Wittgenstein's so-called "picture-theory" of language, wherein he asserts "a proposition is a picture of reality" and again, "a proposition states something only in so far as it is a picture".[4] Wittgenstein's axiom that "what a picture represents is its sense" makes it amply clear how the linguistic deciphering of meaning must work its way through cognitive images, both sonic and visual.[5] In *Tractatus Logico-Philosophicus*, Wittgenstein is also aware that words do not readily register themselves in an imagistic manner:

> At first sight a proposition – one set out on the printed page, for example – does not seem to be a picture of the reality with which it is concerned. But neither do written notes seem at first sight to be a picture of a piece of music, nor our phonetic

---

2   Ferdinand de Saussure, *Course in General Linguistics*, trans. Wade Baskin (1916; New York: Philosophical Library, 1959), 13-14.
3   Saussure, *Course*, 15.
4   Ludwig Wittgenstein, *Tractatus Logico-Philosophicus*, trans. D.F. Pears and B.F. McGuinness (1921; London: Routledge, 2001), 24-25.
5   Wittgenstein, *Tractatus*, 12.

notation (the alphabet) to be a picture of our speech. And yet these sign-languages prove to be pictures, even in the ordinary sense, of what they represent.[6]

As we can see here, Wittgenstein is uncomfortable with a simplistic representational image of reality. Is the image only a mimetic reproduction of the real? How would Murnane's use of image respond to this question of realism? Though cognitive philosophers like Daniel Dennett are critical of an imagistic notion of consciousness, even Dennett concedes that "mental images are in a different space, do not have dimensions, are subjective, are Intentional, or even, in the end, just quasi-images".[7] Acknowledging that these psychic images are not like physical pictures (paintings or photographs), I would call them cognitive images. Cognition as a process makes images emerge from words. Do these cognitive images create a semantic network that is potentially infinite? Can this be a way in which literature thinks the phenomenon of infinity? I will direct this question at the level of literature as a specular or imagistic mode of thinking.

How does Literature Think Infinity through Images?

To approach the question at a fundamental level, let us ask whether literature thinks. If literature thinks in a way of its own, that modality of thought would be different from philosophy, for example, which is principally concerned with the act, the process and the product of thinking. If we consider image in its multi-sensory and cognitive form as a mode of literary thinking, what does it do to thinking in general? As Anthony Uhlmann has argued about thinking in the European modernist novel, there are three different levels at which the literary text conducts a process of thought: "relation", "sensation" and "composition".[8] For him, "these three tendencies are crucial to thinking in literature".[9] Cognitive imagery as a domain is relevant to each of these three processes, as we shall see with Murnane. Images that drive the process of cognition are fundamentally sensory in nature; they have a complex web of relationality and finally their matrix is what creates the compositional fabric of this thinking process. These images thus relate to the three aforementioned inclinations of thought. They are sensory and relational, and impinge strongly upon the compositional structure.

---

6   Wittgenstein, *Tractatus*, 23.
7   Daniel Dennett, *Content and Consciousness* (London and New York: Routledge, 2010), 133.
8   Anthony Uhlmann, *Thinking in Literature: Joyce, Woolf, Nabokov* (London and New York: Continuum, 2011), 4.
9   Uhlmann, *Thinking in Literature*, 49.

To turn to Gilles Deleuze and Félix Guattari, who underline the category of image in thinking:

> The image of thought retains only what thought can claim by right. Thought demands "only" movement that can be carried to infinity. What thought claims by right, what it selects, is infinite movement or the movement of the infinite. It is this that constitutes the image of thought.[10]

The context here is what Deleuze and Guattari call the "plane of immanence" and for them this is not a concept but an "image of thought". Not only do they connect thinking to imagery but they also consider this thinking to be a way of broaching infinity as a structure of thought. So, the movement of thought on an immanent plane constitutes a journey towards infinity. In *What Is Philosophy?*, Deleuze and Guattari famously align philosophy with "the power of concepts" while the literary is seen as a field of "affects and percepts".[11] This affectively layered perceptual domain is the cognitive field of images in thought.

Compared to Deleuze and Guattari, who consider an image of thought to proceed towards infinity, Alain Badiou has a different position. A philosopher, invested in the idea of infinity, Badiou does not consider literary thinking to be an opening towards infinity. In "What Does Literature Think?", Badiou argues that the literary text thinks where its narrative function is paused: "Beyond the fictional world, literature that thinks emerges in the cracks in the story [*la fable*]".[12] Literary thought is thus irreducible to storytelling. It settles in the gaps, left by the text's narrative function. Badiou underlines the notion of "work" in literature to fix it as a production of the finite: "In stark contrast to the infinite variety of experience (which is perfectly obvious), the work of art or literature is the difficult, unlikely production of the finite. And it is precisely this production that constitutes thought".[13]

For Badiou, while experience in general is infinite, a literary text is produced by taking out a part from that infinity. Its work lies in slicing a finite piece from an infinite totality. He evokes a rather simplistic binary where the literary work is "finite" and "artificial" while the "natural" world is infinite. As we shall see with Murnane, the literary text is not merely a finite selection, scraped out of extra-textual infinity. In fact, his texts are transfinite in that they look outward

---

10   Gilles Deleuze and Félix Guattari, *What Is Philosophy?*, trans. Hugh Tomlinson and Graham Burchell (1991; New York: Columbia University Press, 1996), 37.
11   Guattari and Deleuze, *What Is Philosophy?*, 65.
12   Alain Badiou, "What Does Literature Think?", in *The Age of the Poets and Other Writings on Twentieth-Century Poetry and Prose*, trans. Bruno Bosteels (London and New York: Verso, 2014), 133.
13   Badiou, *The Age of the Poets*, 134.

into the margin of the text where it situates its point of closure. In Murnane, this movement of closure is also an opening into the outside of the text. We will return to this play of the textual and the extra-textual at a later point through the Mallarméan dialectic of *a* book that is written and *the* Book of the world that essentially excludes *a* book and can never be completely written.

Badiou deepens the point about literary thinking by asking the question: "if literature is a form of thought, must it not be the thought of that thought?".[14] This critical redoubling of thought makes thought both subject (thinking) and its own object (thought-object, produced by thinking as subject). This meta-thinking is something literature has to meddle with, as it negotiates the infinite multiplicity of experience on the one hand and the structural unity of a particular work, on the other. Badiou calls the former "many" and the latter "One" in his Platonic register. Though he generally maintains the reductive dichotomy of finite text and infinite experience, when it comes to this "meta" aspect of literary thinking, Badiou concedes that literature "asserts that thought is also thought of thought, turning its own thinking, at least in certain places, into a closed area, and a glimpse of the gap between inside and outside".[15] There are parts in a literary text, which he calls "closed areas", where the gap between the inside and outside of a text is glimpsed. This textual limen is a reflective enclosure where thought doubles back on itself and produces a subject of thinking and a thought-object. This margin of the text is at the cusp of inside and outside and thus, potentially, transfinite.

Badiou clarifies that "what literature thinks is both a real marked in language with the seal of the One, and the conditions governing the way that real is marked".[16] At this liminal point, literary thinking not only works towards a unification in the form of sealing the reality that is marked out and portrayed by language, but it also thinks the "conditions governing the way that real is marked" in literary language. This second point is crucial because it brings infinite multiplicity into some sort of relation, albeit tangential, with the literary text. Literary thought does not simply mark out a reality in language. It also thinks through the process through which that reality is depicted and deployed by language. Badiou finally calls it a "double point" in the work of literature which holds both "the symbolic seal of the One" and "the real of the real".[17] Though Badiou thinks that the literary text is a finite emergence from experiential infinity, he also locates a duplicity in this simplistic binary formation. In this "double point", the thought of thought exposes the cusp between inside and outside and reveals an

---

14   Badiou, *The Age of the Poets*, 136.
15   Badiou, *The Age of the Poets*, 139
16   Badiou, *The Age of the Poets*, 136
17   Badiou, *The Age of the Poets*, 139

engagement with the infinite as a manifestation of the way reality is expressed in the language of the text. Reading Badiou's text, somewhat against its grain, I would claim that this doubling of thought ("thought of thought") and reality ("the real of the real") are cognitive images of thinking that open the finite to the infinite.

Cognitive Image in *A History of Books*: Between Reading and Writing

Consider the opening image of *A History of Books*. We see a man and a woman, debating with one another, hitting each other and soon thereafter turning into "a male and a female jaguar, or it may have been a male and a female hummingbird or a male and a female lizard".[18] This scene, taking place somewhere in a Central American town, evokes a "magical realism" which Murnane's narrator discusses in a disparaging manner in the next two paragraphs. The scene is repeated after his dismissal of magical realism as a simplistic literary tradition. This time, the debate and fight of the man and the woman takes place in a Melbourne suburb. Instead of turning into the aforementioned animals, after having sexual intercourse, the woman falls asleep and the man, lying on the bed, watches mental images of "a male and a female jaguar, or it may have been a male and a female hummingbird or a male and a female lizard" (5). Although the entire phrase is repeated after the indictment of magical realism, the corporeal and metamorphic aspect becomes imagistic. The man and wife do not become the animals but one of the two imagines them in his mind. As the narrator clarifies, the animal imagery comes from the man's reading of a book. This reader aspires to become a writer and hence his consciousness attempts to capture the perspective of the writer through supposition. This potential writer wants to create images that have the capacity to surprise him, just as he had remembered the strange images of jaguars and hummingbirds and lizards from his reading experience.

The man begins rationalising the images he has remembered in his mind. He "observes" that it is his wife's undergarment that resembles the skin of the lizard. He also "observes" that "the shining of the sunlight on a few stray hairs at the woman's forehead" brings to his mind the image of the hummingbird (6). Murnane's fiction thus treats the cognitive activity of observational image-analysis as a mental action whereby an image is studied in its relational matrix. After rationalising the relations between his wife and the lizard on the one hand and the hummingbird on the other, the man falls asleep, keeping the connection with the jaguar in suspension. This is where we have the hypothetical third observation that explains the jaguar

---

18   Gerald Murnane, *A History of Books* (Artarmon, NSW: Giramondo, 2012), 3. All subsequent references are to this edition and appear in parentheses in the text.

image. Murnane's narrator treats this third observation as a speculative possibility, to be realised when he becomes a writer of fiction. The narrator refers to "certain secrets known only to writers of fiction" (6) and if the man were to possess these secret tricks, only then he "might have observed" how the fabric of his wife's toiletry bag had a spotted print, making it look like a jaguar's skin. The "conjectured writer might have observed" that the man, asleep on his bed, has the posture of a jaguar, "preparing to leap towards its prey" (7). To extract the critical points from this opening scenario, reading generates mental images which are then cognitively processed, relationally explained by the connection that causes them to return, but there are images left to a hypothetical future when reading would turn into writing. This speculative aspect that characterises the final observation is a passage from the finite to the infinite. The hypothetical preserves the domain of that which does not happen but may happen. This is not an actual infinite but the "may", in all its contingency, which saturates the finite with a gesture towards the infinite.

J.M. Coetzee calls Murnane a "radical idealist" who believes in the reality of mental images, in their complex ideational network of associations.[19] For Coetzee, Murnane has a "topography" of the mind, but no "theory of the mind" because he sees it as nothing beyond a "watchful passivity".[20] As we have seen above, it is not that the Murnanian mind is all passive. Observation is used actively to connect between image and referent and explain the recurrence of an image. In the 1986 article "Why I Write What I Write", Murnane puts great emphasis on sound and hearing. He underscores how hearing his own sentences is central to his composition. While this might return us to Saussure's notion of the "sound-image",[21] integral to the signifier-signified relational structure of the linguistic sign, what is more relevant is how he talks about his sentences, "arising" out of "images and feelings" that "haunt" him.[22] Throughout this essay, Murnane couples images with feelings, which highlights how image is an affective aspect of thinking through sentences. Affect is the bridge between image and language here, but more importantly perhaps, Murnane is arrested by the idea of "shape" or "contour", as his enchanted quotes from critics Hugh Kenner and Herbert Read suggest (26-27). Murnane finds the translation from image and feeling to language generative in a structural way. The process generates new "shapes" and "contours": "I find as soon as I've written the sentence that a new throng of images and feelings

---

19 J.M. Coetzee, "Reading Gerald Murnane", in *Late Essays: 2006–2017* (New York: Viking, 2017), 263.
20 Coetzee, "Reading Gerald Murnane", 263.
21 Saussure, *Course*, 11.
22 Gerald Murnane, "Why I Write What I Write", in *Invisible Yet Enduring Lilacs* (Atarmon, NSW: Giramondo, 2005), 28. All subsequent references are to this edition and appear in parentheses in the text.

have gathered to form a pattern where I had not known a pattern existed" (29). This pattern of imagistic network is the generative aspect of writing as a cognitive activity in Murnane. But is this pattern infinite?

In the second image-scenario in *A History of Books*, we return to the traversable gap between a reader and a writer in terms of another figure who reads and wants to become a writer. He discards his writing if it reminds him of images encountered in books he has read. He wants to invent images through his writing, images that have "never previously appeared" in his mind (8). This is the writer's task but he fails to generate images. "Image" becomes more of an adjective than a noun in Murnane's world as it indicates a self-reflexive distance from the real: "The image-trees were the nearest image-trees of an image-woodland that extended a little way among the image-hills" (13). We know all these are images in the mind rather than actual events, happening in the outside world, but for Murnane, these images are more real than reality. To respond to my question above, image is not so much a representation of the real in Murnane, as it is an *emanation*. It does not reproduce the reality. The image is a reality in itself. It conjures a real through cognition. This is how it maintains a distance from the external real and yet this patch of distance is an ironic bridge. The images of reading in this novella concern the material environment of reading the book as a tangible object. We see four illustrations cut from a book, two patches of dried gum lying on a white page where there was once a coloured reproduction of a painting, pages torn away from a book where the inner margin of a torn page remains like a trace of the tearing act. These images emphasise the materiality of the book-object and the activity of reading. More than the story or plot of a book, what remains with the reader over a certain passage of time are the material details of the book and the experience of reading it.

Image, Book and Memory-Traces: Towards Plasticity and Infinity

Time is important in this fabric of image-memory. Characters in *A History of Books* are obsessed with finding out what they remember of a book, read more than fifty years back. There are images, such as that of a naked woman, which travel from one vignette to another as a generic image-fantasy in the imagination of the usually male readers. After a long passage of time, there is more forgetting than remembering and often there is a temporal indeterminacy regarding the image's first appearance:

> The man seemed to recall a number of images that had appeared in his mind while he had read the work, but he suspected that these images had appeared some years

later while he was reading the biography of the man with the eye-patch [the author in question]. (24)

At one point, Murnane's narrator uses the expression "image-fiction". *A History of Books* is one such "image-fiction" (30). The complex temporality of forgetting and unforgetting builds a cognitive history of reading that creates its own gallery through the pathway of time. With a Borgesian conviction, the narrator says that a "book of fiction could not, by definition, come to an end" (31), and attributes this infinity of fiction to the iterability of reading and re-reading. The logic of fiction's infinity thus lies in "the image-scenery brought into being whenever a certain sort of reader read what a certain sort of writer had written" (31). The narrator calls this an "image-existence" in the mind that defies the simplistic logic of oblivion. Psychologist Douwe Draaisma, in his history of ideas that traces the metaphors of memory, dwells on the book as a significant epochal metaphor for human memory. With the onset of print culture, the book becomes not just a metaphor of memory but also a corrective to the frailty of memory: "What had been entrusted to parchment, whatever had been transferred from the memory of an individual human being into the domain of the written word, escaped transience".[23] Murnane's novella flips this proposition by returning us to memory from the book, rather than the other way around. Whereas the book was a conceptual metaphor that improved upon human memory in the history of human civilisation and modernity, in Murnane, we go back to the fragility of human memory as it reflects back on the book as an experiential object of reading. The book is literalised in Murnane and as it ceases to be a metaphor for memory, we are back to the sea of oblivion that gathers around reading as a memory.

In the Freudian logic, as summed up by Catherine Malabou, "no experience is forgotten. The trace is indelible. The trace can be modified, deformed, reformed – but never erased".[24] It is this "plasticity of psychic life"[25] that becomes crucial in Murnane's reading traces. The fact of forgetting breeds fictions of unforgetting. We go through stages of imaginary embellishment of a mnemonic trace, modified through the passage of time and its plastic subjective counterpart – the ever-changing imagination. Across the vignettes that constitute *A History of Books*, we keep coming across readers, unable to remember anything about a book, read long ago. But the acknowledgement of forgetting soon turns to fleeting images, modified through an imagination that traverses time. The Murnanian network

---

23 Douwe Draaisma, *Metaphors of Memory: A History of Ideas About the Mind*, trans. Paul Vincent (Cambridge: Cambridge University Press, 2000), 32.
24 Catherine Malabou, *Ontology of the Accident: An Essay on Destructive Plasticity*, trans. Carolyn Shread (Cambridge: Polity, 2012), 43.
25 Malabou, *Ontology of the Accident*, 43.

of images creates aesthetic ambivalence as the narrative layers get metaleptically confused. The modification of the memory-trace itself paves the way for such ambiguities. In one vignette, a man, sitting beside a campfire at the base of a cliff, describes to a woman what happens in certain passages of a neglected masterpiece of English literature. The passage of the literary work echoes their own situation, where we see images of a man and a woman at the base of an image-cliff practising how to conjugate the same verb in different ways in the Armenian language.

The book and the life situation of readers and listeners outside the book merge in an uncanny way but the narrative metalepsis (collapsing of layers within the narrative) does not end here. Murnane's narrator traces the same man after forty years, to assess how much he has forgotten of the book. While some of the generic images have stayed with him, he has forgotten most of the details. He remembers a different scene more vividly, which takes us into another part of the book. This other scene constitutes the man and the woman discussing a neglected work of literature as they sit near a campfire at the base of a cliff. As the landscape details and the situation testify, the man and the woman from external reality have been folded inside the book. They are now part of the image-memory of the book, read a long time ago. This is a climactic point for the metaleptic ambivalence. A reader's passionate evocation of reading a book becomes part of his memory of what the book actually contains. Time, in its collusion with fictional memory, generates an image which impresses the man to be a part of the book but it is not. This image comes from life, lived outside of the book. In this process, a mnemonic trace gets modified with time. Murnane's images have this quality of plasticity.

While this notion of plasticity and change throws open the point of infinity, we have another vignette that indicates a proliferation of infinite images. This is a vignette about someone trying to learn a landscape poem by heart. He gets the idea from a book on the poet, read long ago, that the poet "conceived of his own mind as an image-landscape" (37). He starts investing in the idea that the mind is an image, as he begins reciting the poem. If the mind is not just a repository of playful images but an image in itself, this generates a so-called "bad infinity" of endless seriality. The image-mind will therefore generate endless images because it is nothing but an image itself. This is another point where Murnane's network of images has more than a brush with infinity.

To follow up on Draaisma's metaphor of the book of memory, let us note how Daniel Dennett provides an editorial model of consciousness where mnemonic traces are edited, as in the multiple drafts of a manuscript. Murnane's purchase on the psychic traces of reading flips the theory of psyche as a series of reading traces that we find in Dennett's model:

According to the Multiple Drafts Model, all varieties of perception indeed, all varieties of thought or mental activity – are accomplished in the brain by parallel, multitrack processes of interpretation and elaboration of sensory inputs. Information entering the nervous system is under continuous "editorial revision".[26]

Dennett's Multiple Drafts Model traces plasticity of mnemonic traces in consciousness in the form of editorial revisions. Murnane's memory-images speak to this model by indicating constant rewriting and writing over of the same trace in a spectrum of temporal plasticity. However, this is not a simple mapping of the cognitive theory onto the literary text because Murnane engages with the book as an actual object and not as a conceptual metaphor, as in both Draaisma and Dennett. He approaches reading from a point of view of plastic memory-traces, rather than treating psyche as a crystallisation of protean memory traces. The directionality of the critical move is thus from the other end.

The Function of the Image and Specular Thinking

The function of the image in *A History of Books* goes beyond memory-traces that modify, edit and revise themselves with time. The anonymous readers of the mostly anonymous books who appear throughout the novella extend "image-page after image-page of image-fiction" (48). Books read long ago continue to cast image-shadows on their readers as they remain convinced about the relentless activities of the image-personages in the image-world of the book. An image from a book returns at a crucial point in the reader's life for no apparent reason. A letter kept inside a book denotes an important phase in a man-woman relationship. The cover-images of unread or half-read books generate actions. To return to the three aforementioned categories of novelistic thinking evoked by Uhlmann, let us see with one example how "relation", "composition" and "sensation" operate in Murnane's specular mode of novelistic thought. In one vignette, we see a reader speculating about the image of part of a glass marble on the spine of an unread book. He goes to his son's room and brings a jar of glass marbles back to his library, pours them out on the carpet, stands back and observes them closely. His feelings of looking forward to reading the book with the image of the glass marble finds a companion in the feeling generated by the actual glass marbles, rolling on the carpet. This is a readerly act of "composition" to create a cognitive "relation" between the book's image and the real world. Looking into the "many-coloured mass" of the marbles is replete with the "sensation" of visual perception of course (52).

---

26 Daniel C. Dennett, *Consciousness Explained* (New York: Back Bay Books, 1991), 111.

This is an example where imagistic thinking binds the three layers of sensation, relation and composition. The crescendo of this specular thinking, however, arrives in the construction of a conceptual metaphor of the horserace. As the man observes the glass marbles, each seems to him to represent a racehorse. He pushes them around a mat to "see in his mind image after image of the running of a horse-race" (52). He also compares each marble to a book of fiction in his library. He starts "hearing" in his mind the names of the glass marbles, as if they were racehorses and books. Once again, we see the "sensation", making "relations" and generating the "composition" of a dual conceptual image of both horseracing and books. The reader's composition has an intertextual moment when his act with the glass marbles is connected with Herman Hesse's German novel *Das Glasperlenspiel* or *The Glass Bead Game* – a rare mention of a book title in *A History of Books*. The reader's compositional construction of "enacting" the image on the book's spine goes in a direction opposite to that of memory-traces. Unlike the imagistic reiteration of mnemonic traces from the past, this is an imagistic network, rooted in the present. Instead of enfolding the real by the book's textual world, it opens outward from the book into the extra-textual reality.

A book and *the* Book: Partition of Inside and Outside and the Infinite

The various anonymous readers in *A History of Books* are, more often than not, writers as well. This transition from reading to writing consists of an encoding of the real with the world of the text. This image is at the heart of one vignette in which the remembering man remembers his younger self in a lounge room where all the walls, bed, bedsheets, blankets – everything – is covered with pages that have quotes from multiple books of fiction. The space of the room is thus transmuted into a text-scape and for this reader, also an aspiring writer, "fiction" is "superior" to "reality" (63). Unlike the previously discussed moment, here, the directionality is inward and the image becomes a way of enveloping the real with the book. This gesture would remind us of the modernist fantasy of "the" Book in the French poet Stéphane Mallarmé, who used it as a trope of potential totality which is also infinite in nature. This Book with capital B, characterised by totality and infinity, is never to be written but all the books with small b would realise themselves vis-à-vis this Book. Elizabeth McCombie, introducing Mallarmé's poems, defines this infinite Book as "a system of all thought in language".[27] Murnane's metaphor of the book

---

27 Elizabeth McCombie, "Introduction", in Stéphane Mallarmé, *Collected Poems and Other Verse*, trans. E.H. and A.M. Blackmore (Oxford: Oxford University Press, 2006), xx.

returns to the Mallarméan Book "to come" by attempting to completely enclose the real with the textual.

Maurice Blanchot observes, while developing Mallarmé's idea, that "the" Book is "[s]till to be read, to be written, always already written and thoroughly penetrated by reading, the book constitutes the condition for every possibility of reading and writing".[28] This infinite Book is both unwritten and "always already" written. It is the impossible condition of all possibilities as far as turning the real into a book is concerned. Blanchot thus talks about "the absence of the book".[29] For him, writing produces "a" book and by doing so, it "goes toward *the absence of the book*".[30] What Murnane writes is a history for the books that are written but this history is conditioned by an absolute encapsulation of the world into a book which remains impossible. This impossibility that conditions the history of reading and writing finds in the cognitive conjuring of mental images a mechanism of connecting the finitude of books with the potential infinity of the Book *to come*. The image is poised at this crossroads between *a* book and *the* Book. It is at the littoral of the finite and the infinite. It connects and distances the two in the same breath. In Murnane, cognitive image thus becomes a tool to stage this dialectical interplay of the finite and the infinite on the one hand and *a* book and *the* Book, on the other.

The crucial thread that runs through *A History of Books* is the contingency of what a book contains. Reading, coloured by mnemonic images, alters, supplements and adds to the contents of the book. This is how *a* book approaches *the* Book as its impossible totalisation. In one vignette, for instance, an elaborate image of two men and a woman in a swing appears in the memory of a reader. While he knows this image is not from a particular book read two decades ago he connects it with the book because of temporal reasons. The picture of the two men and the woman is an illustration he had seen while reading the book and in time they are located alongside one another in a way that the image is now part of the book. This is how a book reveals its plasticity with temporal movement as memory-images extend it towards what is not an actual part of it. As we have seen above, the metaleptic collapse of narrative layers has a similar effect because it re-renders the real as textual. We encounter a reader, "living in his mind the image-life of some or another image-person who had taken his interest in some or another work of fiction that he was reading" (66). This vicarious image-living is another way *a* book approaches its impossible and infinite totality in *the* Book. A book is lived by the reader as he identifies with its image-personages and the more his own life looks

---

28   Maurice Blanchot, *The Infinite Conversation*, trans. Susan Hanson (1969; Minneapolis: University of Minnesota Press, 1993), 423.
29   Blanchot, *The Infinite Conversation*, 424.
30   Blanchot, *The Infinite Conversation*, 424.

like a leaf from the book, the more the book with small b moves towards the absent but conditioning Book, with capital B. As we proceed, the image attains a double-distance from the real by way of refraction: "In the mind of a man aged somewhat more than sixty years, an image appeared of an image of rays of sunlight appearing in the mind of a young man of somewhat more than twenty years" (74). As we can see, there are two images and two minds here. The first mental image does not connect with anything other than a second mental image. One image can only refer back to another image and no extra-imagistic real referent. This is where the image pushes *a* book towards *the* Book as a form of absent totality and infinity. The infinite is present in this impossible conditioning; it masters, from its absence.

Let us connect the point about the insistence of some reading traces over others with the approach towards the infinite in a movement from book to life which is also an ironic counter-movement of life, becoming *the* Book. In one vignette, a reader remembers only nine words from a book, read long ago. Of the nine, four words constitute the title of a chapter: "*The lunatics hail Clarisse*" (102). For no apparent reason, the reader takes a liking to these words, and so much so that he finds the chapter which has these words to be the most readable and understandable section in a book that he finds difficult to fathom otherwise. The end of the vignette declares that in the said chapter, when Clarisse meets a male lunatic in the fictional asylum, he sets about "*masturbating like a caged monkey*" (103). We are not directly told what the other five words are. But the italics in Murnane's text signal that "*masturbating like a caged monkey*" are the remaining five words, remembered by the reader. If we place these nine words together, we get a full sentence: "*The lunatics hail Clarisse masturbating like a caged monkey*". This sentence, taken out of context and without surrounding details from the book, creates an impregnable density. Who is masturbating? Clarisse, or the lunatics? The singular "*a* caged monkey" implies that it is Clarisse who is masturbating and not the lunatics, but as we know, the book says the opposite. This is the fictional after-life of a sentence, combined from a book, but it shows its plasticity when left on its own to the whims of memory. It comes out of a book but becomes something else on the unreliable terrains of remembrance. This something else is life outside a book, in all its dynamism and flux, but at another level it is also the unwritten Book of life that contains all that was not written and could never be written in "a" particular book. The mnemonic traces connect the finite with the infinite in this case.

A History of Books abounds in vignettes that describe and summarise scenes from either unpublished works of fiction or working notes of an author, regarding a book of fiction he does not expect to write at all. These instances substantiate an infinitesimal movement of writing towards the unwritten and the never-to-be-written. A reader, who is also a writer, finishes an image in his mind that links the author of a famous novel he had used in his published work of fiction. This mental image concerns a male author, sitting at his "image-desk" and writing about his native country. It connects with the female author of the famous novel he had previously used in his published work as an extended allusion. Like himself, he imagines the female author writing about Gondal, her native country, all her life, but none of that has ever been published. But then again, this female author becomes the model for "a famous female character in a famous work of fiction" (109). This tension of "a" book with *the* Book, and of extra-textual life with a text that excludes life outside it, continues throughout Murnane's narrative fragments.

As the reader and the writer, the man and the image-man start merging, *A History of Books* alienates its own status as a book by translating passages from other books, notably a two-volume autobiography in the Hungarian language. The last vignette ends on a familiar note as we see a reader, wanting to internalise the setting of a book in his mental landscapes. The finale where he remembers the ending of a book, read years ago, encapsulates Murnane's tryst with fictional infinity. This infinity is a place "where the land seemed to meet, or even to merge, with the sky, the visible with the invisible, the writer even with the reader, and whatever had been written with whatever had been read" (123). This is a projective vision of infinity in which both the writer and the reader as personas, and the written and the read as materials, have disappeared into one another like the visible and the invisible, creating pure indiscernibility. This absolute unification of the written with the read and the entities that perform writing and reading is impossible, due to the fluidity of self, time and the plasticity of image-meaning and the image-mind. This is an impossible infinity which can nevertheless be conjured as a potential to come. It is an image-infinity.

Conclusion

In this essay, I have followed Gerald Murnane's specular mode of novelistic thinking in *A History of Books* to make an argument about the cognitive image generating the real, rather than simply representing reality in a realistic way. I have suggested that Murnane's fiction formalises reading as a series of plastic mnemonic traces that change over time and sees the book as a dynamic, contingent object, considerably modified by the fictional inventiveness of fragile human memory. We have probed whether Murnane's imagistic thinking can approach infinity as a structure of cogitation and seen how he ultimately arrives at a potential and futuristic notion of the infinite. This infinity is an impossible totality that constantly inscribes and determines the field of possibilities. I have used Mallarmé's notion of the universal Book that can never be written entirely to ground this idea of the infinite. *A History of Books* is obsessed with a serialised history of reading traces of memory that are both retained and modified by the reader's mind across a substantial passage of time. What the novella stages is a relentless tension between what is inside the text and what remains outside it. The partition where the book meets external life and vice versa is the intersectional point of the infinite or the transfinite. Murnane's fiction of cognitive imagery is tasked with tracing this intersectionality. The image for Murnane is the device that enables this play between the finite book and the infinite life outside. His book with small b thus gestures towards the Book with capital B, through the connecting trope of cognitive images.

References

Badiou, Alain. "What Does Literature Think?", in *The Age of the Poets and Other Writings on Twentieth-Century Poetry and Prose*, translated by Bruno Bosteels. London and New York: Verso, 2014, 132-39.
Blanchot, Maurice. *The Infinite Conversation*. (1969) Translated by Susan Hanson. Minneapolis: University of Minnesota Press, 1993.
Coetzee, J.M. "Reading Gerald Murnane", in *Late Essays: 2006–2017*. New York: Viking, 2017, 259-72.
Dennett, Daniel C. *Content and Consciousness*. London: Routledge, 2010.
——. *Consciousness Explained*. New York: Back Bay Books, 1991.
Deleuze, Gilles and Felix Guattari, *What is Philosophy?* (1991), translated by Hugh Tomlinson and Graham Burchell.; New York: Columbia University Press, 1996.
de Saussure, Ferdinand. *Course in General Linguistics*, translated by Wade Baskin. 1916; New York: Philosophical Library, 1959.
Draaisma, Douwe, *Metaphors of Memory: A History of Ideas About the Mind*, translated by Paul Vincent. Cambridge: Cambridge University Press, 2000.
Malabou, Catherine, *Ontology of the Accident: An Essay on Destructive Plasticity*, translated by Carolyn Shread. Cambridge: Polity, 2012.
Mallarmé, Stéphane, *Collected Poems and Other Verse*, translated by E.H. and A.M. Blackmore, with an introduction by Elizabeth McCombie. Oxford: Oxford University Press, 2006.
Murnane, Gerald, *A History of Books*. Artarmon, NSW: Giramondo, 2012.
——. "Why I Write What I Write". In *Invisible Yet Enduring Lilacs*. Artarmon, NSW: Giramondo, 2005.
Uhlmann, Anthony. "Signs for the Soul". *Sydney Review of Books*, July 2013. https://sydneyreviewofbooks.com/signs-for-the-soul/.
——. *Thinking in Literature: Joyce, Woolf, Nabokov*. London and New York: Continuum, 2011.
Wittgenstein, Ludwig. *Tractatus Logico-Philosophicus*. (1921) Translated by D.F. Pears and B.F. McGuinness. London and New York: Routledge, 2001.

10
Reporting Meaning in *Border Districts*

Anthony Uhlmann

As many critics point out, Gerald Murnane challenges how we read, how we think and interpret. The closer one reads him the more profound these challenges appear. I will attempt two things in this chapter. First, I will make some comments on some of these challenges. Second, I will offer a reading of some of the associations of images the work brings together.

In *Border Districts* (2017), the narrator claims that the work he is writing is not a work of fiction; rather, it is "a report of actual events and no sort of work of fiction".[1] He continues:

> As I understand the matter, a writer of fiction reports events that he or she considers imaginary. The reader of fiction considers, or pretends to consider, the events actual. This piece of writing is a report of actual events only, even though many of the reported events may seem to an undiscerning reader fictional. (109)

What comprises actual events, however, are the images, or image-events that occur within the mind of the writer, even when these image-events *only* occur within the mind of the writer. The passage cited above occurs at a moment when, perhaps more clearly than anywhere else in the report, the narrator is imagining what it might be like to be within the mind of a long dead maiden "aunt" or cousin of a friend at whose house he stays when visiting the capital city of his state. He imagines he might be sleeping in the room she slept in. He knows certain things about her, most tellingly, that she was being courted by a young man who went to fight in World War I and never returned. He pictures her associating images that concern a narrative of a possible life she might have led if her suitor had not

---

[1] Gerald Murnane, *Border Districts* (Artarmon, NSW: Giramondo, 2017), 109. All subsequent references are to this edition and appear in parentheses in the text.

died, if she had instead married him and moved with him to a farming district to work for a landowner. The image-events he imagines would, in anyone else's terminology, be called a story, a fictional story. Indeed, it seems doubly fictional, as he is imagining what he supposes she might have imagined while lying awake in the room he imagines she might have slept in. And yet the narrator insists that all of these image-events are actual.

In order to begin to unpack some of the complexities at stake it is usual to quote from a passage, yet it is not possible to quote the passage without explaining the images that link to it and away from it. This is explained in "The Still-Breathing Author" in this volume, where Murnane discusses his process of relating images and presents a diagram setting this out. The narrator tells the story of a Catholic brother from his school who carried a holy card with the image of the Virgin Mary holding two doves to her breasts. This image is associated with Thomas Hardy's novel *Tess of the D'Urbervilles* (1891), since the narrator remembers seeing a photograph of an actress who played the role of Tess in an early twentieth-century film version that Hardy himself was involved with. This actress looks like and so is conflated with the image of the Virgin Mary and the doves. From here the narrator recounts the story of a brother advising the schoolboys (and a version of the narrator is a boy in the class) not to refer to their religious faith when writing essays at university. The narrator then recounts how another younger self avoids studying John Milton's epic poem *Paradise Lost* (1667) at university because he cannot believe in the reality of the imagery, since he has lost his faith in the reality of Christian imagery and beliefs.

There are layers of self that are recounted, and these selves do not all believe the same things. The schoolboy listens attentively without fully comprehending, yet his older self, who is studying at university, thinks the brother is foolish for believing that Satan is real. This same man, the university man, also dismisses Milton for seemingly believing in the reality of his images (of God, Christ, the angels and Lucifer and the fallen angels), when that university man, who has lost his faith, no longer believes in these images. The idea that fictional images are actual has not yet become apparent to the young man who will become the narrator of this report.

The narrator states:

> If the man had recalled the image of the young woman, he might have begun to understand that an image in the mind is itself real, whether or not it may be said to denote some other class of entity; that the dark-haired image-woman standing in the shaft of image-light from the image-window was by then as much a part of him as was any of his bodily organs. He might have begun to understand that even the images that he claimed no longer to believe in – even these were necessary for his salvation, even if they were not more than evidence of his need for saving imagery. (44-45)

That is, for the narrator of this report even images which are not believed in are actual, and as such, are potentially meaningful.

This involves a shift from some of Murnane's earlier works. The idea that some fictional images can be as real as any other thing, however, is consistently in place. My point is that the insights offered by the narrator are elusive and subtle: what seems to be at stake is the possibility of real shifts in understanding between versions of the same self, while something essential is maintained between these selves. The narrator talks about essence in relation to the kind of knowledge that fiction can give one access to. He discusses Marcel Proust and Proust's assertion of the importance of the bond between the writer and the reader, and what the writer might allow the reader to glimpse. In trying to explain this relation, what is given to the reader by writing of a certain kind, the narrator states:

> Today, I content myself with my own formulation of the matter: sometimes, while reading a work of fiction, I seem to have knowledge of what it would be to have knowledge of the essence of some or another personality. If asked to explain the meaning of the word essence in the previous sentence, I would do so by referring to the part of myself (the seeming part of my seeming self?) that apprehends (seems to apprehend?) the knowledge (seeming knowledge?) mentioned in the previous sentence. (54)

The heart of the matter, then, is the feeling of understanding, or meaning, that is given to the reader. The narrator questions whether "feeling" is adequate to this process, and so uses the word "essence". The essence, in turn, seems to be the understanding itself, or the part of the self that is capable of understanding or apprehending the meaningful. What is given, however, is not understanding itself, but seeming "to have knowledge of what it would be to have knowledge". I would suggest, then, that what Murnane calls images are not merely images; rather, they are meaningfulness itself, the feeling of understanding itself. If it is true that Proust uses the word "feeling" to describe this, this word might be made to align with the narrator's point: a feeling of understanding is a seeming to have knowledge of what it would be to have knowledge.

In his monograph *Gerald Murnane*, Imre Salusinszky argues that Murnane's fiction involves "an orderly, progressive unfolding of a set of central concerns that have to do with the relation of the individual mind to the reality confronting it. Murnane's books are about the adventure of consciousness".[2] While the narrator of *Border Districts*, like a woman writer he describes who is also interested in the mind's workings, is sceptical about "some or other fashionable theory of the

---

2   Imre Salusinszky, *Gerald Murnane* (Melbourne: Oxford University Press, 1993), 2.

mind" (115), he sets out to examine or explain how the mind, in effect, creates meaning for itself. It does this through the association of images. As Salusinszky observes, it is difficult to deny that there is "something analogous to philosophical investigation" in Murnane's fiction.[3] In trying to account for the occasional propinquity of the work of artists and philosophers, Gilles Deleuze and Félix Guattari argue that in engaging with the same problem fields the two modes of thinking at times overlap and speak to one another. That is, while artists typically think with sensations or affects and percepts, and philosophers think by developing concepts, artists might from time to time develop sensations (of concepts) that might overlap with concepts (of sensations).[4] This is liable to take place when a writer writes about the feeling of meaning (as Murnane does), just as certain philosophers and cognitive scientists directly attempt to consider kinds of meaning that are felt as much as they are logically understood.

It is no accident then that Murnane's ideas resonate with philosophical accounts of the nature of images and how images relate to understanding. The Ancient Stoics and Spinoza offer contrasting ways into these ideas. The Stoics see perception as involving *phantasia*, or images that are impressed upon the soul like a signet ring on wax. Some of these images carry meaning, but this meaning is only applied to them if the mind "assents" to their truth.[5] So the mind reaches out to the world, in an effort to understand, in the process imbuing that world with meaning. Spinoza does not like aspects of the Stoic system, replacing the concept of the image with that of "the idea". The idea is not a concept, but the very act of understanding itself; that is, it is *the feeling of understanding*. For Spinoza, grasping something is both a knowledge and a feeling at once:

> To have a true idea means nothing other than knowing a thing perfectly, or in the best way. And of course no one can doubt this unless he thinks that an idea is something mute, like a picture on a tablet, and not a mode of thinking, viz. the very [act of] understanding. And I ask, who can know that he understands some thing unless he first understands it? That is, who can know that he is certain about some thing unless he is first certain about it?[6]

---

3   Salusinszky, *Gerald Murnane*, 2.
4   Gilles Deleuze and Félix Guattari, *What Is Philosophy?*, trans. Hugh Tomlinson (New York: Columbia University Press, 1994). See in particular pages 163–200 for the interactions between philosophical concepts and "percepts" and "affects".
5   Josiah B. Gould, *The Philosophy of Chrysippus* (Leiden: Brill, 1970); Andreas Graeser, "The Stoic Theory of Meaning", in *The Stoics*, ed. John M. Rist (Berkeley: University of California Press, 1978), 77-100.
6   Benedictus de Spinoza, *Ethics*, Part 2, Proposition 43, in *The Collected Works of Spinoza, Volume 1*, ed. and trans. Edwin Curley (Princeton, NJ: Princeton University Press, 1985), 479.

The relation of feeling to understanding is further underlined by Spinoza in Part 5 of the *Ethics*, where he states: "the mind feels those things it conceives in understanding no less than those it has in memory. For the eyes of the mind, by which it sees and observes things, are the demonstrations themselves".[7]

So too, comparisons might be made with the theories of contemporary cognitive scientist Antonio Damasio, who sees Spinoza's theories as prescient. Damasio talks of the "feeling of what happens".[8] This emerges from the nervous system reporting back to the brain on the state of the body. Meaning for Damasio emerges from a feedback loop that necessarily involves a sense of one's own being. Damasio develops a distinction between 'emotion' (which is a sensation we have, a preconscious cognitive activity as the brain reports without conscious reflection on the condition of the body). Damasio also calls this a kind of appraisal, and distinguishes it from what he calls "feeling", which emerges after this initial preconscious appraisal has been made and involves conscious reflection on this initial appraisal. This appraisal involves a sense of meaning, that something is meaningful to us.[9] That is, before one consciously reflects upon what is taking place (what Damasio calls feeling), there is already appraisal; in effect, appraisal, and so meaning is, or should be, present at every step of the emotion–feeling continuum Damasio describes. The appraisal mechanism is coextensive with the emotion mechanism, then, at each step. When they are disconnected, which Damasio argues is possible, the consequences for the subject unable to appraise (and therefore experience meaning) due to brain injury are devastating.[10] These processes all involve elements of relation, the association of images or ideas with what is meaningful. While these comparisons would never be exact, I allude to them here to underline the consistency of what Murnane is allowing us to glimpse: that, emerging from the intense observation of the workings of the mind and the images and associations it contains, Murnane offers insights into the nature of what is meaningful, not only for him, but for readers with an interest in such questions.

What is crucial for the narrator of *Border Districts* is that the process of understanding is internal in nature; that understanding comes from within the mind and in some way gives meaning to what it encounters. The narrator tells us he had long wanted to believe "that my mind was the source of not only my wants and desires but the imagery that tempered them" (36). This quotation comes within a passage in which he asserts that the image he has created of the Virgin Mary with her doves and the young actress playing Tess is not dependent on those brute

---

7   Spinoza, *Ethics*, Part 5, Proposition 23, Scholium, 608.
8   Antonio Damasio, *The Feeling of What Happens* (1999; London: Vintage, 2004).
9   Antonio Damasio, *Looking for Spinoza* (London: Vintage, 2003), 62-65.
10 Damasio, *Looking for Spinoza*, 79.

images themselves; rather, they have become something meaningful in his mind and may or may not relate to the external images that initially allowed them to come into being.

To put this another way, he has imbued these images with meaning; or rather, he has felt something meaningful within them, and, through associations that gather fragmentary images in patterns, he seeks to extract meaning for himself, while at the same time creating it for readers. It is for this reason that, as he states early in the report, "I am even more inclined than of old to accept as well founded any supposition likely to complete a pattern in my mind and then to go on writing until I learn the meaning for me of such an image" (2).

What matters is not so much the plausibility of suppositions (what we might call ideas or possibilities), but whether these ideas help him to associate his images in such a way that a pattern might emerge. An example of this can be found in two passages that seem incredible, and yet necessary to the pattern of meaning the work weaves. The second involves imagining that the picture of a female writer he admires shows not her eye, but a marble pressed against her eye (58-60). I will not discuss this second example here other than to say that it allows the narrator to associate this image with the iconography of marbles that runs through all of Murnane's works.

The first describes how he allows himself to believe in a fanciful theory of perception. He explains this as follows: "According to the theory, a person perceives an object of sight by means of a ray of light emitted through the eye of the person. The ray travels outward from the eye and then renders visible the object of sight" (57). The narrator puts this theory in brackets and does not claim to believe it, and yet it allows him to explain something essential to his pattern: that it is the one who perceives who imbues what is perceived with meaning. That this meaning does not reside, objectively, in the thing; that it only comes into being through the eyes of the one who perceives. This is underlined when the narrator takes detailed photographs of the coloured glass at his friend's house in the capital city. Once these photographs are processed, he notices that the meaning he had felt in perceiving the qualities of light through the glass has been lost: "what I missed when I looked at the photographic prints was the meaning that I had previously read into the glass". He then returns to the pattern that is allowed by the odd theory of perception mentioned above. He states:

> And if I could give credence to such an eccentric theory, then I might as well go further and assert that I saw in the glass part of the private spectrum that my eyes diffused from my own light as it travelled outwards: a refraction of my own essence, perhaps. (120)

The narrator, in forming this pattern, is asking us to consider that the process of forming meaning, or feeling the meaningful, involves feeling ourselves within this process of seeming to understand, seeming to find things meaningful.

The Report

In *Border Districts*, the narrator speaks of two other writers who might be considered contemporaries. One was a former priest who worked with the narrator when he taught at university. What annoys the narrator about this writer is his failure to address the question of meaning in his fiction, his failure to offer the images from his mind that might offer a glimpse of how he understood what it meant to believe, before he lost his faith. The second writer is a woman from across the border whom he hears speaking on the radio. This female writer does offer images: of the landscape of her youth, and of a house she imagines purchasing in the country bordering that of the narrator. She wants to purchase this property so that other writers might come to the house and report on their creative processes. What intrigues the narrator about this writer is her desire to address the site of meaning, and to glimpse how it is created. After the fact, after he has begun, it appears that the narrator might be writing the report that comprises the text entitled "Border Districts" to offer to this woman as his contribution to her project of understanding how the mind creates meaning.

Yet *Border Districts* also meditates on the loss of meaning. A motif that recurs is of former priests or brothers or parishioners who abandon their faith in the Catholic Church. What seems of most interest to the narrator now (elsewhere in Murnane's works this has not been so pronounced) is not so much that faith has been lost, rather what goes on in the mind of one who believes, and what happens to the images in the mind when one no longer believes in them. He recounts the story of a woman who loses her faith when confronted by stories of the sexual abuse committed by certain priests and brothers. He wonders about the mental events that accompany the images that used to be meaningful. He wonders if he had asked her about it whether he might have "glimpsed for myself a version of her seeming to see the colour draining from the tall glass windows in the church where she had prayed since childhood" (23).

This takes us to images that are central to *Border Districts*. First, light refracted through coloured glass, which might be the stained-glass windows of a church or chapel, or of a home, both sites to which meaning is likely to adhere. Second, the image of guarding one's eyes, with which the book begins and ends. This second image carries with it the idea of glimpsing, suggesting that the narrator might somehow see more clearly, or encounter meaning more fully, by looking from the corners of his eyes rather than directly. Yet it also carries, at times, the idea of deliberately avoiding seeing things that might distract one from a train of thought that is more meaningful. So the young Catholic brother writes on the back of his holy card that he must "Guard eyes while in town" (158), meaning that he must avoid temptations of the flesh in order to protect his vocation.

So too the narrator "guards his eyes" not just to glimpse meaning, but to avoid seeing what might distract him from it: such as the names of places on signs beside the road which might carry associations that in turn lead him away from the train of thought he hopes to pursue in order to find some or other meaning. Seeing, then, becomes subordinated to the desire to find meaning. At the end of the book the coloured glass motif is reconnected from the Catholic brothers and priests to the world of the boy who will become the narrator.

In guarding his eyes while feeling the meanings carried by coloured glass, he encounters the image, if such there is, that rests within the stained-glass windows, yet which has, over time, become opaque. Yet at the very end he remembers or imagines the images on the chapel at his school. Those images are of representations of brothers of the same Catholic order who teach him: images of brothers who are "looking askance". The narrator claims not to know what this might mean. He states:

> Depicted in the stained glass was the founder of the order of religious brothers mentioned often hereabouts together with the young men who were his first followers. Each young man is shown as wearing a robe of black with a white bib at his throat. None of these details surprised me, but I cannot account for each young man's being shown as having his eyeballs lying to one side: as looking from the sides of his eyes. (163)

In terms of the patterns Murnane has drawn together, however, it is clear that the young men are looking askance because they want to glimpse what cannot be seen directly, and to avoid seeing what will prevent them from seeing what cannot be seen directly: that is, *meaning* itself. After this passage the narrator demonstrates something that has also been underlined throughout: that the meaning that comes through images also comes through the association of images, and that the association of images deepens the meanings that emerge (in part through the images themselves and in part through the associations they are able to bring).

He does this by drawing our attention to other images that have occurred to him, more or less simultaneously, but also sequentially in association with the image of the stained-glass window. First, that he cannot remember being aware of the image in the window; rather, he was only aware of a "certain golden or reddish glow" (163). One might read this as the sign of the narrator as a boy: the glow is the glow of the meaning he felt at that time. While he would lose the referent of this meaning (the trappings of meaning carried by the Catholic order of brothers who taught him) he would still, nevertheless, carry the feeling of understanding, glimpsed in the colour rather than directly in the images portrayed by the glass. Second, in a subsequent paragraph, he tells us this image is associated with two lines from Percy Shelley. These lines end the book:

> Life, like a dome of many-coloured glass,
>   Stains the white radiance of Eternity. (164)

In reading Murnane it often seems that one needs to attend most closely to the associations he builds up for the reader, in order to find the meaning he establishes. It is not clear as to whether it remains valid to move outside this frame. Whether it might be valid to track down the image of the young actress who played Tess, for example (Blanche Sweet), or to try and find the chapel in the small town he describes at the beginning of the book, or the image of the Virgin Mary with the doves, or the followers of Saint Jean-Baptiste de la Salle whose images appear in the stained-glass window. Would this not involve looking directly at something rather than glimpsing it out of the corner of your eye?

A similar concern is there in the quote from Shelley, which is taken from "Adonais", a poem written as an elegy for John Keats. The full stanza reads as follows:

> The One remains, the many change and pass;
> Heaven's light forever shines, Earth's shadows fly;
> Life, like a dome of many-coloured glass,
> Stains the white radiance of Eternity,
> Until Death tramples it to fragments. – Die,
> If thou wouldst be with that which thou dost seek!
> Follow where all is fled! – Rome's azure sky,
> Flowers, ruins, statues, music, words, are weak
> The glory they transfuse with fitting truth to speak.[11]

The resonance with the themes Murnane develops in *Border Districts* here are both strong and equivocal, both particular and abstract. The narrator of *Border Districts* speaks of the images with which meaning is created as fragments that are drawn together as a kaleidoscope draws together its fragments of colour. The

---

11   Percy Bysshe Shelley, *Shelley's Poetry and Prose*, ed. Donald H. Reiman and Neil Fraistat (New York: Norton, 2002) 426.

narrator sees his mind as drawing together these fragments into patterns, which then become meaningful to him. Shelley, looking at the process from the other side, sees death as dispersing the meaning with which the living imbue the world. So too, if the narrator of *Border Districts* ties meaning to the mind or the imagination that finds meaning by associating images and words, Shelley gestures to the Oneness of things, to a nature or divine that encompasses all things. This is something greater than the self, and acts as the ground for meaning.

Is this the opposite of Murnane? There is no certain ground of meaning for Murnane, only "suppositions" in which he does not need to believe. I will end by returning to a passage I have already cited where he talks about beliefs that once gave meaning, which he no longer believes in:

> He might have begun to understand that even the images that he claimed no longer to believe in – even these were necessary for his salvation, even if they were not more than evidence of his need for saving imagery. (44-45)

"Saving imagery" might mean "imagery that relates to salvation" or it might mean "imagery that is preserved". The narrator needs to preserve or guard images that give meaning, and/or the narrator needs images that, meaningfully, seem to offer a glimpse of salvation.

References

Damasio, Antonio. *Looking for Spinoza*, London: Vintage, 2003.
——. *The Feeling of What Happens.* (1999) London: Vintage, 2004.
Deleuze, Gilles and Félix Guattari, *What Is Philosophy?* Translated by Hugh Tomlinson and Graham Burchell. New York: Columbia University Press, 1994.
Gould, Josiah B. *The Philosophy of Chrysippus.* Leiden: Brill, 1970.
Graeser, Andreas. "The Stoic Theory of Meaning". In *The Stoics*, edited by John M. Rist. Berkeley: University of California Press, 1978, 77-100.
Hardy, Thomas. *Tess of the D'Urbervilles.* (1891) London: Penguin, 2003.
Milton, John. *Paradise Lost*, edited by John Leonard. (1667) London: Penguin, 2003.
Murnane, Gerald. *Border Districts*. Artarmon, NSW: Giramondo, 2017.
——. *A Million Windows*. Artarmon, NSW: Giramondo, 2014.
Salusinszky, Imre. *Gerald Murnane*. Melbourne: Oxford University Press, 1993.
Shelly, Percy Bysshe. *Shelley's Poetry and Prose.* Edited by Donald H. Reiman and Neil Fraistat. New York: Norton, 2002.
Spinoza, Benedictus de. "Ethics". In *The Collected Works of Spinoza, Volume 1*, edited and translated by Edwin Curley. Princeton, NJ: Princeton University Press, 1985.

11
What Kind of Literary History Is *A History of Books*?

Ivor Indyk*

This is one of those occasions where I feel I am wearing too many hats, and I am not sure what to do with the excess ones. This is because I am speaking of Gerald Murnane in a number of different roles – as a friend, a critic, a publisher, an editor – though I should admit that Murnane doesn't need much editing, at least in my experience, since what I suggest as an editor tends to get rejected anyway. As he busies himself behind the bar in the room here as I talk now, I cannot be sure whether he's listening, or whether, like the narrator at the beginning of *Border Districts*, he has resolved to guard his eyes, so as to be more alert to what might appear at the edges of his attention.[1] But perhaps the greater discomfort for me, is to talk as both a publisher and as a critic. As a publisher there's a sense of excitement when you're producing a book, a kind of intimacy in the production of it, which as a critic you're not meant to feel; you keep the book at a distance, the better to form a judgement of it. Nevertheless, when I'm preparing a book for publication I do read it critically and develop ideas about it that I think are significant, and should be conveyed to readers, particularly those who have not read Murnane before. I'm only allowed a little over one hundred words, in the blurb on the back cover, to address the reader directly, and there is not a lot one can say there, though there is a lot one wants to say. I have found, especially being here today, that much of what I wanted to say has now already been said, or is being said, as the critical discourse catches up with Murnane's works of fiction, and his idiosyncrasies as an author. And though this makes me feel proud as a publisher, it makes feel humble as a critic, because

---

* I would like to thank Melinda Jewell for transcribing an over-excited talk given from notes into a form that made sense enough to be turned into a written paper, though some aspects of the verbal presentation remain.

---

1   Gerald Murnane, *Border Districts* (Artarmon, NSW: Giramondo, 2017), 1, 12.

it's other people making the points that I would have liked to make, and they are making them more thoroughly than I could have done.

In particular, I have been struck by the speakers who refer confidently to the books published from *Barley Patch* onwards as Murnane's "post-break literature". I felt as a publisher that there was a decisive break between Murnane's earlier books and his later ones, which didn't simply reside in the fact that there was a fourteen-year gap between *Emerald Blue* (1995) and *Barley Patch* (2009). It is thrilling to me that what I only had an intimation of as a publisher is now actually being asserted confidently as a critical fact.

What I would like to do here is explore an intimation I had too about *A History of Books* (2012) when I was working on it. Though Murnane's literary values can seem conservative in their formulation, in practice they work to produce complicated and unsettling effects. Perhaps the best example is his use of the narrator, which, despite its expressed indebtedness to the theoretical prognostications of Wayne C. Booth in *The Rhetoric of Fiction* (1961), nevertheless creates ironic elaborations on a scale Booth could never have dreamed of, and would undoubtedly have been horrified by.[2] Though it presents itself as *A History of Books*, I think of this work as posing a radical challenge, not only to our understanding of how literature works on readers, but to our concept of what a book is. I've often wondered when I'm looking at the orders for *A History of Books*, how many of the people ordering it really think they're going to get a history of the book; and how many of them might be academics or graduate students devoting themselves to research in the fashionable literary discipline to which they might take the title to refer, "the history of the book". This is a discipline which is almost entirely devoted to material facts about the printed book, editions, sales figures, distribution, financial returns, to the exclusion of any interpretive angle or speculative end to which the book might be turned.

What is their reaction when they order Murnane's *A History of Books* and discover how far it is from a material history of the book: that what it actually argues for is a dematerialisation of the book, so that the books discussed in this history never appear as physical entities in themselves, but as scattered impressions, or images which have a hazardous existence in the reader's mind? Sometimes it's just a phrase, or a word that survives. Sometimes it's not even the text itself but a colour on the cover. Or more radically, the way the light was falling on the afternoon during which the book was read. Or the occasion when the narrator remembers reading the book twenty or thirty years before. The book itself disappears, to survive only in traces of thought, or memory, or the outlines of an impression.

---

2   Wayne C. Booth, *The Rhetoric of Fiction* (Chicago: University of Chicago Press, 1961).

This dematerialisation of the book is doubly challenging to me as a publisher and a critic. In my role as a publisher, I'm constantly engaged with and frustrated by the materiality of books – from the detailed attention that goes into their production as printed objects, to the expense and effort involved in their distribution and storage, especially when, as has been the case for Murnane's books until recently, they take years to clear their print runs. As a critic, I have been trained to act as if the literary work is available in its entirety to the critical gaze, as a complex structure held in the mind, present to scrutiny in all its details; and that those who are reading literary criticism about the book, for these readers too, the text is completely available in its entirety, it's simply a matter of referring to the right page or the right part of one's memory. But in fact, I have to accept that Murnane's perception in *A History of Books* is the more accurate one in terms of our experience of reading, and that the book is fundamentally a transient entity, barely recalled in retrospect, even though the impressions and feelings associated with it may persist in some form, often only distantly related to their cause, in the reader's memory or imagination.

It was precisely this sense of the tenuous existence led by the literary book that informed Percy Lubbock's *The Craft of Fiction*, a work which had a strong influence on Wayne Booth's insistence on the importance of the reliable narrator in *The Rhetoric of Fiction*. Lubbock opens *The Craft of Fiction* (first published in 1921) with the following lament:

> To grasp the shadowy and fantasmal form of a book, to hold it fast, to turn it over and survey it at leisure – that is the effort of a critic of books, and it is perpetually defeated ... As quickly as we read, it melts and shifts in the memory ... a cluster of impressions, some clear points emerging from a mist of uncertainty, that is all we can hope to possess, generally speaking, in the name of a book. The experience of reading it has left something behind, and these relics we call by the book's name; but how can they be considered to give us the material for judging and appraising the book?[3]

It was Lubbock's whole purpose to fix the book in the mind, so it could be appraised, as it was later for Booth in his prescriptions about the reliable narrator, which Murnane sets such store by, most explicitly in *A Million Windows*, the work which followed *A History of Books*. As its title suggests, *A Million Windows* is indebted to Henry James' essay "The Art of Fiction" – the progenitor text for both Lubbock's *The Craft of Fiction* and Booth's *The Rhetoric of Fiction*. And yet here is

---

3   Percy Lubbock, *The Craft of Fiction* (London: Jonathan Cape, 1965), 1.

Murnane, relishing the very transience of the book it was their mission to guard against.

It has to be said that there is an Australian, larrikin character to Murnane's challenge to the ontology of the book. It isn't just in *A History of Books* that you see his disregard for the authority of the book as a book. It's also in the way in Murnane's work the book is available for cutting up, for what he calls in the story "The Interior of Gaaldine", the practice of "decoding and gutting".[4] Decoding occurs when the narrator reaches across to his bookshelf, takes a book, and choosing words at random, places them in a vertical column beside a column of names of horses, and then advances those horses in an imagined horserace according to the numerical value previously assigned to the letters opposite their name. The second process, which also barely respects the integrity of the physical book, as its description suggests, Murnane calls "gutting". This is when a piece of direct speech from an arbitrarily chosen novel is placed in a similar fashion alongside the names of horses lined up in an imaginary race, and eventually decides the result of the race, depending on the numerical value attributed to the letters of the words in the excerpted quote. Whereas "decoding" simply moves the horses gradually towards the finishing line in a way which creates excitement and anticipation but never satisfies it, because you never know if or when they're going to get to the finishing line, the numerical values in "gutting" actually determine the finishing order of the horses in the race.

Murnane's term for the second process, "gutting", is deliberately derogatory because he doesn't believe in direct speech as a literary mode of narration, and there's rarely any direct speech in his books. He refers to direct speech as "junk mail" in "The Interior of Gaaldine". Nevertheless, his process of transforming "junk" into race results has produced two voluminous archives documenting two imaginary countries – New Eden and New Arcadia – in terms of their horseraces, the results of those horseraces, the names of the horses, their trainers and their owners. The process of "gutting" and "decoding" might seem like a violation done upon the book, but it works in similar ways to the remembering of books described in *A History of Books*, where it is the traces, the impressions and images, and the connections that might be made between them, that the experience of reading the book is most valued for. In both cases, the book has an instrumental function in offering access to another world of the reader's own imagining. As Murnane's narrator notes in "The Interior of Gaaldine":

---

[4] Gerald Murnane, "The Interior of Gaaldine", in *Collected Short Fiction* (Artarmon, NSW: Giramondo, 2018), 411-16. All subsequent references are to this edition and appear in parentheses in the text.

> I have always been interested in what is usually called the world but only insofar as it provides me with evidence for the existence of another world. I have never written any piece of fiction with the simple purpose of understanding what I might call the real world. I have always written fiction in order to suggest to myself that another world exists. And whenever I have read a piece of fiction that seemed to me worthy to be read, whether the author of that fiction was myself or another person, I have always read with the purpose of suggesting to myself that a world might exist beyond the world suggested by the fiction ... (414)

In similar fashion the "gutting" and "decoding" of books provides the means of access to an imagined world in which horseracing, racehorses and their colours, jockeys, trainers and racecourses, are the fundamental realities. In this sense, you can't really say that the book is being reduced by virtue of its dematerialisation – on the contrary, its generative power has been enhanced.

There's an interesting section in *A History of Books* on Hermann Hesse's novel *The Glass Bead Game*, about which the narrator is also derogatory.[5] This was a book which, as its title and cover suggest – there are images of glass beads or marbles on the cover – promised much to reward the narrator's own obsession with marbles. And so he decides, because it appeals so directly to his own interests, that the book is best not read at all, but savoured in anticipation, rather than in the act. "During the years before he read such a book," – he'd bought it and left it unread on the shelf for ten years! – "he could foresee himself reading a book the contents of which he would not remember after he had begun to read the actual book although he would seem to remember them as having been richer than the actual contents". You have to admire Murnane's flexibility with grammar and syntax here. And as it turns out, when he does read the book, he recalls "not one word of the text of the book, not one image that had appeared in his mind while he read the text, and not one thought or feeling that had occurred to him while he had read". This is a really strong dismissal of the book. Though what he does remember later is "something of what he had formerly hoped to feel whenever he looked forward to reading the book of fiction by the famous German author" (50, 51). Here is a very clear case of a book which is enjoyed "only" in anticipation of its being read, and not in the process of its being read at all – in fact he didn't read much beyond its first pages.

Though this sense of the book, in terms of its anticipatory power, its ability to stimulate expectations and feelings and images, may seem disembodied or removed, there is no doubting its power. In *Inland*, you experience the presence, the powerful influence, of two other books operating within this book on account

---

5   Gerald Murnane, *A History of Books* (Artarmon, NSW: Giramondo, 2012), 48–53. All subsequent references are to this edition and appear in parentheses in the text.

of their remembered images – Emily Brontë's *Wuthering Heights* and Gyula Illyés' *People of the Puszta*. In fact, *Inland* ends with the same paragraph with which Emily Brontë had ended *Wuthering Heights*. This is not the only time that Murnane has borrowed – or taken – words from other authors. *Border Districts* ends with two lines from Shelley's poem "Adonais" – "Life, like a dome of many-coloured glass, / Stains the white radiance of Eternity" – lines which gain extraordinary intensity in the expressive context of Murnane's own preoccupation with light in his last work of fiction. In *A History of Books*, "the man" who wrote *Inland* is given to suspect that the reason why reviewers and critics of the book never noticed that its ending was lifted from *Wuthering Heights* was that,

> even though they wrote fluently and at length about what they called the subject matter or the themes or the meaning of book after book, [they] were like himself in that they were unable to remember more than a few words or phrases from the text of any book that they had read. (107)

Yet those remembered words or phrases, migrating from text to text, exhibit a similar power to Murnane's "decodings" and "guttings", in their stimulus to the imagination.

The big issue that *A History of Books* circles is memory, because everything in it is remembered, and the book is about both the fallibility of memory and its power. The question that is posed by the book as a whole is, what remains? Not just in terms of the reading experience, but more generally as well. The way the book is constructed is to constantly remind the reader of the passage of time. The sections are habitually introduced with variations on the formula, "In the mind of a man": "In the mind of a young man aged about thirty years, an image appeared" (57); "In the mind of a man aged forty and more years" (79); "In the mind of a man aged somewhat more than sixty years" (74); and, towards the end, "In the mind of a man aged nearly seventy years" (96). You cannot but be aware in reading that time is passing and pressing. It is interesting in relation to this temporal pressure, to think of Murnane's assertion in one of his works that there is for him no time, only a succession of places. This implies that the surest way to defeat time is in the accumulation, or the superimposition one upon or within the other, of places or situations, a method which operates in *A History of Books*, and in I think nearly all of Murnane's books – the layering of narrators and places so that memory works, not through time, but through the evocation of one place inside another place, and within that place other places. This is the process of recursion, the embedding of realities within realities, especially those with a strong emotional impact, so that the embedding serves to distance and contain the emotion it recalls. But recursion works in two directions, not only to contain but to expand. Hence the importance of the plain, the mostly level countryside with a line of trees in the distance, which constitutes the mind on which the images produced by reading or from memory appear. "It was not necessary that the setting should be the sort called dramatic or picturesque", Murnane writes in the section of *A History of Books* "provoked" by the reading of a novel by Halldór Laxness, "so long as it was spacious and lacking precise boundaries" (122).

The effect of recursion in *A History of Books* is particularly pronounced because its occurrence is so persistent, each section taking the form of an older man remembering himself as a younger man reading a book. In one of the early sections, the man recalls as a school pupil reading about another young man – so there's a triple recursion – in a book which carries the word Fag in the title, and is set in an English public school, while he sits next to a girl in class who is reading an art book with a naked man as one of the illustrations. The recursions in this case express a complex of feeling about the youthful stirrings of sexuality, both homosexual and heterosexual. The delicacy is in the handling of implication, the half-revelation in the process of elaboration, as if the author himself barely knew what the repeated image, or constellation of images, might contain, until it had been elaborated – which does seem to be the way memory works in Murnane, building connections from fleeting or fragmentary impressions.

This section is immediately followed by another set in a farmhouse surrounded by mostly level grassland in which live three unmarried sisters and an unmarried brother. This is an ancestral setting to which Murnane's imagination returns again and again in his writing, and it holds a strong emotional charge, which requires successive works of fiction to clarify. You do have this sense in *A History of Books*, of Murnane exploring in a dynamic way the images that come to mind in his writing, by associating them with other images, or by pursuing them along different pathways of thought, or by placing them in contexts which are themselves highly charged. And this is where I disagree with Emmett Stinson's argument in this collection, that Murnane's writing is operating retrospectively in *Border Districts*, to place earlier works within a larger sense of his oeuvre. I think of Murnane as working proactively, returning to images in later works which clearly have a charge which he didn't – or couldn't – elaborate on fully in earlier attempts. And so he comes back to them again and again, each time with a little more to add, and a little more. Sometimes this elaboration leads to a very large climax, as in his attenuated exploration of the images associated with the house in the clearing in the forest, and the serving maid who drowns herself in the well, which leads to a stunning revelation of personal tragedy at the end of *A Million Windows*.

I'm one of those who feel that Murnane's work is essentially personal, and that its structural complexity, based on repetition and elaboration, is operating to contain a range of emotions – guilt, embarrassment, anxiety (especially about writing), self-consciousness, shame, grief. And in those instances where the writing moves outwards rather than inwards – joy, elation, or what he calls in the section on *The Fortunes of Richard Mahony*, the "feel of things" (123). To the extent that it consists of embedding and expansion, you can think of this style as baroque, and the sections in *A History of Books*, and more generally in his larger works, may be thought of as working in the manner of arabesques, because of the circulation of and the circling around repeated motifs, the retrieving of different aspects of a perspective, the elaborations, the improvisations on a theme.

Some of the motifs repeated early in *A History of Books* are the town square, the hot afternoon, the girl on a swing – these go from one section to another, they appear in different forms – the sunlit room, the blue hills of West Virginia – carrying echoes from other earlier books as well. There are two in particular I want to refer to here, though I hesitate because Murnane's in the room, but I'm sure he won't mind my referring to them. One motif comes up very strongly in the book: the woman who strikes the man, and the man who strikes the woman in return. It's there in the very first section, in the square in a country in Central America, as remembered from an issue of *National Geographic*. It's replicated later in an upstairs flat in a certain inner suburb of Melbourne. It reappears in an account of a scene at the base of a cliff, in a tribute to George Borrow's novel *Lavengro*. And most hauntingly, and at length, in the emergency ward of a public hospital in Melbourne. Murnane's wife, Catherine, died in 2009, just before the publication of *A History of Books*, and I've no doubt that something of that terrifying, really trying time, is in the writing here, particularly in the repetition of the phrase "crying out", which is part of the motif as it appears in the book in its different transformations.

There is also, and I feel a little less reticent in talking about this, because it's on the public record, the image of the clearing in the forest, which comes up again and again in *A History of Books*, and in earlier works as well. It's one of those images which gains in meaning with each appearance, and its recurrence conveys the feeling that the author is not sure where it's going either, and that its significance is being revealed to him, and to the reader, in the process of composition. The clearing in the forest is associated in a number of ways with the girl who drowned in the well from Gyula Illyés' *People of the Puszta*, an image of extreme potency. The significance of the association between the two images – the girl who drowned in the well, the clearing in the forest – is brought to full expression at the end of *A Million Windows*, when the association's intimations, which first appeared in *Inland*, culminate in the revelation that within the rape of the girl who drowned herself in the well there is a second suspected rape, that of the narrator's own mother, in the house she shares with her mother and step-father in the clearing in the forest.

I referred above to the image of the mostly level countryside with a line of trees in the distance, which relates to the ancestral family home, Murnane's grandfather's house near Warrnambool, and its associated image of the bay or cove beneath steep cliffs, which in turn evokes memories, or is evoked by memories, of reading a novel by one of Murnane's favourite novelists, Thomas Hardy. This in turn draws in other associations – a Portuguese caravel and the legend of the Portuguese ship wrecked off the south coast of Victoria – which can be traced back to the story of the ocean liner in *Barley Patch*. This is an amazing story about a dream in which the narrator swims out to a passing ocean liner and is drawn up onto the deck only to find a cocktail party in progress, with the women in elegant dresses and the men in tuxedos, while he is just wearing a swimming costume which shows his tool and stones to dramatic and embarrassing effect. These associations are underwritten by the narrator's memory of his unmarried uncle, who lives in the house set in mostly level countryside with a line of hills in the distance, and who once told him a story which featured his stones, and hinted at an extreme case of sexual inhibition.

Finally, I would like to mention two other persistent anxieties which run through *A History of Books* and Murnane's work more generally. One is the inability to write, where the narrator presents himself as a failure as a poet, and as a man who has been negligent in his responsibilities to his family, because he has taken time off to write, and hasn't written anything worthy of publication. There is a substantial reality to this anxiety, the fact that *A Lifetime on Clouds* and *The Plains* are both small sections of larger works that weren't published in their entirety, and there's the large failed work *O, Dem Golden Slippers* sitting unpublished between *Velvet Waters* and *Emerald Blue*. And again, the gap of around fourteen years between *Emerald Blue* and *Barley Patch*. The latter begins with the haunting questions, "*Must I write?*" and "*Why had I written?*"[6] so that the anxiety has a real basis, and its recurrence as a motif is not just a rhetorical device – there is an abiding concern there. As there is in the spectre of alcoholism, evident in the sections on Christopher Brennan, John Clare and of course Jack Kerouac. And in insanity, which appears in many of the accounts of remembered books, or their authors: John Clare, Elias Canetti, Robert Musil's character Clarisse in *The Man Without Qualities*, Henry Handel Richardson's Richard Mahony. In part this anxiety can be thought of as a matter of inheritance, in part also as a consequence of solipsism, of the writer's preference, over the visible world, of "a space enclosed by words denoting a world more real by far" (63).

The fear of insanity is most hauntingly expressed in the section on *The Fortunes of Richard Mahony*, the third volume *Ultima Thule*, where Mahony, who has been

---

6   Gerald Murnane, *Barley Patch* (Artarmon NSW: Giramondo, 2011), 3-4. All subsequent references are to this edition and appear in parentheses in the text.

such a huge figure in the previous two volumes, is brought from a hospital for the insane in Melbourne, a completely broken man, and is met on the wharf by his wife Mary, who takes him back to the little cottage next to the country post office where she's working in order to earn a living for both of them. Murnane's narrator concludes that he might have called to mind this series of images "more often than he had called to mind any other images deriving from any other text", and in the context in which this claim is made, one readily believes him.[7] For this leads by association, in the very same section, to a scene in the emergency ward of the public hospital where he has brought his wife, who is crying out in the throes of paranoia, and who will later be confined to a hospital for the mentally ill. And this recalls again, by association, those scenes in the book where a husband is struck by a wife or a wife by her husband.

These are some of the strongest aspects of Murnane's work, but I want to finish by referring to another – the yearning to enter the world of fiction, in which there is the intimation, or perhaps the recovery, of a lost spiritual or religious dimension. Somewhere Murnane writes that he makes of writing what others make of religion, and I think that's true. There's a story in *Barley Patch* which Murnane has acknowledged as a turning point in his writing, and which should be useful for those who are interested in charting the contours of his "post-break" writing. In it the Russian author Turgenev imagines that his characters come to him in a dream and ask him to bring them into the world of his fictions. Murnane's narrator turns this on its head, arguing that Turgenev didn't really get it right, and that on the contrary his characters were appearing in his dream to urge him to enter their world.

This idea that the book, the reading of the book, and writing itself, allows access to another world, a world beyond the visible world, is played out in *A History of Books* in a very funny story about Marcel Proust, drawn from the biography by André Maurois. This relates a dream in which Proust knocks on the door of the palace of the Gods on Olympus. Murnane's version tells the story from the gods' point of view, as they are reclining naked beside their bathing pool during the quiet hours of the afternoon, discussing in an indolent way the sounds of knocking that carry to them faintly from a distant part of the palace. They are inclined to ignore the knocking because, as gods, they're not the kind of people who get fussed about such things, but the knocking goes on and on and on, day after day. So eventually they dispatch one of their number to go to the extremes of the palace to find out what the hell's going on. Finally, the god comes back – having gone to the furthermost reaches of an infinite library in the palace where there's a doorway that had once been built into the wall and then closed up again. He runs back to tell the

---

7   Murnane, *A History of Books*, 85.

others that he's discovered the source of the knocking and "that the person at the door claimed to be the author of an enormous work of prose fiction, although he seemed no more than an asthmatic little poofter from a place called Paris" (113). This is a wonderful example of Murnane's ability to parody his own aspirations, a crucial concern in this case, that the characters that one remembers, or the images that one remembers from reading a work, actually come from another world, and are calling you into that world.

References

Murnane, Gerald. "The Interior of Gaaldine", in *Collected Short Fiction*, Artarmon, NSW: Giramondo, 2018.
——. *Border Districts*. Artarmon, NSW: Giramondo, 2017.
——. *A History of Books*. Artarmon, NSW: Giramondo, 2012.
—— *Barley Patch*. Artarmon, NSW: Giramondo, 2011.
Booth, Wayne C. *The Rhetoric of Fiction*. Chicago: University of Chicago Press, 1961.
Lubbock, Percy. *The Craft of Fiction*. London: Jonathan Cape, 1965.

12
The Still-Breathing Author

Gerald Murnane

I've prepared and delivered this sort of address once before. That was in September 2001, at a conference similar to this in Newcastle, New South Wales. At that time, no book of mine had been published during the previous six years; nor had I written or planned during those years anything that might have gone towards any sort of book. During those six years, the time that I might otherwise have given to writing for publication I had used for adding to my archives. None of the matters mentioned in the previous two sentences was mentioned in my address to the scholars at Newcastle.

I gave a title to my Newcastle address: "The Breathing Author". As soon as I had delivered the address, Ivor Indyk asked if he could publish it in his periodical, *Heat*.[1] My consenting to this was the first in a series of events that led to the publication, by Giramondo in 2005, of *Invisible Yet Enduring Lilacs*, my first book for ten years, *and* to my resuming my writing career, as you might say.[2]

I've been told that the text of *this* address will be published somewhere in due course, and when I compare my situation today with my situation in Newcastle sixteen years ago, I perceive a sort of symmetry. If questioned at Newcastle, I would freely have declared that I had given up writing for publication. Without even waiting to be questioned, I declare to you today that I've likewise given up. After the previous conference, I later went back to serious writing, but no such

---

A version of this article appeared in the *Sydney Review of Books*, 6 February 2018, https://sydneyreviewofbooks.com/the-still-breathing-author-gerald-murnane/. The version published here, working from the original typescript, adds references to material interpolated by the author or excised from the final version.

---

1   Gerald Murnane, "The Breathing Author", *Heat* no. 3 (new series) (2002), 9-31. Republished in Gerald Murnane, *Invisible Yet Enduring Lilacs* (Artarmon, NSW: Giramondo, 2005).
2   Murnane, *Invisible Yet Enduring Lilacs*.

reversal will happen in connection with today's event. At Newcastle, I could not rid myself of the suspicion that I was depriving my readers of one or more books that existed in potentiality, which is a favourite phrase of mine. Here in Goroke, I feel no such thing. When the last of my completed but unpublished works has been published in a few years from now, my readers will be in possession of all that I'm capable of giving them.[3] At Newcastle in 2001, I was not comfortable. I was far from my native part of Victoria; my hotel room overlooked the ocean, which I've hated and avoided all my life; and I was somewhat troubled by my having left off writing for publication. Here today, in the clubhouse of my beloved Goroke Golf Club, surrounded by the splendid vistas of Goroke State Forest, I feel sublimely untroubled. I'm no longer a writer, as that word is usually understood. You might say of me, as someone said of Thomas Hardy after an interview with him when he was about my age, that I've been *delivered* of my books.

I wrote this address in the same way that I wrote most of my works of fiction – the book-length works and the shorter works. During a period of about a week six months ago, I jotted down on loose pages torn from a notebook such thoughts of mine as seemed likely topics for this address. After a week, I had eighteen such thoughts, each on a separate page. Then I did with my pages what the narrator of "In Far Fields" is reported as having done with his manila folders.[4] I strewed my pages on the floor of my room and spent an absorbing half-hour arranging the pages in what seemed like the right order. After this, I numbered the pages 1 to 18, clipped them into a bundle, and set about expanding the brief notes on the page numbered 1.

One thing I did *not* do at any time while I wrote – I did not engage in any sort of research. Nor have I done any sort of research while writing any of my works of fiction. To put a complex matter rather simply, whenever I've written a work of fiction, I've considered it a detailed report of certain of the contents of my mind *at the time of my writing*. I may sometimes have looked into a dictionary or an atlas or a writer's and editor's guide, but I've mostly reported only what I've been able to bring to mind, with no concern to know whether or not my seeming recollections, imaginings, whatever, corresponded to what might be called the facts. While I was writing *Barley Patch*, for example, I reported memories of what had been in my mind while I was reading, more than fifty years before, the novel *Brat Farrar*, by Josephine Tey.[5] While I was still working on *Barley Patch*, Nicholas Birns, of New York City, read the early sections and the references to *Brat Farrar*. He told me

---

3 Author's handwritten interpolation on slip of paper attached to typescript by sticky tape: "Tell 'em what books are to come".
4 Gerald Murnane, "In Far Fields", in *Collected Short Fiction* (Artarmon, NSW: Giramondo, 2018).
5 Gerald Murnane, *Barley Patch* (Artarmon, NSW: Giramondo, 2009). Josephine Tey, *Brat Farrar* (1949; London: Scribner, 1997).

that the novel had been reissued recently and he offered to get a copy for me so that I could check against the published text the meagre details recollected by my narrator. I declined his offer. The narrator's recollections were some of my own recollections, and I trusted them to possess a sort of power because they alone had stayed with me for more than fifty years, perhaps changing or perhaps acquiring embellishments to meet my peculiar needs – because they alone had stayed with me while numerous others had deserted me or had become lost to me. The question why I recall certain of my experiences as a reader while forgetting so many others – that question has concerned me for much of my life.

I'm interested not only in what I recall and what I forget from my reading and writing; I'm interested also in what I remember and what I forget from my own experience. I've kept detailed journals at different periods of my life, and the twenty-eight filing-cabinet drawers that I call my chronological archive are full of long letters and notes reporting with utter frankness what might be called my private life. And yet, I've never looked into that archive while I've been writing for publication. I trust my own mind to provide me with all I need as the occasion arises. Likewise, for many years I've trusted the appropriate part of me to take note from day to day of any experience deserving to be noted.

In this connection, I'll mention three lessons that I've learned from other writers. During the sixteen years when I taught fiction writing at tertiary level, I felt obliged to present to my students the opinions, beliefs, and theories of the widest possible variety of writers. Early in my teaching career, I read all the books in the *Paris Review Interviews* series and took copious notes while I read. I read also numerous published interviews with novelists, poets, and short-story writers. In my first year as a teacher, I searched through the text of *À la recherche du temps perdu*, which I had read a few years earlier, for the many passages setting out the duties and responsibilities of the fiction writer as they seemed to the narrator of the most impressive work of literature that I've read. In each of my years as a teacher, I must have put in front of my students as many as a hundred memorable quotations from a wide variety of writers. If I waited patiently on this cold, squally day in early spring, more than twenty years since I last stood in front of a class – if I waited patiently, I might recall perhaps a dozen of those quotations, but I've recalled already three that I've often recalled during those twenty and more years. The first is from the narrator of a work by the French writer Alfred Jarry. The passage reports the reply of a young poet to his friends after they had rebuked him for cycling through the countryside with his head down over the handlebars when he might have been looking around him for subject-matter for his poems. The reply was to the effect that a poet must have a poor opinion of his own mind if he has to tell it what to take note of.

The second passage is the simple recommendation by the American poet Robert Bly that a writer must learn to trust his obsessions.[6] The third passage is from the narrator of *À la recherche* ... and it can surely be taken as coming from the author himself. It's the simple advice to the writer that his chief task is to learn to read the book being written continually on his own heart.

While I was writing the last few paragraphs, there occurred to me a diagram that I drew on the whiteboard sometimes in class. Early in my adult life, I observed that I was incapable of abstract thinking. (I sometimes surmise that those who claim to think thus are deceiving themselves, but that's none of my business.) I think of my mind, for example, as a vast *place* that I have barely begun to explore and the boundaries of which I expect never to approach during my lifetime. Whenever I've been obliged to travel into unfamiliar territory in this, the visible world, I've studied maps in order to feel connected with the places where I feel comfortable. I often think of my own life as a very long dotted line with fearsomely complicated twisting and turnings on an enormous map. Many of my works of fiction have begun as diagrams. The diagram that I sometimes drew on the whiteboard was meant to show my students the way in which many of the pieces of fiction literally took *shape* in my mind before I began the actual writing. And the most common shape that occurred to me was a version of this.[7]

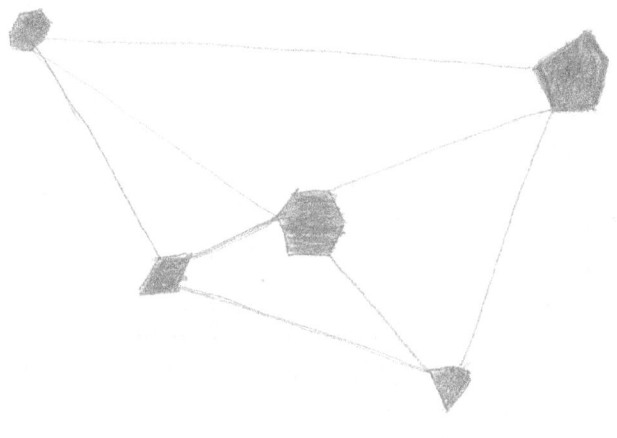

---

6   Author's handwritten interpolation on slip of paper attached to typescript by sticky tape: "I think I can say that I am well supplied with ..."
7   This image is reproduced from Gerald Murnane's typescript.

Each polygon might represent a single image or a simple topic or theme. Of course, the number of polygons would be different for each piece of fiction. The five shown here would be the average number for a piece of short fiction of five thousand words or more. The central image would often, but certainly not always, have been the first to occur to me. Occasionally, the central polygon would have been missing to start with but discovered later, while I was actually writing the piece of fiction.

I would sometimes, during the planning of a piece of fiction, see my polygons and connecting lines as a map of some or another remote district of my mind, with the polygons suggesting townships and the lines suggesting roads or rail lines. Sometimes the diagram might seem to represent a solar system, reminding me that my mind comprised not only varieties of my favourite level landscapes but a starry firmament overspreading them. Or sometimes, in a mood to reduce things to their simplest terms, I would see a diagram as the narrator of "In Far Fields" would have claimed to see it: as proving that his mind consisted only of images connected by feelings.

I mentioned above that the central polygon in the diagram is sometimes missing to start with. This reminded me to mention something that has occasionally happened to me as a reader of my own work. During the first months after I've completed a work of fiction, I feel drawn to read it at least once. After that, the urge soon passes, and I can't recall having read more than isolated extracts from any of my books after their publication.[8] My chief feeling when I handle one or another of my published works is of weariness – I don't care to recall any of the effort that went into the writing of the work. Sometimes, however, during an early reading of the finished typescript, I discover a measure of meaning that I was unaware of while I wrote. Such a discovery produces in me a surge of elation. I feel confident that my theories have been vindicated: that my mind truly is a landscape still not adequately mapped while the firmament above it contains suns or stars yet to be discovered.

As for the question, what is the *meaning* that I've claimed to have discovered, I can answer it very simply. *Meaning*, for me, is *connection*. A thing has meaning for me when it has a connection with another thing.

I have at least as many unworthy feelings as the next person, and my vanity drives me sometimes to google my name followed by the word *author* and to feel proud of the sheer number of reviews of my books and articles or essays about them written by persons such as yourselves.[9] I hardly ever read the reviews or

---

8 Author's handwritten interpolation on slip of paper attached to typescript by sticky tape: "I tried and failed @ B[alla]rat".

9 Author's handwritten interpolation on slip of paper attached to typescript by sticky tape: "my smart phone".

whatever for the simple reason that I find them mostly incomprehensible. This is not meant as a rebuke to the authors of the items. The fact is that I see my books from a standpoint wholly different from the reader's standpoint. Take my book *The Plains*.[10] For the common reader and the scholar alike, the words of the title denote a text of about 35,000 words. The meaning of that text may be debated, but the text itself is a fixed entity. For me, the text of the published work is sometimes far from my attention when I respond to the sound or the sight of the title *The Plains*. Sometimes, I don't even think of my third published book as being called *The Plains*. Instead, I think of it as having the title that I first gave it and defended for several months until my publishers wore me down. That title was *Landscape with Darkness and Mirage*. Sometimes, the title of the published work brings to my mind some of the 90,000 words of the unpublished work of fiction *The Only Adam*, of which the text of *The Plains* was once part. Sometimes the words *The Plains* bring to my mind my interview with one or another of the three publishers who rejected *The Only Adam*. Sometimes the words *The Plains* bring to my mind the view of the straggling cotoneaster trees on the northern boundary of the backyard behind a certain house in the Melbourne suburb of Macleod. I wrote five of my first seven published books sitting at the kitchen bench in that house and staring often at those straggling trees. My mood while I wrote was usually a mild despair. I was many times ready to accept that what I was writing would never be published.

These memories and more make up the wealth of meaning that I attach to those two simple words *The Plains*. I should refer in passing to the fact that the title is the only title from among the thirteen published books of mine to include the definite article. I wish I had the time to try to explain my extreme dislike of titles beginning with the definite article. As for the complicated textual history of *The Plains*, one day, long after my death, some diligent scholar may put together from my copious archives the huge literary entity that is the true denotation for me of those simple words *The Plains*. In the meanwhile, I urge you good folk to go on with your interpretations and your surmising. I'm grateful for your interest in my works. I wish, however, that some of you would hold back from some of your boldest speculations and categorisations. I'm thinking of the scholar or commentator who seems to believe that my published works comprise a sort of program: an orderly progression from one sort of writing to another. I would never deny that trends and developments can be found in my writing, but I assure you that for most of my writing life I could see no further than the book I was currently working on. Sometimes, when I had finished one or another book, I had to wait for months before the outline of my next book began to take shape in my mind.

---

10   Gerald Murnane, *The Plains* (1982; Melbourne: Text, 2012).

Remember, too, that my first seven books had four different publishers and that I made significant changes to the original texts of my first three books at the insistence of the publishers. I would never claim that I was hindered during the writing of any of my books by the demands of any publisher, but when each of my books had reached the form of a finished typescript, I was already prepared to have to make changes if the publisher insisted.

One other matter has sometimes bothered me. A certain sort of scholar has labelled me as though I belonged to some sort of school of writers or some like-minded group. Two labels that come to mind are *fabulist* and *postmodernist*. Such terms have little or no meaning for me. I've said already that I have much trouble with abstract thinking; if challenged to choose a label for myself I'd call myself a technical writer. I mean by this that my work as a writer is to search for the sentences that will most accurately describe the mental imagery that is my only available subject-matter.

I thought of myself as a writer from the age of sixteen. I wanted to be an undistinguished primary school teacher or public servant by day and a committed writer after hours.[11] I thought of myself at first as a poet. I even had a few poems published in obscure publications. In 1962, at the age of twenty-three, I turned reluctantly away from poetry and began what I would have called at that time a novel. It took me all of twelve years to get my first book-length work of fiction completed and published. During those years, I often found myself unable to go on with my fiction-writing and compelled instead to write page after page in my journals and notebooks about what I would now call the theory of narration. That phrase would never have occurred to me in the 1960s while I argued frantically for and against choosing fiction or live theatre or film scripts as the most effective means of bringing to light what seemed my unique subject-matter. It seems strange to me now that I could have seriously considered the claims of film or live theatre when I later lost all interest in both to the extent that I haven't watched a film or a live play for nearly forty years. Not only have I long since turned against film and theatre, but for many years I've preferred not to read what I call theatrical fiction or film-script fiction, by which I mean fiction seeming not to have a narrator; fiction seemingly written in order to create for the reader the illusion that he or she is witnessing actuality.[12] At some time in the early 1980s, which were my early forties, and almost certainly while I was writing *Inland*, I felt no longer reluctant to have my fiction recognised for what it truly is: an honest account by an utterly reliable

---

11 Author's handwritten interpolation on slip of paper attached to typescript by sticky tape: "racks, iron maidens, I feared Uni would harm me".

12 Author's handwritten interpolation on slip of paper attached to typescript by sticky tape: "A leafless branch scraped and scraped against the window. The blind was drawn, but the glow from a streetlight faintly lit the bedroom".

narrator of what most presses on him at the time of his writing.[13] At different times, I've devised terms for my sort of fiction, which makes no pretence to be anything but the reports and postulations of its author. I've sometimes claimed that my fiction is *true fiction* and at other times that my narration is *considered narration*. The first of these terms implies not that my fiction is autobiography but that it truly reports the contents of my mind. The second term implies that the reader can learn only what the narrator, in his wisdom, has consented to impart along with his interpretations and, perhaps, his prejudices.[14]

The following paragraphs contain brief autobiographical notes. I've chosen to report a few things about myself and my lifelong interest in what some might call the world of the imagination or the world of the mind but I call simply the invisible world.

My memory might be called phenomenal but erratic. I can recall the colours carried by every winning horse at the first race-meeting I attended, which was at Mornington in 1953, but my adult sons often remind me of notable events in our family during the 1970s and 1980s – events that I cannot recall, even after having been reminded of them. Those decades, by the way, were the period of my life when I was most devoted to my writing.

My first memory is of listening to the moaning sound made by the wind in overhead wires under a sky filled with fast-moving dark clouds midway through my third year. A memory from about the same time is of my staring at the striking scarlet blossoms of a certain flowering creeper. I believe my lifelong interest in sounds and colours is linked to my having been born with no sense of smell.

In my first memory of myself writing something other than a school task, I am drawing up a list of names of professional footrunners that I watched at a recent sports meeting. I am in my eighth year, and preparing to have the footrunners represented by glass marbles in a race of my own organising. The marbles will be rolled across a linoleum-covered floor and the results of the race recorded in writing.

In my fourth year, and not long before I learned to read and write, I stood sometimes concealed between a garden shrub and the brick wall of my parents' house and talked at length to an imaginary person that I addressed as Mrs Frickey. I wish I could recall the origin of her surname. I clearly recall her appearance but I can recall no actual person that she resembled. She was kindly disposed towards me and willing to listen to me with much interest and concern. I reported to her

---

13 Gerald Murnane, *Inland* (1988; Artarmon, NSW: Giramondo, 2013).
14 Author's handwritten interpolation on slip of paper attached to typescript by sticky tape: "On the eve of his 40th birthday George Firth lay sleepless until after midnight. Information that only a reliable N can give".

many of my daily doings but not as though she were some imaginary playmate. She was of my mother's generation and I tried to impress her by using what I thought was adult language.

Often in my childhood after having been impressed by some or another *actual* item, I would use pencil and paper and a combination of diagram and text to record the details of a *replica* of the item. In my eighth year, for example, I saw a row of aviaries stocked with parrots and cockatoos, and in my twelfth year I visited the Melbourne Aquarium which was then in the Carlton Gardens. After these occasions, I drew intricate diagrams of rows of bird-cages and fish-tanks and I wrote lists of the creatures occupying them. I imagined that my adult-self was the owner of the pretend-aviary and the pretend-aquarium. But this was no simple self-aggrandising daydream. My chief pleasure while I wrote and sketched was not my imagined opulence in the future. I was much taken by the possibility that I could call into being, with only pencil and paper, a mental space that might eventually expand until I found myself confused, disorientated, lost even, among details of my own devising.

By far the most elaborate of my efforts to improve on actuality have been to do with horseracing. I refer you to the chapter "They're Racing in the Antipodes" in *Something for the Pain*.[15] You'll find there a brief account of my latest attempt to create what might be called an alternative world of horseracing. The world came into being in 1985 and continues to the present day. It began as a few pages in a manila folder and now occupies two filing-cabinet drawers. From the time of my early childhood, the vast horseracing industries of Australia and New Zealand have fascinated me. I've spent countless hours indulging my passion for horseracing. And yet, incredibly, all this was not enough. Five times since my early childhood, I've tried to bring into being an imaginary country or, in the case of the Antipodean Archive, two imaginary countries in which a profusion of racecourses, horses, trainers and jockeys satisfies me as the vast industries mentioned above have seemingly failed to satisfy me. Of my five attempts, the first was, not surprisingly, the simplest. Only a year after I had learned to read and write, I recorded the names of about a dozen imaginary racehorses. I've always regretted that I lost or destroyed all the records of that enterprise and of the three subsequent improvements on it. And yet, remarkably, I still recall a few names and a few sets of racing colours from the records that I haven't set eyes on for fifty years and more. Fragments of my created countries have outlived in my mind whole slabs of memories of the real world, as we call it. I should add that my early attempts to document private racing networks were in every instance discontinued only because I could not find the time to maintain them.

---

15   Gerald Murnane, *Something for the Pain* (Melbourne: Text, 2015).

When I ask myself what is the relevance of my horseracing worlds to my fiction, several matters come to mind. First, in 1993, I made the decision to give up fiction writing for the time being and to use the resulting free time for adding to my Antipodean Archive. My last book was to be *Emerald Blue*.[16] I needed to write only one or two more pieces of short fiction to have a collection of publishable size. The piece that I wanted to end the book was to be called "The Interior of Gaaldine", which I intended to be a coded message to the reader. "The Interior of Gaaldine" is a complicated piece of writing that even I, its author, cannot readily spell out, but it presents itself as an account of a man – perhaps on another level of fictionality from the narrator and the female character who interacts with him – who devotes his life to an enterprise such as my Antipodean Archive would have become if I had devoted *my* life to it. Without re-reading the text, I can't recall exactly the message encoded in "The Interior of Gaaldine", but I would have wanted to suggest to the reader that imaginary worlds such as the Brontës' Gondal and Gaaldine must surely share a common boundary in the minds of their delineators with the place that might be called the landscape of fiction, by which I mean the scenery that comes to mind when the delineators are reading or writing fiction. In this connection, I used sometimes to say, by way of explaining my having given up writing for publication, that I had crossed the landscape of fiction and had emerged on its far side and had found myself fully occupied and contented there.

In this connection, also, I can offer a variation of a statement that I've made in print at least once before, the statement being that whereas Richard Wagner once claimed, so I believe, that all art aspires to the condition of music, I claim that all art, including music, aspires to the condition of horseracing. The passage of fiction that has impressed me more than any other occurs near the end of *À la recherche du temps perdu* and reports the effect on the narrator of his having stood inadvertently on two paving stones of different heights. A passage that comes a close second, to use racing parlance, is the ending of *World Light*, by the Icelander Halldór Laxness.[17] When I first read each of these passages in context, that is, after having read the whole work for which the passage was the conclusion, I felt at first what I'll call a surge of feeling such as many a reader of the passage might have felt. What next happened to me has surely happened to a few readers of Proust or Laxness or of any other author of literature. I saw clearly in my mind what is sometimes called by racegoers a blanket finish. The term originated with some long-forgotten race-caller who used to say, when four or five or more horses were approaching the winning-post in a bunch, "You could throw a blanket over them

---

16 Gerald Murnane, *Emerald Blue* (Ringwood, Vic.: McPhee Gribble, 1995).
17 Halldór Laxness, *World Light*, translated by Magnus Magunsson (1969; New York: Vintage, 2003).

all". *Tamarisk Row* contains several passages explaining the effect on the narrator of a blanket finish. I discovered early in life that the ending of a work of fiction could work on me in the same way that the finish of a horserace could work. I supposed for many years that only the reading of fiction could affect me thus, but when I was writing *A History of Books*, and after I had composed the last few sentences, which refer to the ending of *World Light*, I discovered that the act of "writing" could call into being an image of a blanket finish no less compelling than the images that arose from my reading.[18]

I've spent much of my life pondering on the mysterious ways in which fiction has affected me – both as a reader and as a writer. No one should be surprised to learn that I've several times left off reading and writing fiction in order to learn more about those blanket finishes that appear during more intense periods of reading and writing – to learn the names of the horses and of their riders and the colours they carry; to learn the plans and the dimensions of the white-railed racecourse where horses and riders fight out their desperate finishes; to learn what sort of suburban scenery or level countryside can be seen from the upper decks of the grandstands overlooking those racecourses ... I'll quote here the sentence that I used as the epigraph for *Barley Patch*.[19] The sentence comes from *Doctor Sax*, by Jack Kerouac: "The Turf was so complicated it went on forever".[20]

For much of my early life, I supposed I would never marry but would remain a bachelor and celibate. Until my late teens I was closer to a bachelor uncle of mine – a younger brother of my father – than I was to either of my parents. He was a sort of hero to me, and a version of him appears in several of my works of fiction. But he was not the only unmarried celibate among my relatives. Of my father's eight siblings, five never married. One of my father's paternal aunts and her husband had eight children of whom five also remained unmarried. I grew up believing bachelorhood or spinsterhood to be not unusual. The surname of my father's unmarried cousins was Goonan, and I mention them in *Something for the Pain*. As a boy and a young man, I envied the three Goonan bachelors. They owned a large grazing property on the southern edge of the Western District of Victoria, which is one of the landscapes that I had in mind while I was writing *The Plains*. They even owned racehorses. I never saw any books in their house during my few visits, but that did not prevent me from imagining that a well-stocked library occupied a room in a distant wing of their large house. In my late teens, I entertained a daydream that had me ensconced in their library, sometimes reading or writing and sometimes peering out at the level grasslands of the Western District. In the

---

18 Gerald Murnane, *A History of Books* (Artarmon, NSW: Giramondo, 2012).
19 Murnane, *Barley Patch*.
20 Jack Kerouac, *Doctor Sax* (1959; New York: Grove, 1994), 91.

daydream, I was a long-term house-guest of the Goonans. My parents had sent me there after I had finally suffered the terrible nervous breakdown that had seemed to threaten me for much of my youth. My parents thought I needed only rest and quietness, but I had been inspired by the monastic atmosphere in the rambling house on the western plains and I dashed off each day in the library one after another of the poems that had been for long pent up in me. I had learned from my father's bachelor-cousins that the single life kept a man wavering between a state of mild deprivation and one of vague hopefulness, and I had discovered in the daydream that this way of life gave rise to heartfelt poetry.

I've always been an erratic reader. You would be much surprised if I listed for you some of the acclaimed works of literature that I've never read. You might be equally surprised if I listed for you some of the little-known works that have greatly affected me. However, I read very little nowadays. My library, which I spent much of my life putting together, is in far-away Melbourne, and I seldom do more than look at the spines of books when I visit the son of mine who cares for my collection. In my bed-sitting room in Goroke, I have space only for my small library of books in the Hungarian language and my equally small horseracing library. I read from one or another of these libraries at meal-times. Near my desk are three volumes of poetry, their authors being Thomas Hardy, John Clare, and the Australian Lesbia Harford. Sometimes in the late evening, after I've been drinking my home-brewed beer, I read aloud a poem or two. Most of my free time I spend adding to my Antipodean Archive or playing on my fiddle the tunes that I've composed as settings for the many Hungarian poems that I know by heart, or golfing.

I suspect that I'm unusual among my fellow-writers in that I have no interest in politics or social issues. I read two newspapers daily but only for the financial news and in search of what might be called gossip or scandal. I have not listened to radio or watched television for more than a half hour at any time since the early 1960s. I gave up my Catholic religious beliefs at the age of twenty but I am not a materialist. I regard the theories of Charles Darwin and Sigmund Freud as baseless speculation. I describe myself on the census form sometimes as an animist, sometimes as a pantheist, and sometimes as a follower of Richard Jefferies, the nineteenth-century English writer. I have no belief in any sort of personal God but I am utterly confident that the invisible part of me will survive the death of the visible part.

Before television changed the reading habits of many Australians in the late 1950s, one of the thriving publications that provided what I call entertainment-fiction was the monthly *Australian Journal*. In the rear pages of that publication was a section for children, who were enlisted as Journal Juniors. In my tenth year, I sent several poems and short prose pieces to the editor of the Journal Juniors pages but with no success. I sent my pieces not so much for the satisfaction of being published but rather to attract the attention of a certain girl of my own age, whose name and address I forgot long ago, although I recall that she lived in Queensland. (This added to her attractiveness in my eyes – not because I had any interest in Queensland but because there was no likelihood of us meeting in the foreseeable future.) The girl's contributions were published often and were of a standard far above the average published items. I suspect nowadays that her writing was doctored by her parents or some complicit adult, but in my tenth year she was the first version of the female who is my ideal reader. This personage has been never more than a blurred image in my mind and I have no wish for her to be otherwise. As I write these words, she may be a mere child or still unborn, but the desire to have her one day ponder my words in the hope of learning what gave rise to them – that sort of desire has sometimes kept me writing when no other motive would have done so.

I'll make a few last sweeping statements that might explain how my books came to be written or how I think of them. Every one of my books *had* to be written. I was always a part-time writer with no need to earn money from my books. This left me free to write what I chose when I chose. But the word *chose* is misleading. I never felt as though I was choosing my subject-matter. Rather, my subject-matter, sometimes clear and compelling and sometimes vague and elusive, always sought me out: took my eye; winked at me; disturbed me; lodged itself painfully in the heart of me and gave me no rest until I had turned it into sentences.

Here's something I wrote recently for a friend of mine. "Don't think I was able to write my books because I was wise. No, I wrote my books because I was ignorant. I've never truly understood the meaning of my experience. I've never understood people, least of all females. I've spent much of my life *speculating* about the real world, as it's usually called. My books are a partial record of my speculations."

And yet … (almost everything I've written has deserved to be qualified by that phrase) and yet my books, when I stand them side by side or pile them on top of one another, seem to demand some sort of categorisation. At such times, being unable to think in abstractions and always inclined to conceive of thought as occupying space, I consider my collected works as a map of one of the outer regions of my mind, a region that I was driven to explore in search of the racecourses that proved to lie even further off.

In 1952, Brother Julian Watson was preparing fifty and more boys in Form Two at De La Salle College, in Malvern, for the Victorian Junior Scholarship. When preparing us for the question on the English paper requiring us to report our response to a previously unseen poem, Julian gave us a simple piece of advice. I took no special notice of the advice and may not even have followed it. Forty years later, when writing "In Far Fields", my teacher's words came back to me when I happened to be asking myself whether my books might be said to consist of some sort of basic matter, some literary equivalent of sub-atomic particles. Julian had told us to be sure to write in our exam answers that the poem under consideration produced in our minds vivid images and strong feelings.

Images and feelings ... I'll end by reading the title poem of a collection of my poetry that I hope to see published by Giramondo next year.[21]

Green Shadows

You'd think a man who's nearly eighty,
who buried his parents and his brother,
who nursed his wife through a year of suffering
from terminal cancer, and who once had to wait

for fifteen minutes in an emergency ward
while they went on trying to restart the heart
in one of his sons (they did it at last) —
you'd think such a man would be able to call

on reserves of strength or something whenever
he felt that second-hand pain or grief
that you feel for someone else in deep
trouble. You'd think so, but I've resolved never

again to look into *Green Shadows: A Life
of John Clare*, by one June Wilson,
Hodder and Stoughton, nineteen-fifty-
one. I was able to read it right

through in the eighties; I couldn't not
learn the facts about one of my saints.
But today, while I read, I recalled again
what was ahead and I couldn't read on.

---

21 Now published, as Gerald Murnane, *Green Shadows and Other Poems* (Artarmon, NSW: Giramondo, 2019).

Of course, I tried the usual ploy:
I told myself that they were all dead;
that their sufferings long ago came to an end,
but I knew all along I could never avoid

the truth I'd discovered when I first
engaged with texts: the self-evident fact
of there being no reader nor subject-matter —
only images and feelings in a sort of eternity.

References

Kerouac, Jack. *Doctor Sax*. (1959) New York: Grove, 1994.

Laxness, Halldór. *World Light*, translated by Magnus Magnusson. (1969) New York: Vintage, 2003).

Murnane, Gerald. *Green Shadows and Other Poems*. Artarmon, NSW: Giramondo, 2019.

——. 'In Far Fields', in *Collected Short Fiction*. Artarmon, NSW: Giramondo, 2018.

——. *Something for the Pain*. Melbourne: Text, 2015.

——. *A History of Books*. Artarmon, NSW: Giramondo, 2012.

——. *Barley Patch*. Artarmon, NSW: Giramondo, 2009.

——. *Invisible Yet Enduring Lilacs*. Artarmon, NSW: Giramondo, 2005.

——. "The Breathing Author", *Heat* no. 3 (new series) (2002): 9-31.

——. *Emerald Blue*. Ringwood, Vic.: McPhee Gribble, 1995.

——. *Inland*. 1988; Artarmon, NSW: Giramondo, 2013.

——. *The Plains*. 1982; Melbourne: Text, 2012.

Tey, Josephine, *Brat Farrar*. (1949) London: Scribner, 1997.

Contributors

Shannon Burns is a freelance writer and member of the J.M. Coetzee Centre for Creative Practice at the University of Adelaide. He is currently working on a critical biography of Gerald Murnane.

Mark Byron is Associate Professor in the Department of English at the University of Sydney and an Australian Research Council Future Fellow. His current project, "Modernism and the Early Middle Ages", has produced the monograph *Ezra Pound's Eriugena* (Bloomsbury, 2014) and a dossier co-edited with Stefano Rosignoli on Samuel Beckett and the Middle Ages in the *Journal of Beckett Studies* 25.1 (2016). He edited *Ezra Pound's and Olga Rudge's* The Blue Spill*: A Manuscript Critical Edition* with Sophia Barnes (Bloomsbury, 2019), and the essay collection *The New Ezra Pound Studies* (Cambridge University Press, 2019). He is the current President of the Ezra Pound Society.

Luke Carman is the author of *An Elegant Young Man* (Giramondo, 2013), which was awarded a NSW Premier's Literary Award and shortlisted for the ALS Gold Medal. In 2014 he was named *Sydney Morning Herald Best Young Novelist*. His latest book is *Intimate Antipathies* (Giramondo, 2019).

Arka Chattopadhay is Assistant Professor of Literary Studies in the Department of Humanities and Social Sciences at the Indian Institute of Technology, Gandhinagar. He works on psychoanalysis, modernism and world literature. His first monograph *Beckett, Lacan and the Mathematical Writing of the Real* has been published by Bloomsbury in 2019.

Tristan Foster is a writer from Sydney. His short story collection *Letter to the Author of the Letter to the Father* was published by Transmission Press. *926 Years*, co-written with Kyle Coma-Thompson, is forthcoming from Sublunary Editions.

Suzie Gibson is a senior lecturer in English literature at Charles Sturt University. She has published widely in national and international journals and volumes in the fields of literature, philosophy, film, and television. Both her publishing and teaching cover a number of textual forms and disciplines including traditional and experimental literature and philosophy.

Ivor Indyk is Whitlam Professor in the Writing and Society Research Centre at Western Sydney University. He was the founding editor of *HEAT* magazine and director of Giramondo Publishing, and co-founder of the *Sydney Review of Books*. He has written on many aspects of Australian literature, art, architecture and literary publishing, including a monograph on David Malouf published by Oxford University Press.

Brigid Rooney teaches Australian literature in the Department of English at the University of Sydney. She has published widely on twentieth century and contemporary Australian literature and co-edited scholarly collections on such topics as Christina Stead and Australian literature as world literature. She is the author of two monographs: *Literary Activists: Writer-Intellectuals and Australian Public Life* (University of Queensland Press, 2009) and *Suburban Space, the Novel and Australian Modernity* (Anthem Press, 2018).

Emmett Stinson is a Lecturer in Writing and Literature at Deakin University and the author of *Satirizing Modernism* (Bloomsbury, 2017) and *Known Unknowns* (Affirm Press, 2010).

Samantha Trayhurn is a Doctor of Creative Arts candidate at Western Sydney University. Her research forms part of the ARC funded "Other Worlds: Forms of World Literature" project. Her work has been published in *Westerly*, *Overland*, *LiNQ Journal*, *Hecate*, and *eTropic*.

Anthony Uhlmann is Professor of Literature at Western Sydney University. He is the author of two monographs on Samuel Beckett, *Beckett and Poststructuralism* (Cambridge University Press, 1999) and *Samuel Beckett and the Philosophical Image* (Cambridge University Press, 2006). He has also published a monograph on modernist literature, *Thinking in Literature: Joyce, Woolf, Nabokov* (Bloomsbury, 2011). His most recent monograph is *J.M. Coetzee: Truth, Meaning, Fiction* (Bloomsbury, 2020). He is the author of a novel, *Saint Antony in His Desert* (UWAP, 2018).

Index

abstraction 110–110, 117–118, 121, 175
affect 88, 128, 131
Andersson, Lars 1
Antipodean Archive 49, 171, 172, 174
Auster, Paul 94
Australian literature 21, 25, 97
autobiography 29–36, 139, 170–176

Bachelard, Gaston 74
Badiou, Alain 128–130
Banville, John
   The Sea 85
Beckett, Samuel 94
   The Lost Ones 89
   Molloy 89
Bendigo, Victoria 68, 70, 72, 74, 79, 89, 92
Bergman, Ingmar 121
Bernhard, Thomas 94
Binelli, Mark 4
Birns, Nicholas 49, 90, 101, 164
Blake, William 94
Blanchot, Maurice 137
Bly, Robert 166
Booth, Wayne C. 37, 45–50, 46, 152
Borges, Jorge Luis 108
Borrow, George 158
Brady, Eugene 35
Brennan, Christopher 159
Brontë, Emily 74, 82, 172
   Wuthering Heights 79, 81, 87, 156
Buell, Lawrence 69

Burns, Shannon 2, 5, 10

Canetti, Elias 159
Carlyle, Thomas 94
Carman, Luke 5, 69
Catholicism 2, 10, 35, 68, 72, 115, 122, 142, 147, 174
de Certeau, Michel 72
Clare, John 159, 174
Coetzee, J.M. 3, 4, 9, 38, 131
cognitive science 3, 127
colour 2, 30, 72, 170
Craven, Peter 93

Damasio, Antonio 145
Darwin, Charles 174
death 81, 95, 103–105
Deleuze, Gilles 128, 144
Dennett, Daniel 127, 134
Derrida, Jacques 94, 95, 96
direct speech 154
Dostoevsky, Fyodor 94
   Notes from the Underground 94
Draaisma, Douwe 133, 134

eco-criticism 69
elegy 93, 94–96
Éluard, Paul 39, 80
Emerson, Ralph Waldo 94
Eriksson, Ulf 1
Eurasian steppe 98, 103
exclave poetics 97–105

exile 97
existentialism 18, 25–27, 25
eyes 25, 69, 86, 115, 120, 148, 149, 151

Fawkner, H.W. 1, 96, 96
female 39–43
film 120, 121, 169
Fitzgerald, F. Scott
   The Great Gatsby 118
Fletcher, Angus 67
Foster, Tristan 4
Freud, Sigmund 33, 34, 94, 133, 174

Gaaldane 74
Garner, Helen 21
Gelder, Ken 65, 93
gender 35, 39–43, 93, 132
Genoni, Paul 1, 2, 97
geography 64, 67, 77, 81, 85
Gillett, Sue 93
Giramondo Publishing 9, 10, 163, 176
glass 21, 55, 57, 72, 120, 135, 146–150, 147, 156
global literature 97
Goroke, Victoria 3–5, 9–11, 25, 27, 31, 122, 164, 174
grasslands 85–106, 122, 157
Guattari, Félix 128, 144

Hardy, Thomas 11, 164, 174
   Tess of the D'Urbervilles 79, 142, 145, 159
Harford, Lesbia 174
HEAT 3, 163
Heidegger, Martin 88, 96, 96
Hesse, Herman
   The Glass Bead Game 155
Hobson, Sydney Courtier 72
horseracing 2, 32, 49, 83, 99, 118, 136, 154, 170, 171–172, 172, 174
horses 98–101
Hungarian language 100–101, 139, 174
   Hungary 77, 78–81, 86, 87–91, 94

ideal reader 35, 39, 90, 118, 147, 175
Illyés, Gyula
   The People of the Puszta 79, 80, 93, 100, 102–104, 156, 158

imagery 2, 10, 11, 66, 74–75, 82–83, 97, 126–140, 158
   and cognition 127–136, 140, 141–147
imaginary countries 171
implied author 2, 30, 37, 45–60
Indyk, Ivor 3, 5, 9, 10, 163
irony 49

James, Clive
   Cultural Amnesia 16
James, Henry 107–123
   The Ambassadors 108, 109–123
   The Golden Bowl 108
   The Portrait of a Lady 107
Jarry, Alfred 165
Jefferies, Richard 174
Jenkins, Henry 72
Joyce, James
   Dubliners 88

Kafka, Franz 94
Kappus, Franz Xaver 14
Keats, John 149
Kefala, Antigone 21
Kenner, Hugh 131
Kermode, Frank 17
Kerouac, Jack 22–25, 69, 159
   Doctor Sax 173
   On the Road 22
Kind, Tom 47

La Trobe University 63, 82
landscape 109
Laxness, Halldór 157
   World Light 172
Lerner, Ben 4
linguistics 126–127, 131
London Review of Books 17
Lorrain, Claude 72
love 95, 104
Lubbock, Percy 153

magical realism 130
Malabou, Catherine 133
Mallarmé, Stéphane 129, 136, 139
Manne, Thomas
   The Magic Mountain 85

Index

marbles 2, 10, 135, 155, 170
marriage 173
marriage 31
Maurois, André 79, 91, 160
McCarthy, Cormac
  Blood Meridian 85
McCombie, Elizabeth 136
Melbourne 68, 72, 77, 79, 86, 87, 89, 91
  as allegory 94
Melville, Herman
  Moby-Dick 85
memory 75–77, 82, 87, 94, 105, 115, 125–140, 156–158, 164–165, 170
Mental Places (film) 11
Merleau-Ponty, Maurice 120
Merri River 92
metafiction 69, 70–74, 76
migrations 100, 100
Milton, John
  Paradise Lost 142
modernism 110, 117–119, 127, 136
Moonee Ponds Creek 92
Mowbray, John
  Feversham's Fag 10, 157
Muller, Hans-Harald 47
Murnane, Gerald
  A History of Books 10, 37, 38, 125–140, 152–161, 173
  A Lifetime on Clouds 1, 76, 159
  A Million Windows 21, 39, 46, 66, 70, 107, 121, 157, 158
  Barley Patch 2, 13–27, 39, 40, 68–77, 102, 152, 159, 160, 164, 173
  Birds of the Puszta 89, 90
  Border Districts 25, 45–60, 45, 70, 109, 115–117, 122, 141–150, 157
  Emerald Blue 2, 31, 33, 46, 152, 172
  Green Shadows and Other Poems 176
  Green Shadows and Other Poems 43
  In Far Fields 46, 164
  In Praise of the Long Sentence 17
  Inland 2, 39–42, 77–83, 85–106, 122, 155, 158, 169
  Invisible Yet Enduring Lilacs 3, 24, 48, 86, 163
  Kerouac in Bendigo 23
  Landscape with Landscape 2, 31, 83, 122

  Last Letter to a Niece 37, 41
  O, Dem Golden Slippers 159
  Something for the Pain 83, 171, 173
  Stream System 63–83, 77, 82
  Tamarisk Row 1, 31, 70, 76, 173
  The Angel's Son 100
  The Breathing Author 3, 11, 32, 45, 88, 163
  The Cursing of Ivan Veliki 86, 99
  The Interior of Gaaldine 49, 74, 154, 172
  The Plains 1, 45, 55–59, 65, 97, 108, 109–123, 159, 168
  The Still-Breathing Author 11, 37, 37, 39, 43, 107, 117, 121, 142
  The Three Archives of Gerald Murnane 49
  Velvet Waters 31
  Why I Write What I Write 131
  With Perished People 35
Murphy, Julian 87, 96
Musil, Robert
  The Man Without Qualities 159
mysticism 108, 122, 122

narrative voice 1–3, 15, 27, 29–31, 33, 35, 45–50, 65–66, 80, 86, 104
New York Review of Books 4
New York Times Magazine 4
New Yorker Magazine 4
New Zealand 72, 171
Nietzsche, Friedrich 94

Ondaatje, Michael
  The English Patient 85

Paris Review 4, 165
Patagonia 86
phenomenology 96, 120
photography 108, 110, 127, 146
postcolonialism 97
postmodernism 65, 169
Proust, Marcel 72, 79, 90, 91, 143, 160, 165, 172
psychoanalysis 11, 33, 89, 94, 133
publishers 10, 121, 151–161, 163, 168
Pynchon, Thomas
  Vineland 17

Read, Herbert 131

reading 15–21, 101, 104, 125–140, 143–147, 152–161, 172, 172, 174
realism 65, 127, 132
regionalism 86
religion *see* Catholicism
Richardson, Henry Handel
   The Fortunes of Richard Mahony 158, 159
Rilke, Rainer Maria 90
   Letter to a Young Poet 14
Robbe-Grillet, Alain 88, 94
romanticism 117–119, 122
Roth, Philip
   American Pastoral 110

Salusinszky, Imre 2, 3, 79, 81, 93–96, 143
Salzman, Paul 65
Sartre, Jean-Paul 94
scale 68
Schopenhauer, Arthur 94
sentences 17–17, 72, 131, 169
Shelley, Percy Bysshe
   "Adonais" 149, 156
sound 131, 136, 170
South Dakota 86, 90
Spinoza, Baruch 144
steppe *see* grasslands
Stinson, Emmett 2, 70, 157
suburbia 68, 68, 79
Sundin, Lena 96
Sydney Review of Books 107

Tasmania 72
teaching 165
Tey, Josephine
   Brat Farrar 164
time 132–135, 156
topology 67, 71, 73, 77–80, 79, 85–106, 131
translation 95, 139
Turgenev, Ivan 160
Tyndall, Philip 32

Uhlmann, Anthony 10, 38, 70, 125, 127, 135

Wagner, Richard 172
Walton, David 32
Warrnambool, Victoria 68, 72, 92, 159
waterways 90, 92
White, Patrick 21, 80
wind 96, 170
Wittgenstein, Ludwig 94, 126
women 27, 35, 37–43; *see also* gender
Woolf, Virginia
   The Waves 85
Words and Silk (film) 32
world literature 97
Wright, Alexis 9

Yates, Frances 75

www.ingramcontent.com/pod-product-compliance
Lightning Source LLC
Chambersburg PA
CBHW081826230426
43668CB00017B/2389